NYPD GREEN

A MEMOIR

LUKE WATERS

WITH PATRICK RYAN

TOUCHSTONE
New York   London   Toronto · Sydney   New Delhi

Touchstone
An Imprint of Simon & Schuster, Inc.
1230 Avenue of the Americas
New York, NY 10020

First Touchstone trade paperback edition February 2017

TOUCHSTONE and colophon are registered trademarks of Simon & Schuster, Inc.
For information about special discounts for bulk purchases, please contact Simon
& Schuster Special Sales at 1-800-456-6798 or business@simonandschuster.com.

Manufactured in the United States of America

10 9 8 7 6 5 4 3 2 1

The Library of Congress has cataloged the hardcover edition as follows:
Waters, Luke.
NYPD green : a memoir / Luke Waters.—First Touchstone hardcover edition.
pages cm
"Originally published in 2015 in Ireland by Hachette Books."
Summary: "In the tradition of bestsellers like Blue Blood comes a book that takes us
inside the New York City police department and offers a glimpse at the grit, the glory, and
often the absurdity of police work in the Big Apple—this time, through the eyes of an Irish
immigrant who spent more than 20 years as one of New York's Finest, in an account that
"will make you sit up, stay up, and keep reading" (Ed Conlon)"—Provided by publisher.
1. Waters, Luke. 2. New York (N.Y.). Police Department—Officials and employees—
Biography. 3. Police—New York (State)—New York—Biography. 4. Irish Americans—
New York (State)—New York—Biography. 5. Immigrants—Ireland—Biography. I. Title.
HV7911.W367A3 2016
363.2092—dc23
[B]
2015018923

ISBN 978-1-5011-1901-9
ISBN 978-1-5011-1903-3 (pbk)
ISBN 978-1-5011-1902-6 (ebook)

To my wife Susan
and our children, Tara, Ryan, and David

CONTENTS

CONTENTS

GLOSSARY

        ADA: assistant district attorney
        ATF: Bureau of Alcohol, Tobacco, Firearms and Explosives
       AUSA: assistant United States attorney
        B&B: buy and bust
          CI: confidential informant
         CO: commanding officer
        CSU: Crime Scene Unit
        DEA: Drug Enforcement Administration
         DT: detective
        ECT: Evidence Collection Team
        EMS: Emergency Medical Services
        ESU: Emergency Services Unit
        GTO: geographical targeting order
        IAB: Internal Affairs Bureau
        IRS: Internal Revenue Service
      "Lou": Lieutenant
         ME: medical examiner
        MOS: member of service
      NITRO: Narcotic Investigation and Tracking of Recidivist
              Offenders system
        NMI: Northern Manhattan Initiative
       OCCB: Organized Crime Control Bureau

GLOSSARY

OP:	observation post
OT:	overtime
PPO:	probationary police officer
RICO:	Racketeer Influenced and Corrupt Organizations Act
RMP:	Radio Motor Patrol
RTCC:	Real Time Crime Center
RV:	rendezvous point
SWAT:	Special Weapons and Tactics
TAC:	tactical assignment
UC:	undercover
VFS:	Violent Felony Squad

PROLOGUE

APRIL 2008

"Central, stand by; ten-thirteen, stand by!" I call tersely into the handheld radio. The police channel which crackled with coded updates moments ago is silent.

Thousands of police officers pause, waiting for my location.

Those nearby will respond immediately with lights blazing, sirens wailing, pistols drawn to the most serious of all calls: "Officer needs assistance."

Updates on my position have to wait. My attention is focused on the large Hispanic man who has broken away from his three friends, the sunshine glinting off his chrome semiautomatic pistol. He raises it towards the crowd of men, lead pipes held aloft, who are approaching him and his companions—and he pulls the trigger.

People scatter in all directions, including the gunman and his crew, who pile into a silver SUV which accelerates away from the curb with a squeal of tires. I take off on his tail, my cherry light, beloved of Kojak, beside my Kevlar vest and NYPD jacket in the trunk. Whatever I am about to face, it will be alone—while I handle this hot pursuit my partner is off duty, nursing a cold bottle of beer, working on tomorrow's headache. So for now it's just Luke Waters along with Messrs. Smith & Wesson.

I know that I need to call in my location, but I struggle to juggle a gun in one hand and a radio in the other while steering the bouncing Buick as the speedometer needle tickles a hundred miles per hour and street signs blur.

"Okay, Bronx Homicide, 165 and Westchester . . . fuck! . . . Central, silver Lincoln, New York plate, 165 pursuit . . . Da-vid-Frank-Will-iam . . . 627 . . . 167th Street . . . Lincoln Navigator . . . 167 and Intervale . . . 167 and Boston Road . . . Crotona Park . . . Fulton Avenue . . . shots fired! Shots fired! . . ."

My car struggles to keep up with the SUV, and I pray that we don't hit another car or a mother pushing a baby carriage as we blaze through lights and intersections, the driver in the Lincoln desperately trying to shake his pursuer.

"Claremont Parkway . . . southbound on Third Avenue . . . male Hispanic in a white T-shirt with a silver semiautomatic pistol . . . southbound on Third Avenue 170 . . . ten-thirteen." The gunman suddenly pulls to the side of the street and jumps from the car.

I'm out of my vehicle and running, crouched and frantic.

"Get the fuck on the ground! Eighty-four Washington and 170."

The radio goes silent again. Throughout the South Bronx every cop on duty waits for another update. I take a moment to catch my next breath, thankful that it's not my last.

"Bronx Homicide: negative on shots fired at MOS," I gasp into the Motorola handset. The cavalry has arrived.

The Lincoln is pulled up on the curb, its occupants lying facedown, breathing heavily through mouthfuls of asphalt and tar as they are cuffed by the officers already on the scene. I lean against the wall, my suit drenched in sweat, just knackered, offering a prayer heavenwards and a thumbs-up to the NYPD helicopter hovering above the rooftops.

Washington Avenue is now crawling with dozens of cops, some in uniform and others with shields pinned to their shirts and jackets. Their pistols are pointed at the impetuous and foolhardy men and they scream at them to lie still, their abandoned cruisers flashing red, white, and blue across the startled street.

The perps' stupidity is good for the overtime, and the OT is the lifeblood of every detective. Cynical? Probably. But ultimately, that's the way it really is.

For cop and criminal alike, it's not about that silver Lincoln pulled over on Washington Avenue or a guy with a gun who got his ass arrested. It's about the game, the chase, the pictures of Presidents Lincoln and Washington and Founding Father Benjamin Franklin landing in your wallet at the end of the month. It's about the cash hidden in some bus station locker or tucked away in a pension plan at the end of your career. Just depends which team you played for and the rules you played by. It's all about "the green," buddy.

Welcome to the land of opportunity. Welcome to the maddest, baddest, most exciting couple of square miles in the entire US of A, where crime really can pay if you stay lucky and play your cards right.

Welcome to the South Bronx, baby.

CHAPTER ONE

BANG! YOU'RE DEAD

"What are you lookin' at? Get in that bread van now, you little bastard, before I blow the head off of ye!"

In my twenty or so years as a New York police officer I put about one thousand people behind bars. I worked on so many armed robbery cases that I lost count. But you never forget the first time you face an armed criminal. It was the summer of 1975 and I was just nine years old—and, to judge from the eyes staring out of the balaclava, my career in crime fighting was destined for a premature end. My fate rested with this criminal whose finger hovered on the trigger of a sawn-off shotgun, both barrels waving in my face.

Eighteen inches separated me from life and death. My lips moved wordlessly. I didn't budge an inch. It wasn't that I was a tough guy or that I didn't want to cooperate. It's just that nothing below my waist seemed to work anymore—with the exception of my bladder, that is, which had just sent a long stream down my trousers, trickling into my left shoe.

We stood there, staring at each other for what seemed like an age, until my brain suddenly rebooted and my legs finally got the message, sending me squelching and stumbling towards the back of the delivery truck. I clambered in and joined a baker's dozen already held hostage, the door slamming behind us with a heavy clang as the gunman snapped the lock into place.

My future career in law enforcement was a million miles from my mind right now. A toy silver six-shot revolver lay under my bed alongside my shiny plastic policeman's badge, filed in a shoe box with a Swiss Army knife and a thirdhand copy of *Playboy*. If my mother ever found them, she wouldn't need a gun to sort me out.

I was outnumbered, outgunned, and out of my depth. An hour earlier I had been stacking cans of Heinz Spaghetti Hoops in my father's tiny corner shop on Russell Avenue in Dublin's inner city. My mother, Sheila, was sweeping the stockroom as my fourteen-year-old sister, Bernadette, cleaned down countertops, waiting for my dad, Vincent, to return from the local bakery distribution site. In those days, he—like all of the local merchants—used the bakery depot as a bank to exchange coins and pound notes for larger bills. But that night Ireland's most dangerous man decided to make a withdrawal of his own.

Da wasn't back yet and Ma's patience was wearing thin. Da had driven our ancient Ford Escort one hundred yards up the road and turned the corner into JMOB—the Johnston Mooney & O'Brien bakery distribution site. It was a fifteen-minute round trip at most, so even allowing for the chat with his delivery pals and all the bluster, my mother sensed that something was wrong. Bernie took matters in hand by kindly volunteering her baby brother for the rescue mission.

"Good idea. Get over there and see what the holdup is, Luke," Ma said, unwittingly prophetic in her turn of phrase. "And tell your father that if I miss my bingo tonight, I'll kill him."

I skipped down the street between the cracks in the pavement, whistling a song as I descended the short ramp into the yard. I made the sharp left turn, as I had done countless times before, stepping right into the two dark circles of a twelve-gauge shotgun.

At first I assumed the whole thing was some elaborate practical joke and grinned at the man on the other end. I was surprised at his roughness as he shoved me across the yard past the row of electric trucks, humming steadily as they recharged for the deliveries next morning. We stopped in front of a knot of half a dozen masked raiders, dressed in black and, like the sentry, all armed.

Their sudden explosion of curses and threats made me feel about as welcome as Santa in September. The raiders had carefully cased the joint and knew the high walls surrounding the site would give them the time they needed to empty the bulging company safe. But my unscripted appearance caused some of them to panic, never a good sign in a man with a long criminal record and an illegally shortened shotgun.

"What's yer name, ye little bollix? What are you doing here? Where's your ma and da? Who's goin' to come lookin' for ye?" one of them said calmly. He seemed almost amused by the sight of a schoolboy in short pants surrounded by a semicircle of irate armed robbers, desperate men who realized that with my mother, or more likely the guards, next on the scene they were cooked.

"Right, lads. We're banjaxed, thanks to this little bastard. Time to go," the leader said with a sigh, shooting me nothing more dangerous than a grin as he ordered them to bundle me into the back of the van with my father and the employees. Meanwhile, he walked over towards my dad's car.

We strained our eyes to peer out through the vents of our

wheeled cell. Through the descending dusk we could just make out the last raider piling into the Ford. For the first time ever, it took off with a single turn of the ignition and a squeal of tires, and presumably a stream of curses, as the frustrated thieves were forced to leave all the dough behind.

They had even missed out on the consolation prize. The gunman who had ordered Da to hand over his car keys hadn't thought of searching him. Vincent had hidden the shop takings of about three hundred pounds behind a shelf of half-baked rolls. He retrieved the stash with a gleeful chuckle and joined the other men booting the lock, which popped under the battery of boot leather.

Half an hour later the place was crawling with detectives, some taking notes, others taking our footwear, which was sent to the forensics lab for analysis. My first brush with criminals proved more than an early lesson in crime scene investigation.

Standing there, shoeless, in urine-soaked shorts, I learned nothing about forensics but a little about life. It's all about luck and being prepared to take a chance. My mother did miss her bingo jackpot that evening but she was probably the most fortunate woman in Dublin. Nobody was ever charged, but the police told my father that they were sure it was the work of Dublin's most significant crime gang. In my years on the Job, I would question a lot of armed robbery suspects, but my first interrogation had been carried out by Martin Cahill.

The man who would become infamous as "the General" rose from the miserable conditions of his childhood in the worst slums in the city to become one of the few "ordinary decent criminals" to defy the IRA, robbing banks and jewelers in multimillion-pound holdups, even stealing priceless Dutch masters in art heists which horrified and fascinated the nation in equal measure. His exploits sold a lot of copies of the *Evening Herald* and inspired a couple of Hollywood biopics.

The General died as he had lived, gunned down by an IRA hit man on his way to return a copy of *A Bronx Tale*. Tellingly, the movie chronicled the life of a youngster who, despite the temptations, managed to stay on the straight and narrow. Cahill was shot almost eighteen years after the day he and his brothers stood pointing shotguns at a terrified child.

(In another strange coincidence, one of the actors from *A Bronx Tale*, Lillo Brancato, Jr., would later cross my path. Hopelessly broke and addicted to drugs, he shot an off-duty NYPD officer dead after a botched burglary. As fate would have it, I ended up discovering the shooting range where he and his crony practiced, complete with the mercury-tipped "cop killer" bullets he boasted of specially preparing before the shooting— evidence which would destroy his claims that the murder was a tragic, spur-of-the-moment mistake.)

I was born in October 1965 to Sheila and Vincent Waters, who, despite their modest means and raising our family of six children in a shoe-box-sized house, taught us that respect for others begins with respect for yourself. I grew up the second youngest of the six—three boys and three girls—in our version of the "Wild West": Finglas, complete with horses, guns, and natives armed with bows and arrows. Finglas was one of a number of areas which had sprung up to replace the bulldozed slums of the inner city, which had bred people like the Cahills. Our housing estate was better than many, but it was far from perfect— in some ways like the New York housing projects I would visit years later, but on other levels far different.

Drugs and guns fuel crime in the USA—when I was young,

narcotics were unheard of in the community, and cooperation with the Gardaí was the norm, not the exception.

Finglas has a reputation for being edgy, and it was much the same in my day: horses roaming freely on public parkland opposite our front door adding a realistic touch to the games of cowboys and Indians; children plaguing the deliverymen by grabbing on to the backs of their vans "for a carry" as they dropped off bread, milk, or bags of coal and sacks of dark, damp turf—in an era before central heating, the only way our parents kept the home fires burning, in the process blanketing the streets in smog for six months out of the year.

The Waterses had a far longer record with the law than Martin Cahill, but on the right side of it. Both my grandfathers had spent their careers in the Dublin Metropolitan Police and An Garda Síochána, a tradition followed by many of my cousins, and my older brother, Tom, would go on to serve as a sergeant in the force.

I formed a lot of close friendships through those years, and one ultimately would drag me to the USA. Paul Hurley was raised in a house identical to ours, but from an early age he was obsessed by the idea of moving to America. He eventually opened a string of Irish bars in New York and made a name for himself in one of the toughest businesses in the city.

My 1970s summers were spent on endless games of football in the streets, doing poor impersonations of Johnny Giles or Brian Mullins. I had no problems making friends and keeping them, although my social skills didn't transfer into the classroom of St. Kevin's, where I proved a consistent student—equally poor at everything.

I would happily play hooky if Sheriff Sheila hadn't deputized my brothers, Vincent and Tom, to walk me the half mile to the front gates for our nine a.m. start and another seven hours of torment. My brothers were my keepers. And if they were busy, my two older sisters did just as well.

Bernie and Lucy not only took me to school, but on my ma's orders stayed with me after school. They helped me with my "ecker" (slang for "homework" in my neighborhood), trying in vain to explain the mysteries of math and the Irish language. I would listen, nod, chew my Bic Biro to a pulp, and fill my copybooks with fiction, hoping that the teacher wouldn't pick on me. Mostly I got away with it.

Ireland was a different place then, a different world, where joining the guards, the army, or the civil service was the height of most parents' ambitions for their children: secure, pensionable jobs for life, entry decided on your performance in the Leaving Certificate; university education was not even discussed. Sports or music offered the only real alternative in our neighborhood—if you were lucky you did the same job as your father or, failing that, you emigrated.

If anyone from our estate did make a name for themselves, it was as a member of the Dublin team in Heffo's Army[1] or, if really lucky, they were signed by an English soccer club, like my schoolmate Ronnie Whelan, who starred for both Liverpool and Ireland. Northsiders U2 showed us all that unlikely dreams could come true and along with Springsteen provided the sound track to my formative years—the pictures came from movies and television.

Heroin had started to gain a stranglehold on a few working-class communities by the time I left St. Kevin's for the nearby Patrician College Secondary School.

---

[1] Kevin Heffernan (nickname: Heffo) was a famous Gaelic football player in the late 1960s whose fans were known as Heffo's Army.

Finglas was still untouched by its evils—the only drugs on offer were cigarettes, loose Woodbines smoked furiously and furtively behind the sheds lest my father spot the telltale signs. Despite the fact that he smoked a pack a day, he'd have killed us if we were caught.

Patrician College had opened its doors a decade earlier to cater to the influx from the new estates, and my years there totally changed my attitude towards education. I was helped in no small measure by mentors like Brendan O'Reilly, an excellent teacher, who did everything to encourage me when I said I wanted to follow in the family tradition and join the police. My schoolwork improved dramatically, but I still struggled to play catch-up with Irish, which I needed to pass if I was to get through the gates of the training college in Templemore.

My neighbor Hurley couldn't care less about the Leaving Certificate. He had his sights firmly set on the USA, and New York in particular, an ambition echoed in almost every house on Kildonan Drive and in the entire country in the late 1970s.

My father made front-page headlines himself shortly after the abortive JMOB raid when he was involved in another holdup: a raider walked into the shop and demanded the takings. My father grabbed the man's revolver and the gun went off, the bullet narrowly missing Da's head. The Martin Cahill wannabe took off out the door, with an irate shopkeeper a yard behind threatening him with a can of Batchelors beans.

My old man was unhurt, but not for long once my mother found out the details. His careful attempts at a cover-up were somewhat undermined by the interview he enthusiastically gave to the *Evening Herald* and which appeared on the front page. That was my father. Lying was not in his DNA. Neither was lying down.

Holdups, cons, and scams of all kinds were part of life in Haughey's Ireland. The IRA used crime as a way to buy Semtex to bomb the Brits; ordinary criminals stole as much as they could to fund their retirement plans. With the top rate of income tax close to 60 percent and one in five adults unemployed, many otherwise decent people also became lawbreakers. Cash in hand, a nod and a wink, the black economy thrived.

Competition for a place in the Garda College was fierce, but my brother Tom had already made a good impression within the force—which would have helped my application if I hadn't failed my Leaving, Irish proving the stumbling block. "Luke, if you really want the guards, repeat the exam. What's another year? Nothing over a career," Tom advised me over a pint in the local pub.

This time I had to study without the help of Brendan O'Reilly, who surprised us all by emigrating to New York, armed with nothing more than a set of brushes, a color chart, and a dream. It turned out that Brendan's work would be inspired more by Dulux than any Dutch masters, as our old teacher switched from correcting piles of copybooks of dull prose to applying coats of brilliant white emulsion to the walls of new-builds along New York's Long Island, a business which thrives to this day.

Hurley soon followed him over, just another young buck sweeping the floor of a bar for five dollars an hour, but before long he was already making a mark on the city we would both call home for the next couple of decades.

The only difference was that he knew it long before me. My sights were still firmly set on becoming a police officer in Dublin, and while Paul packed his bags I stuffed job applications into the postbox. I got lucky, landing a job as a security guard at Mostek, a U.S. computer company, in Blanchardstown. I made about £120 a week, more than my brother earned as a rookie pounding a beat in Dublin. I worked almost every hour that God sent and I paid the price when my results arrived. I had failed Irish for the second time.

If I was smart I would have followed the advice of Tom and Vincent and stuck with the security work, but I had inherited my father's stubborn streak. I decided to resit my already-repeated exam the following June and hit the books whenever I could.

I sat my dreaded Irish exam for the third time and spent an anxious couple of months waiting for the results. This time around the markers must have taken pity on me: somehow I scraped a pass and my application to An Garda Síochána was back on track.

My family's service clearly helped my application and I made it through the initial interviews. That left just the medical—but that was months away. I quit the security job and took the bus into the travel agency on O'Connell Street. Airline ticket in hand, I went down the street to the Bank of Ireland and changed my punts into U.S. dollars, the bills identical in size and color. Then I rang Hurley to tell him I was coming over to New York on holiday. Or at least that's what Immigration would mark on my paperwork.

In reality I was heading to pick up some casual labor until I undertook my vocation that September in Templemore, County Tipperary.

On November 16, 1985, I waved the family goodbye and boarded an Aer Lingus 747, which touched down at John F. Kennedy International Airport some seven hours later. The trip changed my life forever.

CHAPTER TWO

LONG ISLAND ICED TEA

Everything is different about this place: the money, the people, the big yellow taxi in which Hurley and his new girlfriend, a Swiss blonde named Brigitte, wait for me. In the U.S. the grins, the girls, the cars—everything is bigger, bolder, and brighter. We pull out and take our place amongst the red Cadillacs and green Camaros which vie for space on the bustling freeway, honking horns furiously at the cabdrivers who gesticulate out the window, giving neither an inch nor a damn.

Feck it, even the traffic jams here are glamorous.

As we headed towards Manhattan I caught my first glimpse of the city at night—skyscrapers standing out like a jagged mountain range, their looming shapes set against navy skies. We pulled off the I-495, went through the toll plaza, and on into the blinding brightness of the Midtown Tunnel for a one-mile trip under the East River.

New York City was overwhelming to me: strange sights, sounds, and smells, yet still somehow familiar from movies and TV cop shows like *Kojak*. As we pulled up in Manhattan, I stared in fascination at Telly Savalas's real-life counterparts sitting in their NYPD Plymouth Gran Furys, making sure nobody shot one of the tourists and gave Mayor Ed Koch a coronary.

My Finglas neighbor Hurley had just graduated from broom jockey to barman in O'Reilly's Townhouse on West Thirty-fifth Street and Broadway, just yards from the Empire State Building. It was a prime spot for a traditional Irish bar and O'Reilly's had been doing good business under the management of Eoin O'Reilly, who had emigrated a generation earlier. And he, like so many Irish bar owners, would offer an immigrant not only a job, but also a lead on somewhere to stay.

I crashed on their customer couch for the first few weeks. From there I bunked with Bill Donohoe, an Irish-American regular at O'Reilly's who was always happy to put a newcomer up on the sofa of his small apartment on West Thirtieth Street. I spent the days taking in the sights of my new home, a city even bigger and more impressive by day—a world away in every way from recession-riddled eighties Ireland.

There was a confidence in the air, a belief that here anyone could be anything they wanted to be with hard work, determination, and luck. It's a lie, but a seductive one. I had always been confident, figuring somehow I could get where I wanted if I stuck at it. For the first time I found myself surrounded by people who felt just the same.

Hurley didn't have a work visa, but he was a man with a foolproof plan, which he explained over a pint of Guinness. He assured me the lack of paperwork wasn't much of a problem. He might not have a Social Security number, but his aunties and cousins had birthdays, so he used those to make one up and urged me to do the same. Like countless other illegals, Hurley had been left well alone to get on with things, do his shift, and pay his taxes. The Immigration Service didn't seem to regard anyone with a bit of a brogue as a priority. And so my pal was earning as much in a day as I made doing an eighty-hour week back in Dublin.

Within a month of my arrival, Hurley tipped me off that his boss's brother, Connie, was renovating his bar, Finn McCool's in Port Washington. It was in a quiet Long Island suburb on a direct train line. Hurley figured Connie might be softhearted and soft-headed enough to hire me as a barman, so I gave him a call.

The elder O'Reilly gave me a chance and tolerated my mistakes as I learned on the job. The first thing to learn in the bar business in NYC was how to mix cocktails. Back home it was a pint or shorts, but in Long Island the preferences and practices were different. While every place had its share of beer drinkers, there was a steady demand for bright, mixed drinks with paper umbrellas. So my studies commenced as I learned how to mix a Manhattan, shake a martini, and not to laugh when someone asked for Sex on the Beach.

I poisoned plenty of the New York Mets baseball fans who frequented the bar, particularly on game nights, high-fiving after every score. I worked alongside Brendan Larkin from Belfast and Gerry Carroll, who had helped Offaly deny Kerry the five in a row a couple of years earlier.

I worked hard, but nowhere near as many hours as back in Dublin, and I saved as much as I spent, wiring my mother hundreds of dollars at a time. Sheila Waters became suspicious of my sudden change in fortune and about what could be paying me so well. "Ma, I keep telling you, a lad can earn a lot as a barman. There's no recession here, not like back home. I'm as honest as they come!" I explained in a Times Square call box, hooked up to the unlimited international line for a grand total of five bucks.

"Son," Sheila would say, "tell the truth! And for the love of God, stop dealing drugs! Just say no!"

Her scruples didn't stop her from putting the cash away in Finglas Credit Union, though—Ma was nothing if not practical.

Summer '86, and Finn McCool's was attracting more and more baseball fans. Friday afternoons were quiet before the match-day onslaught and I usually got to drive the boss's Mercedes to the bank for the change we'd need later on. But one Friday was different.

I had given the boss's car keys to his wife and she still wasn't back, so we had no wheels. The only other person in the joint was a local barfly everybody called Sid, a hefty Hispanic-looking man, not much older than me. He would hang out with his pals, a giant black guy called Darren (or maybe Daryl—I could never remember) and another named Larry or Lenny, chatting up women, knocking back beers on the house, and talking about sports. Sid had a solution to Connie's conundrum. He tossed me a set of keys.

"Hey, take my wheels, kid. They're parked out front. You can't miss 'em."

I stepped out onto the street expecting to see a junk pile of a Ford or Chevy. The road was deserted except for a top-of-the-line red convertible sports car. So I went back into the bar to break the news to Sid that his car must be gone, towed or stolen.

"Wh-a-a-t? Are you for real? Someone stole my Porsche?"

"Porsche? Oh, that's yours? No, it's still there. Thanks again, Sid," I replied.

I skipped out the door before he could change his mind about loaning a thirty-thousand-dollar convertible to a twenty-year-old newbie from Dublin. As I cruised along Shore Road, I put on Sid's sunglasses and let the cool breeze blow through my hair. With three thousand dollars in a bag beside me, Dublin was, in every possible sense, thousands of miles away.

A few days later the hometown team was on TV yet again and the customers were packed wall-to-wall. It didn't really register with me that a few of the regulars were missing, including the guy with the Porsche. But hey, next thing, there's Sid on the telly! I was thinking he must be as good at bumming tickets as he was drinks and had talked his way into the best seats in the stadium. But the next shot proved me wrong—it must be a guy who looked like Sid, my barstool regular, because he struck out one of the other team's batters, sending Shea Stadium and all our customers into a frenzy. The camera panned to the Mets' bench. A few of the other guys looked like our customers, too.

"Connie, isn't yer man there on the telly the image of that Sid? You know, the guy who loaned me the Porsche?" I shout over the noise. "And isn't that his mate Darren? Darren Orange?"

Connie had one eye on the TV but turned and stared. "You're kiddin', Luke? Tell me you're kiddin'!" Connie pleaded.

A roar went up in the bar as the Mets stole another base.

"Luke, that 'guy who lent you the Porsche,' as you put it, is El Sid. You know, SID FER-NAN-DEZ?" Brendan Larkin shouted at the top of his lungs as the fans chanted Sid's name in drunken unison.

I nodded, pretending to understand, but Connie knew . . .

"He doesn't have a clue, Brendan! He's a pitcher, Luke. And the 'other guy' isn't Darren, you moron. It's DARRYL STRAW-BERRY. The other fella with them is LARRY-FECKIN'-DYKSTRA, you feckin' eejit! They're the biggest stars in the city. They're the reason why half of Long Island is drinking here and keeping us all out of the poorhouse!" the boss said in exasperation. These regulars whom I had barely heeded were the Yank equivalents of Liam Brady, Frank Stapleton, and Paul McGrath.

For some reason Connie didn't fire me that night, either, and I was still in my "holiday job" when my mother phoned to tell me I had been called for my Garda medical. For all intents and purposes, this meant I was in the force and my dream of becoming a guard was about to become a reality. But in the States, other dreams—ones I never knew I had—were coming true. Coming out of dreary Dublin in the 1980s, I had arrived in the land of plenty, where I could make a thousand dollars a week, not to mention that the weather was great, the girls gorgeous, and they loved the Irish. Americans made us feel truly at home.

The decision was an easy one. My future was in the bar business, and NYC would be home for the foreseeable future. I would have to be an idiot to give all this up to join the guards. That's what I told myself.

I didn't know that a few years later an unlikely idea would form in my restless mind. Maybe, just maybe, I could still live out my Irish dream of entering the force, but it would be right here, reborn in the USA. All I had to do was figure out some way of becoming a citizen. Hey, how tough could that be?

CHAPTER THREE

FRANKIE MAYBE

The greatest detective there never was wants an answer, and he's tired of waiting.

"So, what happened to that martini? Like I just said, straight up, with a twist," the heavyset bald man instructs. "In a glass. Anytime this century . . ."

That's New York City for you. Just wait long enough and the world will go by, or maybe even sit down and order a drink. Telly Savalas has to wait, too, but only long enough for me to pick my jaw up off the counter and reach for a bottle of gin and a glass with a slice of lemon. I steady my shaking hand as I pour my childhood hero his martini.

"I . . . I have to tell you, I grew up a huge fan in Ireland, Mr. Kojak!" I finally blurt out.

"Good to hear, kid," Savalas says, solemnly accepting my handshake. Forever the showman, he goes straight into character, the rest of the staff and customers at Brews on East Thirty-fourth Street unable to quite believe the impromptu performance they are about to witness.

"Irish, huh? Who'da guessed? Okay . . . so you claim you're a *Kojak* fan. Then you tell me, mister, what was my captain's name in the show?" the superstar challenges, turning on the tough-guy act. I reply immediately.

"Captain McNeil—Frank McNeil—played by Dan Frazer." The words roll off my tongue.

"Say! You are a fan, kid. Top marks. Well, you know you can't have a show about the NYPD without an Irishman, right? So we got an Irishman. Now, can I get that martini from an Irishman? Guy could die of thirst over here!"

Savalas would be dead soon enough, within a year, in fact, but on that afternoon he was full of life and looked exactly the same as he had on our TV fifteen years earlier. He took the time to chat about the show which had offered us, in days of two-tone, two-channel TV, a tantalizing taste of what life in that exciting, faraway city was surely all about: good guys and bad guys, black and white, crime and punishment. As I wiped imaginary streaks off the glasses, my star customer chatted about his New York, a city where he grew up as a son of Greek immigrants: a tough city, where he studied cops as he worked selling them newspapers and shining their shoes to help the family finances. This city which allowed an ordinary kid to lead an extraordinary life and pursue an unlikely dream. I didn't tell him that I had already decided to follow in his footsteps—not on the screen but solving homicides, just like Kojak and McNeil.

My short stay stateside lasted longer than I had intended, and five years flew by as I worked in half the watering holes in Manhattan. The first couple of years I was illegal, but in 1988 the Donnelly visas, offering green cards to successful applicants, were released on a phased basis and, at first, were viewed with deep suspicion by many undocumented workers. A lot of people swore it was all a scam, designed by the Man to help Immigration flush us out, arrest us, and ship us all back. But the cynicism soon disappeared once it was clear that the Irish were on a roll, winning almost half the first ten thousand visas on the list. This achievement was all the more remarkable when you realized thirty-five other countries were also included.

The trick was to fill out as many applications as humanly possible—I must have completed about three hundred forms, and other applicants far more, which we returned from as many different locations as we could, driving all night across several states before dropping them in U.S. mailboxes along the way, just in case they were applying geographical quotas. I got lucky once more, and in February 1988 I took my seat on a packed Aer Lingus jet to travel back to the U.S. Embassy in Dublin. I had to do an interview and a medical assessment, both of which I needed to pass in order to get that sliver of green plastic. The jumbo was full of illegals from across the States and every one of us knew the high stakes in this game.

After a short reunion with my family, I wasted no time in getting down to the U.S. Embassy in Ballsbridge. It seemed that others were even more anxious to get an early start, and when I took my place in line I was eighth in the queue.

It was a quirk of fate which would decide my future.

One by one the seven people ahead of me were called up for their face-to-face chat with a humorless bureaucrat through three inches of security glass, and although I could only hear one side of the conversation it was clear the interviews were no mere formality.

Several applicants, including a couple of men my age, wiped tears from their eyes as they tramped dejectedly towards the door and past the U.S. Marines and onto the street outside, their lives altered indelibly by a shake of this Midwest Bertha's head. All the interviews took about the same time, and I noticed how long into the conversation it was that the body language started to change. I realized that everyone was faltering at the same time, and presumably on the same question.

A young woman in her early twenties was ahead of me and when her name was called I slipped into her seat to get a better eye, and ear, on what was being said. I was just close enough to make out her answers. She slipped up at the same point in the interrogation.

"Oh. Well . . . I suppose, I have a few things to sort out here, but I . . . well, I could probably be there by the end of the year and start looking for anything I can get, ma'am," the applicant replied, with a look in her eyes hovering midway between hope and desperation. Within a few moments she, too, departed in tears.

Bawling never got you far in Finglas. Neither did brawling when it wasn't a fair fight. The key to getting ahead was to do it to them before they did it to us. It would be wrong to tell a lie here in these official circumstances—but telling the truth would be a tactical error.

The time had come to lie like a hoor.

I took my seat and cruised through the routine questions, the official noting my replies, until we came to the Dealbreaker.

"So, Mr. Waters, if your application is successful, when will you move to the USA and what will you do when you get there?" Iceberg dead ahead.

"Ma'am, I will be over in your fine country in a week, and all I want to do is to serve. I am thinking about joining the U.S. military. Marines, maybe?" I responded, remembering the stone-faced guard at the entrance.

Bertha's smile almost cracked the thick security glass, as she ticked a box with a flourish.

There and then, I was sworn in. I had beaten the odds once

more and soon received one of those coveted Donnelly visas. While the celebratory drinks flowed with family and friends in the local pub over the next couple of days, the significance of what I had achieved didn't really sink in until I touched down on U.S. soil again, this time a fully legal new arrival, and handed the officers the envelope which Bertha had given to me.

"Hey, you guys. I got a winner! Give the guys here a wave, buddy boy. You're a star, 'cos believe me, you jus' won the lottery!" the Immigration official said as he broke the seal, the smile on his face replayed across the faces of his colleagues.

I never did make it to Marine boot camp, but I didn't feel too bad about taking liberties in Ballsbridge that day.

In truth, I did toy briefly with the idea of signing up at the U.S. Armed Forces recruitment booth on Times Square, but by then I'd started dating Susan Murtagh, having met her in a bar in Queens. She was a Cavan girl from a farming background who, like me, had arrived as an illegal with little more than a couple of phone numbers. After some tough times, Sue put herself through nursing school and worked for an agency which provided staff for infirm, well-to-do clients in their own homes. Ultimately she settled into a good position looking after the Raos, an Italian clan long resident in Spanish Harlem. Her job was to care for Vincent and his wife, Annie, who lived next door to their famous restaurant, which they still ran. The place had been in the family for three generations and would eventually pass to their nephew, a singer and actor named Frankie Pellegrino, who had worked there for thirty years.

In contrast, my work situation had taken a turn for the worse and now I was picking up shifts in different bars back in the city. By 1993, I was tired of it—the time had come to throw in the bar towel and see if I could rekindle my dream.

My early experiences with Irish and U.S. officialdom had proven how important it was to read the small print, so I pored over every line of the application form for the New York Police Department between serving shots in Kennedy's Bar. I paid particular attention to the reminders that failure to disclose any fact would see your application filed in the wastepaper basket. Thanks to Senator Donnelly, I was officially a new arrival, so I carefully cross-checked every answer to make sure that the fiction I was committing to paper read like reality.

My police recruiter, Julian Jones, a genial black detective, was helping me through the process. He had no idea that the man he had in front of him was a long-term illegal alien who had consistently bypassed U.S. Immigration controls and had also facilitated the entry of other lawbreakers into America. As if that weren't enough, I had to persuade my father to declare that between 1985 and 1988 Luke Waters had been stacking the shelves in his corner store in Dublin, not pulling pints in Long Island and Manhattan. Da is an honest man, so it was with the greatest reluctance that he backed up my story, and then only because he knew how much all of this meant to me.

The Job left nothing to chance, and I was careful to supply only work references which corresponded with the details I had given to get my Donnelly visa, but the staff down at One Police Plaza went back as far as my school days in St. Kevin's, checking everything in minute detail. In time I got a letter telling me to report for my medical examination, conducted in assembly-line style with dozens of other applicants, which was when my luck took a downturn.

I had taken up running again to get my fitness back and was in the best shape since my school days, but when I lay on a trolley and the nurse attached electrodes to my chest, their leads plugged into an electrocardiogram (ECG) machine which would uncover any defects that would render a candidate ineligible for service, she discovered that I had a heart murmur.

Well, maybe I had a heart murmur. She couldn't be sure and mumbled something about how she had to speak to the doctor. That's when I nearly had a heart attack.

"Oh . . . Hmm. I see. I really don't like these numbers. Any history of high blood pressure in your family, Mr. Waters?" the physician said with a frown as he flicked through the results.

I explained to him that barmen picked up germs as easily as they pocketed tips, and I had arrived with a chest cold and coughed my way through the test, which might account for a false reading. I begged for another chance, confessing that I had an excellent record in passing exams the third time around, but Doc Savage shook his head and instead told me to take two aspirin and call a cardiologist in the morning.

I called Frankie Pellegrino over at Rao's Restaurant. He gave me the name of a guy on Park Avenue in Manhattan with terrible handwriting who would be highly insulted if you called him "Doctor" instead of "Professor" until he saw your check for four hundred dollars. I arranged an appointment for the following week, which I breezed through, and I dropped my clean bill of health down to Julian Jones. He confirmed that I had now passed all the required checks, and the only thing that remained was a single sheet of paper—the one with official seals and official signatures.

"Luke, you know you need to be a citizen to come on the Job, but once you can get that paperwork down to me you're good to go. I will have you in the very next class at the NYPD Academy, brother," he said warmly, shaking my hand.

Jones's congratulations were welcome but premature, because securing citizenship was the biggest obstacle I had faced so far.

Try as I might, there was little I could do to move things forward, and unlike the military, who would yank anyone out of civilian life irrespective, the department insisted that you must already be an American citizen and produce irrefutable evidence of that fact before you could see the inside of the academy. You had to be a legal resident for five years before you could even start the process—and my first few years behind the bar and below the radar did not count.

One day I was over at Rao's, my home away from home, to visit my girlfriend.

"So, Sue has been telling me about this difficulty, Luke. You wanna be a cop, right?" Frankie Pellegrino said with a wave of his fork, as we all sat down for a late dinner, a Rao's ritual when the last customer had been sent on his way.

I nodded as I passed the pasta to Annie, who was sitting beside Sue, dressed in her trademark white cashmere slacks, gold sandals, and dark-tinted spectacles, a thin cigar in the holder between her fingertips. Meanwhile, her nephew, between mouthfuls, offered to reach out to someone who could help get my difficulties resolved. He told me to ring him early the next day when he was at his desk.

When I telephoned Frankie to remind him about the citizenship issue, the call went well—he had already made a few inquiries and passed along a number for someone who might be able to help me out. It was Al D'Amato. The eccentric Republican senator was a real mover and shaker in politics, locally and nationally, who realized that the bigger picture was made up of a thousand tiny brushstrokes.

I called the number and his secretary explained that her boss was looking into it. The senator would be back to me as soon as possible with news of how my application was progressing. Less than twenty-four hours later she rang me back and instructed me to call a woman known only as "Mrs. X" down in Brooklyn who, she said, had my file. Good detective work is about wasting no time in following up on a lead.

"Hello. My name is Luke Waters, ma'am, and I was told to call you by—"

The voice on the other end interrupted before I could get any further. "No names. I don't know who you are. And I don't know what this is about. Here is what I do know: Be down here at eight a.m. tomorrow. Bring your paperwork. Goodbye."

I could have been offended but, in truth, I didn't care about Mrs. X. I just wanted to get my citizenship and become a cop; and I wanted to repay Frankie Pellegrino for his help in making it happen.

I turned up early the following morning at the U.S. Post Office and Courthouse in Brooklyn, a well-known landmark thanks to the 120-foot-high square tower in one corner. I climbed the short flight of steps, walked through the main door, and followed the signs to the reception hall, which was buzzing with anticipation and excitement.

Some of those present had endured great hardship to make it there, in many cases literally selling everything they possessed and laying their lives on the line to cross mountains, oceans, and deserts in the hope of making it to the USA, arriving penniless, with no contacts, and without a word of English. By comparison I'd had it easy, but my relief was no less heartfelt as I stepped forward to the desk, sliding my Irish passport and my green card over to the official seated there. He glanced up to check that the picture matched the face in front of him before scanning through his printout of names, his blue pencil searching the list for Waters.

The federal employee paused, checked my passport again, and scanned the names for a last time before clearing his throat to break the news, and my heart.

"Sorry. You're not on my list."

I was stunned, but stayed calm and chose my words carefully before replying, telling myself that it was probably a typing error. Surely I hadn't come this far to fail at the final hurdle.

"Can you check again, please? My name must be there," I replied, my heart now thumping even faster, as my mind rushed through the possibilities.

"No. I'm sorry, sir. Your name is not here. I can give you a telephone number to follow up on the matter, but there's nothing I can do for you," he replied firmly, easing my forms back. I slid them over again. He stared at me and once more slipped them across.

I smiled and ping-ponged them over once more.

I played my final hand.

"Look, there must be some mistake. Can you talk to Mrs. . . . er . . . Mrs. . . . ?"

The guy looked at me blankly. The name of the dame tantalized the tip of my tongue.

"Is Mrs. . . . X here? She's dealing with my case."

The clerk cracked a smile for the first time that morning, maybe that week.

"Uh-huh. Why didn't you say so earlier, Mr. Waters? I'll call her down right away."

Two minutes later a middle-aged black lady walked from

the elevator with a sheet of foolscap in her left hand. She completely ignored me as she leaned over to talk to her colleague.

"Waters. Luke Gerard Waters. I have the file. Just add his name to the list for now. We'll update it later." The clerk did exactly as he was instructed.

"Congratulations, Mr. Waters. You're good to go. You need to join the line for the swearing-in ceremony. Just take a seat. Your name will be called. My apologies for the delay," he said, cracking another smile.

Mrs. X looked up at me for the first and only time, pursing her lips as she handed over the sheet of paper she had been holding. She didn't offer congratulations, just a parting comment, as much a warning as a casual observation.

"I don't know who you are," she said, looking me in the eye, "but this isn't right."

I stared after the woman as she walked back towards the elevator, our meeting brief but, for me, unforgettable.

I turned over the sheet of paper she had just handed to me. I saw the watermarked certificate, complete with letterhead, seals, and signatures.

I joined the next group being sworn in, men and women from the four corners of the world, every color, creed, and hue represented in our ranks. We took our Oath of Allegiance, hand on the Bible, and were officially welcomed to the ranks of the Land of the Free and the Home of the Brave. Spontaneous applause broke out and flashbulbs lit the air as we were engulfed in a sea of tiny Stars and Stripes.

I was now proudly hyphenated—reformed, redeemed, reborn in the USA, now "Irish-American." A Freeborn Man of the USA.

CHAPTER FOUR

SHOOT THE THUG

It's October 1993 and I'm out near the beach in the middle of a downpour.

I line up the sights on my pistol and squeeze the trigger twice in quick succession, sending two lumps of 9mm lead into the chest of the stocky man in the pale yellow tracksuit who is pointing a gun straight at me.

"Hmmm. Not bad," says Kenneth Weiver, sourly surveying my efforts. "Ha! Hey, looks like I spoke too soon, Luke. Ya boy is still alive."

Brutish, determined, and short on conversation skills, the target, aka "the Thug," I'm pointing at has been hanging around the NYPD firing range for almost thirty years. The facility is out on a peninsula called Rodman's Neck, which juts out from the Bronx into the Long Island Sound. Whoever this thug is, he's bulletproof. He's harder to kill than a summer cockroach. Turns out he's made of cardboard, and replaced for each shooter, which explains his longevity.

My fellow probationary police officer (PPO) curses the instructors and me under his breath and steps into the firing line, putting his rounds right on target. He removes his ear protectors and reloads a fresh magazine, only to earn a barrage of abuse from the nearest instructor.

"Weiver! Yes, you! Whadda ya think you're doing? Who showed you to reload like that? No, don't tell me, because guess what? I don't care! This is how we do it, which means it's how you do it. Got that?" the cop snarls, drawing a magazine from the pouch on his belt and holding it in the heel of his hand before sliding it into the grip of the gun.

There was one way to do things on the range: their way. Our instructors couldn't give a damn about the couple of years you may have spent in a sheriff's department in Missouri, your past experience with the U.S. National Guard, or the little silver-crossed semiautomatics with the words "Pistol Expert" you might have proudly worn in the Marine Corps. You were now in the hands of the NYPD. If you had picked up any skills anywhere else, you had better drop them pretty quickly.

This presented a problem for about one-third of my group: Company 13, Academy Class of 1993, who had served in either the military or a smaller police force before being accepted into the NYPD. We had all recently entered a run-down facility on 235 East Twentieth Street, beginning six months in the classroom, in the gym, and on the shooting range, where our instructors sought to forge us into members of New York's finest.

When the letter from the NYPD had dropped through my letter box, informing me that I'd be going to the academy in two days, I didn't celebrate. This might seem perverse, given that I'd put so much into making my dream come true, but my case supervisor, Julian Jones, had been clear about it. He warned me to stay out of bars, to avoid police contact, to get a haircut—in short, to behave as if I were going into the military, which was what the academy was: a boot camp for police officers.

"Okay, who's got experience? How many of you have fired or

owned a gun or done any firearms training?" one of the instructors asked, clipboard in hand, as he scanned our ranks.

"Everyone, huh? Oh, no?" He smiled as a couple of hesitant hands reluctantly rose. "You two, down the back row. You don't got no experience?" Only two recruits had never fired a firearm before: a baby-faced brunette and a six-foot, two-hundred-pound Dubliner.

Amazingly, shooting was a skill which I found easy to learn, only because I knew nothing about it. An expert showed me what to do. I listened carefully and did it exactly as I had just been shown, working so many rounds through my newly issued weapon that I lost count after the first couple of thousand. I never took my eye off the bull's-eye and managed to hit it a couple of times. I was good at it but didn't take for granted that I was being trained to kill if needed.

The range was a busy place. Every officer had to qualify at Rodman's Neck twice a year and the facility was also used by the New York City Department of Corrections and the members of our SWAT team, the Emergency Services Unit (ESU), who did a lot of extra training with specialized weapons.

Limerick native Steve Morrissey, a longtime weapons instructor, told me later about a few of the more unusual shooters who turned up from time to time, men and women who were numbers, not names, who stepped out of vans wearing ski masks and put every round in the bull's-eye before being whisked away to their deep undercover work inside criminal gangs and terrorist organizations.

Most of our academy coursework was done in the classroom, however, and lectures always began with the same two words: "At ease." The next lesson became equally repetitive as Instructor Cassidy would walk to the blackboard and begin to creak out the phrase with a stick of white chalk.

"The law. Know it. Love it. Live it and breathe it." He would step back to survey his efforts with satisfaction, pause to slap his hands together, and smile at the empty desks in the front.

Although barely older than me, Cassidy was definitely old school when it came to study, and if you didn't hit the books every evening you would regret it the next morning. In reality, he was pushing an open door. Every one of us was anxious to learn as much as we could over the next six months.

The curriculum dealt with every aspect of law enforcement. Police Science was taught by Instructor Downey, covering everything from filling out accident reports to the correct way to toe-tag a dead body. Instructor Velez was in charge of Social Science, which was commonsense stuff such as dealing with the public, community relations, and other practical issues. She clearly had a soft spot for Weiver, who looked like Charlie Sheen but didn't behave like him.

The physical element of training was just as important as the mental, and a high level of fitness was expected of all cadets: the series of runs, press-ups, and jumping jacks would be familiar to anyone who has undergone basic training with the military. All recruits, male and female, were taught to box, and later to use equipment like the PR-24 nightstick, a development of the regular police stick which features an extra handle at right angles near the end of the baton, creating an "L" effect. The PR-24 is excellent if used properly and can serve as an outer arm guard to block swings by a club, lead pipe, or machete, or be moved in a sweeping motion to take a suspect's legs from underneath them. We were shown how to punch with the tip, which concentrates huge force into a surface area no bigger than a coin, with devastating results, particularly against vulnerable points of the body, a technique inspired by martial arts.

An even better tool on our utility belts was the aerosol can of pepper spray, which contained oleoresin capsicum (OC), originally developed to ward off bears in remote parts of Canada before being taken up by the NYPD, too, for use against human attackers. The spray used an extract from chili peppers to cause intense pain—we were warned not to use it on crazy people or pit bulls.

We learned how to search a perp, pat them down for weapons and contraband, and handcuff them, another essential class for any cop. If a police officer thinks a suspect poses a threat, they will always try to restrain them behind the back on both wrists as soon as possible, because although a foot or an elbow which connects will hurt, a hand clasped around a broken bottle, knife, or gun will kill.

We were organized into "companies" which were as diverse as possible. I was one of about a dozen Irish-born cadets but our numbers were spread out, as were the other ethnic groups, in our massed ranks. The average age in my company was about twenty-two, so, as we were a bit older, PPO George Walz, his girlfriend Sherry Silbert, Kenneth Weiver, and I naturally gravitated to each other over the coming weeks.

Sue and I were living in an apartment in Woodside, Queens, a popular neighborhood amongst the Irish for generations, and each morning I dressed in my uniform, similar to that worn by the NYPD patrol officers but gray in color, and grabbed a quick breakfast before catching an early train at Roosevelt Avenue to make the seven a.m. roll call in Midtown. Like all the other recruits, I walked in the door and stepped up to the large Stars and Stripes dominating one side of reception, saluted the flag, and paused briefly in front of the giant NYPD insignia, with the motto, "Enter to Learn, Go Forth to Serve," before I headed over to the muster area for morning inspection.

From the very start they wanted to learn about our backgrounds, and one of the first tasks was to select a leader. Instructor Downey stepped forward and introduced himself.

"Okay, Officers. I need a show of hands. Who here has previous military or police experience?" Several hands popped up, including one attached to the arm of George Walz, who, because he was the oldest, was made company sergeant. My pal smiled weakly, cursing his luck, faced with the prospect of the forty-four other recruits running rings around him for the next twenty-five weeks. It wasn't long before one of our recruits would cause concern for not just poor George, but also the Brass down at the Training Bureau.

Company Sergeant Walz put us into formation at roll call one morning.

"Everyone is present and accounted for, sir—except PPO Sanchez," he reported, snapping a salute to Downey, the most laid-back of our instructors.

"Don't worry about Sanchez," he said. "She won't be joining us anymore . . ."

Participation in the regular random drug test was not optional. Anyone could be selected and we found out a little later that Sanchez had produced a positive sample the previous morning—her career was over before it had even begun.

On the Job a positive test sees you fired, without exception. Cops who take drugs are corruptible, undependable, and unwanted.

The real highlight of the academy was our Emergency Vehicle Operator's Course, a two-week class conducted at the Driver Training Unit in Floyd Bennett Field, in Flatbush, southeast Brooklyn. We got to hurl along abandoned airstrips with JFK International Airport in the background and the NYPD Aviation Unit as near neighbors. The aim was to learn how to drive as fast as possible and as safely as possible, and we put on helmets before sliding into a Chevy Caprice—two cadets to a cruiser, with the instructor yelling instructions from the backseat as we took the sharp turns.

The atmosphere was more relaxed than on the range, and a lot more fun, as I put my foot to the floor of the car, hitting over a hundred miles per hour on stretches. The real challenge was to move the two-ton sedan through curves, as I wove in and out of rows of cones which simulated the sort of scenario we might see out on the street. That's when the unexpected happened.

I was in the driver's seat, belting along the old landing strip, when an NYPD helicopter flying above the car suddenly descended and landed right in front of us.

"Hit the brakes!" the instructor yelled, and we slowed to a halt a few yards in front of the chopper, as the pilot, dressed in a helmet, leather jacket, and sunglasses, jumped out. He gave me a thumbs-up and walked to his passenger door, which was flapping half ajar—he slammed it shut, then stopped in front of our car and snapped us a salute. The cop jumped back into the aircraft, starting up the rotors and taking off again, soon disappearing into the distance as we stared enviously from the car.

"Now that, guys," our instructor said with a sigh of admiration, "is a vehicle."

Of the twenty-eight hundred cadets who entered the academy at the same time as me, twenty-two hundred graduated as police officers. I was amongst them. The program had been challenging, and we learned a lot in the twenty-five weeks, making us as prepared as we could be for what awaited us on the streets, although the real training would only begin the day we arrived in a precinct.

I fulfilled my lifelong dream in March 1994 when I took my place with the other cadets, our gray uniforms replaced by immaculately pressed dress blues, for the graduation ceremony in Madison Square Garden. Mick O'Rourke, from County Leitrim, Mary McDonagh, from County Waterford, and Sean Quilter, a County Kerry native, graduated along with me, and up in the gallery their families joined my old Finglas neighbor Paul Hurley and his wife, Fionnuala. My parents, my brothers Tom and Vincent, and Sue were all there. Ma and Da were proud that I was following in the family tradition, although they were nervous about my becoming a New York cop and wearing a gun, even though they knew it was part of the Job. As the years passed, they would become used to the gun and to my regular appearances on the news at various crime scenes, although they never fully relaxed about it. Parents worry.

As the formalities ended, a roar went up to rival any title fight and our white gloves flew into the air.

After we'd posed for pictures and raised more than a few glasses to toast our future successes, we transferred across the five boroughs, and we would soon drift apart. The occasional Christmas card or retirement party would bring back rose-tinted memories of the boasts and predictions of the Fightin' Irish, NYPD, Class of '93.

CHAPTER FIVE

DOG DAY AFTERNOON

My first few months as a full-fledged member of the NYPD, and everybody is happy. Except me. For an ambitious rookie, to be standing on guard duty outside Boutros Boutros-Ghali's luxury townhouse on Sutton Place—just off Fifty-seventh Street—is just about the worst job in the entire city.

Don't get me wrong. Sutton Place is swanky. Just a few weeks earlier Princess Margaret, sister to Elizabeth II, the Queen of England, spent several days as a houseguest of one of Boutros-Ghali's neighbors, while the diplomat Jean Kennedy Smith and movie stars such as Sean Connery and Sigourney Weaver are amongst the well-connected residents. These blocks are home to some of the richest and most powerful people in New York City. But I joined the police to make a difference and had hoped to be sent somewhere with problems, a neighborhood where I could make a name for myself.

Sutton Place isn't exactly a high-crime zone. It isn't a low-crime zone, either. It's a tow-away zone. A go-away zone. An absolutely-no-crime-under-any-freakin'-circumstances-you-got-that? zone. It is, not to put too fine a point on it, cop hell.

And six months earlier it had all started so promisingly.

The day after we'd finished at the academy, we each received word of where we were to be posted. Initially, the news that I was to play nursemaid to the influential residents in the United Nations district of Manhattan didn't faze me. I had chosen Midtown because I'd worked in bars there and was familiar with the place. Little did I know what a nightmare choice I'd made.

I reported for duty on my first day carrying so much gear that I staggered, rather than swaggered, into roll call at 6:55 a.m. The telltale smell of overpolished leather let all the veterans know they were in the presence of an overenthusiastic rookie.

Underneath my carefully pressed uniform I wore a Kevlar bulletproof vest, which, reassuringly, would stop the five hundred pounds of force delivered by a small-caliber pistol round, with only a 5 percent risk of inflicting a broken rib. It comes with a 100 percent guarantee of weight loss, too, as you sweat like a racehorse in the hundred-degree heat of a Manhattan summer.

On my hip was that newly purchased service Smith & Wesson 9mm pistol, holstered to a utility belt on which I had my two spare magazines, a radio, pepper spray, a PR-24 nightstick, and a flashlight. When anyone with bars on their collar or stripes on their sleeve walked by, raising my arm in a salute left me so exhausted I needed to get my breath back. Strangely the bosses I passed in the corridor seemed to have missed the memo from the chief of patrol that they had a future star in their midst.

Sergeant Brian O'Leary came over to personally shake my hand. "Welcome to the 17th Marines, Waters!" he said with a smile, as I introduced myself to the lads, who shook with laughter. One clapped, sarcastically. It didn't take me long to get the gag. A grizzled veteran later confided that the only real Marine around this place was our bullet-headed, barrel-chested CO, now retired from the military. This precinct was known as a "deadhouse," populated mainly by "hairbags." It's a phrase which became popular in the 1950s, in reference to the well-worn woolen uniform pants of the era. The crime stats were so low in this corner of the Big Apple that they made policing the Garden of Eden look action-packed. Being assigned to the 17th was paradise for time-fillers simply "wearing the bag," turning up in uniform day after day, week after week, answering routine calls, as the months melted into years and dragged into decades, until suddenly it was time to retire and pick up that fat pension.

When roll call rang out that first morning at 7:07 a.m. I looked around the muster room to see what fate awaited me if I didn't make my mark and ensure I got moved to a place where people abused the laws, rather than obeyed them.

It was weeks later that I hopped behind the wheel of a Radio Mobile Patrol (RMP) car and pulled out into traffic with Sergeant O'Leary sitting beside me, taking off at speed to make my first arrest. It wasn't a kidnapping, a rape, or a murder, just a routine 10-31 call at one of New York's most famous addresses, but it was still my first arrest and I was determined to make the most of it.

Jimmy Jones was a career burglar who was first handcuffed in NYPD squad cars when I was still chasing my brother Vincent across the fields on horseback in Finglas. Jimmy had been nabbed by security officers at a thousand-foot tower of glass, brick, and steel on 405 Lexington, the Chrysler Building. As we pulled up onto the sidewalk outside the famous landmark, the tires on our Ford squealed in protest, followed by a similar exclamation from O'Leary.

"Whadda you doin'?" my sarge, a stickler for routine, demanded, half turning in the seat to shoot me another glare. It had become his mantra over the last couple of days, curbing my enthusiasm as he urged me to do the same with the Crown Vic, now parked across the pedestrians' path.

"Luke, kid, how many times I gotta tell you? Park the car legally. Take your time. There's no rush on here. Security got our guy collared."

I nodded in agreement, grabbed my notebook, and sprinted in the front entrance before he could even open the passenger door.

We got to the security office, and I read Mr. Jones his Miranda rights ("You have the right to remain silent . . .") before hooking him up—placing him under arrest—pausing occasionally for effect. This was what it was all about. My first collar! Fighting crime, living the dream. O'Leary rolled his eyes heavenwards.

Jimmy had a rap sheet as long as Grape Ape's arm, but unfortunately for me he was more inclined to exercise his mouth than his right to remain silent, and he took us on a whistle-stop tour of the injustices perpetrated upon him by the Man.

"You guys ahways on my ass. I's innocent—innocent, I tell you! Ain't goin' to jail again, you hear me? Ain't goin', man! I is I-N-N-O-C-E-N-T. Gonna fight this all the way!" Jimmy warned.

He was, it seemed, innocent. This time, just like all the others.

"Cops! The Man, he always the same! I 'member first time I's ever stopped by some dumb rookie like you, sonny, back in '68. Or was it in '69? Anyway, it was right after JFK got hisself shot. Or maybe it was his brother . . . No, it was the Reverend Martin Luther King. Anyway—"

"Mr. Jones, Mr. Jones, Mr. Jones," O'Leary interjected, sounding as if he were about to burst into song. It was a lament to the lame-asses he had to deal with. "Officer Waters here has told you—in some . . . some detail—that you have the right to remain silent. Please shut the hell up."

My supervisor took advantage of Jimmy's need to draw breath to bring my attention to one or two shortcomings in my arrest technique.

"Luke, a friendly word of advice: you gotta stop watching *Kojak*. This is not *Law & Order*. Just do the job!"

Jimmy opened his gob once again, and like an athlete now fully warmed up, he hit full speed as he whinged about nothing in particular.

"*Kojak?* You think this is television, eh, rookie? Where cameras at? He-he-he! You funny. Rookies! I heard they did TV here, way back, man. Anyhow, you guys got nothin' on me. Nothin'! Cops! Let me tell you, firs' time I was arrested, back in '76. Or maybe it was '77 . . . No, it was the time Reagan got hisself shot. Anyway, back in the day, that was a frame-up, too. I was innocent, I tell you. I-N-N-O-C-E-N-T! Some cop planted a bag . . ."

My sergeant let out a groan as Jones—who was now up to the late eighties in his life story—was led back to the car. It was hard to tell which one of us was trying his patience more.

I was pretty naive when I joined O'Leary's 17th Marines, and I got greener still with envy when my academy classmates, who were posted to some kip of a station, boasted of dodging bullets, catching kidnappers, and single-handedly taking on Chinese triad gangs armed with deadly throwing stars. And those were the more believable stories. I knew it was all nonsense, but the Job was proving a massive anticlimax, and so far I had managed to make a mess of a simple arrest of a motormouth burglar.

O'Leary realized that he had made a mistake taking me under his wing, so he wisely decided to put me someplace where I couldn't wreck his career as well as his head. And that's how I ended up on one of the many static guard posts he had to fill in a precinct alive with UN dignitaries.

Standing on the corner of East Fifty-Seventh and Sutton Place was to be my assignment for the next, oh, twelve months.

By the third week outside Sutton Place the monotony was so complete that if I was shot on duty someone else's life would flash before my eyes. Such were the random thoughts that ran through my mind as the hours passed into days and weeks in the safest, dullest posting in the entire five boroughs. Until one afternoon, that is . . .

"Pardon me, Officer, what are you going to do about that?" she inquired in a haughty tone, nodding in the direction of the small, sterile, immaculately kept garden which looked out on the tugboats steaming under the Queensboro Bridge, temporarily devoid of life apart from a guy standing, arms folded, a long leather strap wrapped around his forearm and a look of utter boredom etched on his face, click-clicking to his dog in between puffs of a cigarette.

Twenty yards away our perpetrator—aka Fluffy—urinated against a car before panting heavily and shamelessly exposing his hairy ass to our gaze.

"Officer? Am I not being clear? There is a sign on the park which states no canines of any sort shall be allowed to roam this area. Officer . . . ?" my complainant continued, eyes narrowing as she pointed to the Park Service's notification in white letters on a black background which normal people with lives are too busy to pay any attention to. "Waters," I added helpfully. "Officer Waters, ma'am, 17th Precinct."

"So, Officer Waters, what are you going to do?" the old lady said, voice full of expectation.

Humor, that was what was needed here. A little levity to send this auld biddy on her way with a smile on her face. Good for community relations.

"Ah. Indeed. But, umm, well, you know, maybe little Fluffy there can't read?" I suggested, with a sympathetic sigh. "Sure, what can you do, ma'am? The city is gone to the dogs!" Forty-five minutes later, a Ford Crown Victoria RMP shuddered to a two-ton halt at the curbside beside me.

"What's the word, Sergeant McHugh? Not time for my break, is it?" I said with a puzzled expression.

"Fuck you, Luke! I'm glad you're smiling, kid, 'cos you won't be for long. I gotta haul your ass back to the House. What in Christ's sake have you done? Get in, on the double! This other idiot will take over for you," he shouted from the driver's seat, as the passenger door flew open and a fellow rookie jumped out.

"Buddy, I got no clue what you done," the sarge said helpfully, "but when you screw up, you don't do it by halves. Don't think I ever seen Smolka so angry."

My heart went cold. Bruce Smolka. The Manhattan Mussolini. Shite.

"Maybe . . . sure, maybe it's a promotion. You never know," I replied hopefully.

"I look like a detective to you, Officer Waters? But I can guarantee you this, buddy. They're gonna bounce ya, and bounce ya hard," my driver replied, burying his hand in the car horn.

All too soon the car pulled up to the station house, and I jumped out and walked through the door, heart pounding. Lieutenant O'Shea, who had barely glanced at me over the previous six months, stood near the front desk, arms folded, slowly shaking his head from side to side as I tried to sneak past. He didn't speak, just nodded in the direction of the stairs.

The whole time I was thinking—but, for once, not saying—they have finally found me out and I am moments away from a one-stop trip to JFK and a one-way ticket home. My several years as an illegal alien must have been discovered and my training, job, and entire life are going to be shredded as I am shipped back to Dublin. It was exactly forty-nine steps from that desk to Smolka's office and I counted every one as I began the brief journey that I was thinking would end my equally short career until, pulse racing, I arrived at the door. It was open.

Smolka was fuming. At first he stood there without saying a word: his distinct military bearing and close-cropped hair gave away the fact that, though retired, he was still United States Marine Corps to the core.

"Who do you think you are, Waters?" Smolka finally bellowed with the enthusiasm of a drill instructor placed in charge of a bunch of conscientious objectors. "Well? Who are you?"

My lips moved wordlessly.

"I'm waiting. You know what, Waters? I know who you are, mister. And I should not know who you are. I should not be aware of your miserable existence in my station or on the face of this earth! Think you can tell a big shot like Mrs. Heinz—Missus Heinz, the ketchup queen of the entire US of A—'Maybe the dog can't read'? Maybe the dog can't read! You worm! You shithead! You are going to regret this. You're through at this precinct, you waste of space. Through!"

That was the point where he got really upset—as I tried to hide my relief.

Ten minutes later I filled an empty Cheerios box with my personal effects, took my spare uniform from my locker, and slammed the door, along with my time in the 17th Precinct, shut.

There was just time to wave goodbye to the lads in the muster room before collecting a little piece of white paper from the desk with details of my transfer to the Manhattan South Task Force, effective immediately. Unbelievably I had, in all but pay, been promoted.

Determined to turn over a new leaf, I reported for duty a little early the next morning, intent on keeping a low profile, determined to stay out of trouble.

"Hello, ma'am. Officer Waters, transferred from the 17th Precinct?" I said to the female cop on the desk.

The sergeant wasn't only uniformed—she was well informed, and stood up from her seat, without replying, cupping her hands around her mouth and shouting back over her shoulder: "Inspec-tor? He's h-e-e-e-r-r-r-e!"

As if on cue, two men appeared at the top of the stairs. The older of the two was Inspector Fry and the man to his left, Sergeant Wolf. Introductions from my side appeared unnecessary.

" 'Fluffy the Dog,' eh? The ketchup lady, right? Park's gone to the dogs, eh? Ha ha! You clown, Waters! We've been waiting to meet you all morning!" said Fry warmly, the edges of his grin forcing his dimples against his earlobes as he extended a handshake, while my new sarge sent my uniform tie into orbit with a thump on the back.

"You're our boy, all right, 'Fluffy'! The rookie who got Mrs. Heinz pissed! Haven't laughed so much in years. What a comedian! You 'ketchup' fast!" Wolf howled, as he joined in the laughter echoing around the dingy halls of my new home. News of this Manhattan transfer was music to my ears, and it remains one of the biggest breaks to happen to me in my career. I had started out in a deadhouse, ended up in the doghouse, and now was being welcomed to an "A-house," an active station where you could make a name for yourself. Some luck.

CHAPTER SIX

PICK A POCKET OR TWO

"Señor, por favor—perhaps you help me, no?"

The skinny Hispanic kid with broken English and beat-up sneakers is friendly and polite as he hands you a printed business card. It's the name and address of a lawyer, neither of which you recognize though you live just around the corner, and you're struggling to explain this to him when a passerby, dressed in a sharp suit and carrying a briefcase, pauses to offer his help.

Pedro, as the youngster is named, explains as best he can that he has a ticket with several of the winning New York State Lottery numbers, worth, he thinks, about five thousand dollars, and needs this lawyer to help him because he is an illegal and can't cash it in himself.

The sharp-suited newcomer is skeptical.

"Look, there's a bodega on the corner where we can run the ticket, opposite that Bank of America. Let's check it and if it's on the level, well, maybe we can help you out, amigo." Two minutes later, having asked the bodega owner for the winning numbers, you have established Pedro doesn't have a five-thousand-dollar winning ticket. He has a five-million-dollar jackpot winner—but not for long, if the shark in the suit has anything to do with it. Out of earshot of the kid, the guy with the briefcase suggests a partnership. As it happens, his briefcase is full of cash—he's on his way to lodge a sizable sum for a business client. He will front Pedro the five grand he still believes he has coming to him, provided you can cough up your half straightaway, which is the minimum he has to lodge on behalf of a client within the hour. Hell, you'll both take two-million-five from the deal. It's a win-win.

You call Pedro back and carefully examine the ticket. It's perfect, right down to the lottery slogan, "Hey, you never know." But you do know. You know very well that you can't let this opportunity slip through your fingers, so you ignore that little voice in your head and nod to your new partner, who smiles before turning to open the briefcase, offering the kid five thousand of his client's money, telling him that you will cash in the ticket, just to help him out.

Pedro's face lights up like Cinco de Mayo, and he calls down the blessings of numerous Catholic saints on your heads before skipping off with a backpack full of green back to Tijuana or whatever godforsaken place he belongs.

All you have to do now is go to the bank and pay your partner back his half share before you cash in the ticket, but as you cross the road he starts to panic at the thought of his client checking his account, finding zero, and dialing 911. Better that you hold the ticket, he suggests.

"You seem like an honest Joe, but I need something as a good-faith gesture. Give me—what—five thousand? You owe me two and a half thousand anyway, and I can lodge it uptown for my client right now. It means we are both happy, and we can meet up later at the lottery offices after I finish in the bank."

You empty your savings account, and your partner passes you the ticket, along with his business card, pausing to hastily scribble down your name, number, and address from your driver's license, telling you he'll call you later, before shaking hands, hailing a taxi, and heading uptown.

The curtain falls, but it will be a few hours before you realize your role in this revival of that celebrated Manhattan melodrama, the "Spanish Lottery Scam." Once more it has been its usual runaway success.

It's probably not much of a consolation, but countless others have played the sucker, too, from bus drivers to nurses, doctors, professors, and lawyers, because greed is no respecter of IQ or education.

Not everyone is motivated by money, but a really good grifter, as a scam artist is sometimes known, has myriad variations for most of his little dramas, reading your prejudices and preconceptions like a book and seamlessly weaving them into his narrative. Sometimes your own honesty and civic pride will be used against you because these men and women are students of psychology, and history, too. Times may change but human nature, both good and bad, remains basically the same.

Although most NYPD cops deal with fraudsters at some stage, the Job has a number of specially trained units for tracking down these criminals, and seven months after being bounced out of the 17th by Smolka, I found myself joining the Pickpocket Squad, based in the NYPD's Manhattan South Task Force on West Forty-second Street.

The remit of our small close-knit team, which was made up of six keen, motivated cops and our sergeant, Brian O'Leary, another graduate of the 17th, was simple. We were encouraged to act on our initiative, with a particular emphasis on activity on businesses on Fifth Avenue, such as Saks, Tiffany, and Cartier, and the rich customers who patronized them.

Brian had become very knowledgeable on these scam techniques from previous arrests and was in charge of the unit. He partnered me up with Jack Jaskaran, another recent academy graduate, while Tommy Byrnes was paired with Michael Edwards—both had strong Irish roots. Nick Palmari, an Italian whose father had been on the Job, partnered a female Hispanic cop called Judy Sena, who was as sharp and as tough as the best of us. O'Leary split his time between the streets (with us) and the office.

We all carried ASP nightsticks (expandable batons), pepper spray, and guns. And we had Nick, a man-mountain who was big since he was little. Palmari stood six feet six inches tall and spent most of his off-duty time in the gym. With him on the team the one thing we never had problems with was wannabe tough guys, which was important because on the street you could never back down. The Pickpocket Squad was not likely to be as dangerous as my first few months at Manhattan South, which I'd spent on riot duty. But these scammers were no less damaging to the city, its reputation, and its visitors and residents alike.

The idea for our unit was to mingle with the thieves, observing our targets from a variety of angles and positions, a difficult assignment since most were so subtle that we were lucky to spot them "dipping" a passerby. Those street thieves were highly sophisticated. They used everything from children to distract their victims to mechanical clamps hidden inside specially modified suitcases which would be placed over a target bag or purse. Often the person who took your wallet would be just one member of a four- or five-strong crew whose philosophy could be summed up in three words: "Distraction, then extraction."

"Steers" acted as spotters for the crew, selecting victims in the crowd of tourists who stopped to admire buskers, who may or may not be members of the crew, or locals queuing for a bus.

One of the team would shout, "Someone just stole my wallet!" while the steer watched people pat their pockets, checking that theirs was still in place, before signaling a "stall," who would bump this "mark" to distract them while a "hook" lifted the wallet with a featherlight touch, often palming it back to another member of the team in case he or she was stopped and searched.

All six of us in the squad dressed in smart-casual attire, trying to blend in as much as possible with these criminals and their intended victims, generally acting on intuition rather than intelligence, scanning faces in the crowd and watching body language to spot our perps. We often targeted people by sitting on the steps of St. Patrick's Cathedral, eating an ice cream, and watching the drama unfold in front of us. The idea was to watch cars pull up at the red lights, and if the occupants "acted like perps"—looking out the windows at the pedestrians passing by or staring too closely into parked vehicles, for instance—we shadowed them, waiting until they pulled their scam.

Then we pounced, returning to their car later, where we often recovered a trunk full of stolen property from their earlier efforts.

We were on patrol one morning, walkie-talkies under our jackets, earpieces fitted, when Judy's voice broke the static.

"You guys see that? The well-dressed Hispanic dude in the blue jacket just dipped that old man—over at the taxicab! Smooth as silk."

Judy was the only one who had spotted the booster, but we knew our perp had indeed pinched a wallet when he discreetly slid it back into the old-timer's jacket. It might have been an attack of conscience, but Jack Jaskaran, a Guyanan who was raised in Jamaica, Queens, and had plenty of street sense, didn't believe in coincidence.

"Don't make sense, Judy," he said with a frown. "Nobody dips a mark and then puts back the wallet. Let's follow these assholes."

My partner Jack would retire a captain with a couple of degrees, including a master's from Harvard, certainly one of the smartest cops I ever met, and early on we learned that his gut instinct usually proved correct.

We shadowed our targets, two respectable-looking Hispanic men in their thirties, both from behind and from up front. Two of the team kept the rest of us informed over the walkies, dropping back after a couple of minutes to let another two take over. Our suspects wasted little time in heading into Saks, a one-block-long, stepped wedding cake of a store which has attracted brides-to-be from around the world in search of that perfect dress since it first opened in 1924.

Jack and I showed our badges to a manager and were escorted to the security room while Judy and the three other guys posed as shoppers, sticking close to the two suspects as they picked out armfuls of designer clothing and took their place in line.

"Can you tell your girl to go through with this sale, but if they hand over plastic, get her to place it faceup on her till where you guys can focus in on it?" Jack suggested to the security camera operator, who selected the appropriate screen and picked up the house phone.

The sales assistant did as the supervisor instructed, and as her colleague zoomed in I jotted down the number. I called our direct line to American Express—the card on the screen belonged to a man whose date of birth was a match for the man in his sixties whose pocket was picked. Jaskaran let out a chuckle.

"That's why they returned his wallet! All they wanted was the plastic. If they had taken everything he might have noticed and canceled that card."

The duo we arrested that day were slick and very professional, typical of the many South American thieves we nabbed on a regular basis, men and women who spent more stolen money on clothing and accessories every week than we made in a month. We dealt with thieves and con men from all over the world, but Colombians were amongst the best, partly because they're amongst the best-looking—more proof of the research which shows people believe "what is beautiful is good." How we view others is largely based on their appearance and the sound of their voice, rather than the words that come out of their mouth.

We were on patrol another morning soon after when we spotted a car pulled up outside a branch of Chemical Bank, a chain which would later become the cornerstone of Chase Manhattan.

The vehicle was a nondescript rented sedan, the preferred mode of transport for out-of-town grifters, but what tipped us off was that the man behind the wheel was behaving more like a getaway driver than a chauffeur. At first we suspected that we might have stumbled on a bank robbery, although Midtown gridlock made that unlikely.

Sure enough, when his well-dressed passenger emerged a few minutes later he was carrying neither a gun nor cash, but he was nervously glancing left and right. When he slid into his car I jumped out of ours, allowing Jack to tail them while I hurried back to ask the manager a few questions.

"The Colombian gentleman? Everything was in order, Officer Waters," the pin-striped official said with surprise.

"He just changed some traveler's checks—three thousand dollars, if I recall. Routine transaction for us here in Chemical Bank. What's the problem?"

"We don't know—yet," I replied.

Through my earpiece I heard Nick and Judy report that the Colombian gentleman and his driver had just pulled up outside another branch, so Jack followed him inside and spotted our guy turning another three-thousand-dollar check into cash. This was repeated again at another Chemical Bank: the same transaction, the same sum. We decided we had enough to stop them and, pending an investigation, arrest them. So we let them return to the car and approached cautiously.

Con artists usually don't carry guns, but you have to assume they will try to resist arrest and we didn't want any shots fired in Manhattan. This was not the Bronx, and Mayor Giuliani actually cared about what went on in this part of his city, so we pulled our vehicles in behind and in front of our target car and boxed them in before jumping out, pistols drawn.

"Police officer. Show me your hands. Do it now!" yelled brick-house Nick.

"Policía! Todos ustedes pongan sus manos arriba! Rapido!" Judy added aggressively a couple of times from behind her Glock, just to keep it multicultural. I got such a fright I nearly put my hands up, too.

We took the prisoners over to the nearest precinct and I read them their Miranda rights before arresting both men on charges of fraud, which was enough to hold them for interrogation. Pretty soon the details of the ruse emerged.

One of the gang had read a magazine article in which an official at Chemical Bank highlighted the customer-friendly attitude of the large retail bank, explaining that branches were authorized to cash up to three thousand dollars without the usual time-consuming questions. Armed with this knowledge, our perps would go into an American Express office in Bogotá, buy, say, fifty grand or more in checks, and wait a day before reporting them stolen.

As soon as their money was reimbursed they would then hop on the next flight to JFK, wasting no time in cashing the checks at various Chemical Bank branches, confident that the details hadn't filtered through from the company.

Sometimes the scammers were even cops, or at least appeared to be. June 15, 1996, found us driving down Scam Avenue, shimmying and sweltering in ninety degrees of summer sunshine.

The air-conditioning of the Crown Vic was on full-blast when Jack spotted a pistol-sized bulge under the suit of a well-dressed, sober-looking black male in his mid-thirties strolling along the sidewalk.

"Gotta be an MOS," he said. "What the hell? Let's pull him over, anyway."

There are forty thousand police officers in New York, almost all of them carrying handguns, on and off duty, and when you add in state troopers, feds, and plainclothes military police, you realize that there are a lot of people who are entitled to pack a piece, without even taking into account ordinary citizens with carry permits.

As a New York City police officer you are legally entitled to stop, question, and frisk someone if you have reasonable suspicion that they are carrying a gun, but our suspect was relaxed and cooperative right from the start, and as my partner predicted it looked like we had simply stopped an off-duty cop.

"It's okay, guys, I'm on the Job," the man said as we took

out our badges, his lips parting in a smile which showed a gap between his two front teeth.

"The Job? What job would that be?" I echoed, playing the Dumb Mick. On the street, knowledge is power, and you learn early on not to give up information that may give you an edge. Most of my neighbors had no idea what I did for a living in my twenty years with the department, though some knew I worked for the city in an office somewhere.

"Same job as you guys, of course." The pedestrian grinned. "I'm Gene Harrison, NYPD detective."

"Oh, yeah. No problem, Detective Harrison," I said in response. "You know the routine, though, we still have to check."

"Sure," Harrison replied. "Do ya thing."

The atmosphere was relaxed as Jack shaded his eyes from the bright sunshine, peering at the credentials the man had just handed him. Harrison's badge and laminated photo ID card, which were carried by all MOS, seemed identical to those in my own pocket. Well, maybe not *identical*. Our badges were silver and his was gold.

"Where do you work out of?" I asked, more by way of casual conversation than interrogation.

"I'm with OCB," he promptly responded. Wrong answer.

Everyone on the Job has heard of the Organized Crime Control Bureau, composed of half a dozen divisions, including Gangs, Auto Crime, and Narcotics, where I would soon transfer as part of another street team targeting drug dealers in Harlem. But "OCB"?

It's "OCCB." A mistake? Maybe. But no Cold War Soviet agent ever claimed to be a citizen of the USR or CCP.

Every occupation has its own language. On the Job the 17th Precinct is always "the Seventeenth" and never pronounced

"The One Seven," whereas, for example, the 43rd Precinct is always called "the Four Three," never "the Forty-third," and so forth. Why? I have no idea. But more than once a police impersonator has given himself up by making these simple mistakes.

Jack immediately picked up on this man's slip of the tongue and shifted position to stand behind our subject, shaking his head.

"Gene, we have to make sure you are who you claim to be. What's a . . . hmmm . . . okay, what's a 'ten-sixty-three'? Humor me."

Every rookie knows that most important of radio codes, "Officer on a meal break," but Harrison hesitated, and beads of sweat gathered in the creases in his forehead as he broke my stare.

"What's with all the questions, you guys? We're all cops here," he blustered, his voice now tense, his body language defensive.

"We gotta make the OT. You know how it is with the OT."

"Sure. Yeah. We all gotta make the OT," he replied unconvincingly.

"Do me a favor, Gene," I replied, moving swiftly to close the distance between us before Officer Dibble turned into Quickdraw McGraw and reached for that bulge on his hip. "Just put your hands behind your back and relax while we sort this out."

I leaned over to take the gun which had originally attracted our attention.

The bulge turned out to be a pair of police handcuffs but Gene wouldn't be needing them today. Jack had loaned him his pair.

A lot of New Yorkers hate the police, but some people develop a fascination with the Job which can go from a fun pastime to an all-out obsession. Every year a special unit within Internal Affairs named Group 51 investigates dozens of cases of guys using fake badges and imitation uniforms to pull off robberies, rapes, and murders.

When Jack handed me our suspect's credentials I still couldn't see anything wrong. The photo was certainly Harrison, with his name and tax number, under a laminated cover, and his badge seemed exactly like the real thing.

"Look at the tax code again, Luke," Jack urged. "It starts with the wrong number. And there's something just wrong about that picture, too, man, but I can't figure what."

Back in Interrogation we examined the photograph once more, and the truth finally dawned. Every cop, irrespective of rank or assignment, wears a uniform for their ID photo. Harrison? He was in a shirt and tie.

We later found out that his card was genuine, or it was when it was issued to his dad, who had since retired from the Job. Our perp had swiped it and added an old Social Security number, before relaminating the fake identification. That just left his shield. I had really struck out on this one. Unbelievably Gene had hacked it from the faceplate of an old bowling trophy which Pop had won in an NYPD tournament, and although as fake as a three-dollar bill it had passed inspection by two experienced street cops.

Although I was kept busy with our unit, I could still be called in for riot duty with the Rapid Response Team at any time, which was what happened in the wake of the arrest of Abner Louima in August 1997. The follow-up investigation made headlines around the world as the NYPD was forced to ask itself some uncomfortable questions.

Louima, a thirty-year-old Haitian immigrant, was in a gay Brooklyn nightclub when a fight broke out. He and other patrons intervened, and when the cops responded a scuffle ensued, during which one officer, Justin Volpe, was sucker-punched. Convinced the Haitian was responsible, Volpe arrested him and beat him on the drive back to the 70th Precinct. Later he sexually assaulted him by shoving a plunger handle up his rectum, causing serious internal injuries which the officer later suggested were caused by rough sex prior to the victim's arrest.

At first I was skeptical reading about Louima's claims, convinced that it was an attempt to set up cops, whom I could never imagine torturing a handcuffed prisoner in that manner. But it soon emerged that the man was telling the truth. When the news broke there was outrage, particularly in the black community, fueling protests which spiraled out of control as thousands of men, most armed with plungers, took to the streets, heading across the Brooklyn Bridge, threatening to use them on us and wreck City Hall.

Every trained officer was mobilized, handed a riot helmet, nightstick, and a four-foot-long pliable ballistic shield, before being ordered to hold the masses at a perimeter set up several streets back from the building. When I stood in the front lines bracing myself for the onslaught, I looked to the left and right and found faces as full of fear as my own as the protest, which had now degenerated into an uncontrolled, screaming mob thousands strong, streamed towards our position.

We were all carrying the L-shaped PR-24 nightsticks we had trained with in the academy, but I had also packed my collapsible ASP baton, and I had no sooner unsnapped it when a lieutenant roared over the chants, now just yards from where we stood, "Put that shit away, you! Let them vent! Stand your ground, but let them vent! They have a right."

The surge continued to ebb and flow for the next couple of hours, as first threats and later plungers flew through the air, and the appeals by the Brass over loud-hailers telling the mob to disperse were ignored. We eventually got the order to push the ringleaders back towards the bridge, and a diversionary riot soon developed in an attempt to lure the remaining cops away from City Hall. The Brass decided to march us towards the scene and back up the guys already there, who by this stage were engaged in one-on-one pitched battles with protesters. When the orders to disperse were ignored yet again, we waded in, too, driving rioters back with the shields and swinging with our PR-24s as if our lives depended on it, which, for a while, they did. It took time but we ultimately regained control.

Louima later sued the city and our union for the assault, winning $8.7 million in damages. Justin Volpe was sentenced to a lengthy prison term for his part in torturing him, while cops Charles Schwarz, Thomas Bruder, and Thomas Wiese were fired. The case made world headlines, leaving me in total shock that this could happen to someone in police custody and that the perpetrators were the sort of men I served alongside.

Quite honestly, when this story first broke, I thought, Here's another person looking to blame the police. But when Justin Volpe pleaded guilty to the crime, my heart bled for Abner Louima, because I found it so hard to believe that one of my own had done this terrible thing. There was a general air of disgust in the NYPD, a real sense of "lock him [Volpe] up and throw away the key."

Sadly it would not be the first time I felt let down by people whom I, or any other officer, would have supported through thick and thin.

CHAPTER SEVEN

WHEN YOU'RE IN, YOU'RE IN

"Yeah, I think your countrymen are right, there, Officer Waters. You are done."

The captain sits there, stroking his gigantic chin, as he stares across the table at me in an anonymous back office at One Police Plaza, a place where careers and reputations crash and burn.

I was done, all right. The guy had been grilling me for more than half an hour, in the process killing off my chances of a hard-earned transfer. The plan has just stalled.

"You didn't got a lotta answers for me today, but now, maybe you got a question for us?" he suggests.

I had a question for him, all right, but it wasn't one he was expecting.

I'd strolled into the building an hour earlier, full of optimism, hoping that a combination of bluff and my contacts up the food chain might get me through the interview about four years earlier than my arrest record warranted. But so far the day has been a disaster, thanks mainly to this Italian boss who is one of three on the interview panel.

Sitting to the left and right of this capitano are a couple of other "White Shirts," as Brass above the ranks of lieutenant in uniform are called, but unlike his two Irish-American colleagues,

65

who are part of the plan to get me transferred, this other boss is playing it straight down the middle.

His determination to go through every line of my application is muddying my plans to skip the line for a transfer over to Narcotics, which was using federal money and OCCB expertise to train more people in an attempt to get a grip on the growing problems up in Washington Heights, which had become the front line of the war on drugs. The move is a crucial step to getting my gold shield ahead of time.

"Actually . . . yes, sir, I have got one question, for you," I say to the capitano. "I've worked with quite a few Italian officers, all fine bosses, but I haven't met one with an answer for this. It's . . . er . . . well . . . something which has always troubled us Irish lads. Sir, can you explain to me why Italy is shaped like a boot and not like a shoe?"

Murphy and Sullivan suddenly sit bolt upright in their chairs. They know the punch line but can't believe that this nobody is about to finish the worst interview in NYPD Narcotics history with a crack about the guy who stands between him and the job he's chasing.

"Why is Italy shaped like a boot and not like a shoe? Hmmm. I have no clue. That, I do not know, Waters. Maybe . . . an Irishman can tell me," the capitano muses cautiously, smelling a rat and shooting a quick glance at the lads to either side before looking me directly in the eyes.

For the first time today he gets a straight answer.

"Well . . . because you can shove a lot more shit into a boot than into a shoe, Captain!" I reply before Murphy and Sullivan beside him steal my line.

The other two Micks are in no condition to do anything.

Both have abandoned all semblance of seriousness and

now lie half collapsed in their cheap seats, roaring with laughter. Sullivan looks like he needs a doctor.

Capitano just sits there shaking his head as the other members of the interview panel try to recover, but the look on his face sends them into further hysterics, as they all know full well that this story will be around the department within the day. Although I have the last word, he has a smile on his face, too.

He will have the last laugh.

A month before making my short-lived comedy debut in police headquarters, I'd sat with a pint in Kennedy's on Second Avenue to take a long, hard look at my career, realizing that four years out of the academy, and with two years in the Pickpocket Squad under my belt, the time had come to make a move. My dream was to get out of the patrol car, and I could see my friends moving on, getting promoted . . . My good friend Nick Palmari had become a DEA agent, and I thought it was time for me to move up the ladder. So I did what we all do when we need an edge. I called my rabbi.

The man I reached out to was the biggest Mick of us all, or rather the biggest Mike—Inspector Michael Collins, a rabbi, as we called our close advisors in the NYPD, and a cross between a cousin and a mentor to a lot of guys like me. He was well known for favoring anyone with a reputation as a good worker and an "O" or "Mac" at the start of his surname, helping them get a lead on a decent assignment within the department. As long as they didn't make the mistake of using the term "Irish-American" in his presence.

Collins was raised in Brooklyn to two immigrant parents who had come over in the 1950s, and he originally wanted to join the fire department but instead trod the well-worn path to the police academy. He took great offense at anyone suggesting that just because he wasn't "off the boat" it made this six-foot-five-inch, 270-pound cop any less of an Irishman.

On the Job the inspector was known as a "gentleman," a cop synonym for a stand-up guy, a colleague admired and respected, the very opposite of the Empty Suits who dominated the Puzzle Palace, the popular name for our headquarters in One Police Plaza, where policy was formulated and grudges fermented. The NYPD was and remains a political minefield, and without a guy like Collins, a young cop's career progress was slow. Just like on Capitol Hill, contacts were key, from where "juice"—influence—flowed. This inspector would retire in 2009 as a deputy chief, his rise up the ladder largely due to a combination of his considerable persuasive skills, good eyes and ears in the precincts, and a bigger list of contacts than any hack or politician.

It was far too early in my career for this promotion, and I needed Mike Collins to reach out on my behalf if I was to have any chance of making my skinny résumé stand out amongst the thousands of heavyweight applicants for the few Narcotics spots available. On the phone he was sympathetic but he stressed that, though he would do what he could, he was making no promises.

I started the ball rolling by picking up a Career Program Transfer Application and, not for the first time, getting in touch with my creative side. Officially, promotions at my rank level were on a points system based on arrests, and typically it would take a cop about seven years of active police work to hit the numbers required for a place in Narcotics. At this stage I had around sixteen medals for service (worn as colored ribbons on the breast of a uniform jacket for ceremonial occasions), and reading through the application I was reminded that each of these was worth 0.02 of a point, but no matter how much I calculated it, I was way short of the target. At this rate even if I had the Congressional Medal of Honor it wouldn't bring up my scores high enough to make the cut. Yet, ever the optimist, I figured that I could wing it if I could get off to a good start. Assuming that the interviewers didn't do something very technical, like actually read my application.

I got a phone call from Narcotics to come down the following morning to headquarters, and I arrived in my one good suit, showered and freshly shaved. I was directed to a small, glass-partitioned office at the end of a hallway, passing an army of plainclothes and uniformed MOS along the way.

I paused briefly at the door and sneaked a peek at the three men in white shirts on the interview panel, all at the same rank level, waiting for me to enter.

Inside, the introductions were made and, shaking hands with Captain Murphy and Captain Sullivan, I couldn't help wondering if Mike might have reached out to one or to both. I was so fascinated by the size of the gigantic chin on the Italian capitano that I instantly forgot his name—something with a vowel at the end—but as he gestured to me to take a seat it occurred to me that he might be the guy Inspector Collins had called on my behalf.

Two minutes into the interview it was clear that he was no soft touch, unlike the other two men, who nodded and smiled no matter what I said, while their Italian counterpart kept flicking over my paperwork and paying far too much attention to the nonsense I had filled in the blank spaces.

My total score—at least officially—came to 16.1 points.

"One thing I don't understand, Waters. You got only four years on the Job, right? So, how come you got so many points?"

he mused with a puzzled expression, gesturing to me to come around to his side of the desk to look at the form, which I dutifully did.

I was at a loss on the question of how I'd managed to squeeze seven years of active police work into about forty months of hooking up pickpockets and arresting scam artists in Manhattan, and our chat was rapidly turning into an interrogation, despite the efforts of the other two plants to smooth the wrinkles.

"So, you got a answer for this?" he said suspiciously, underlining "Dept. Recognition" with his pen, beside which I'd listed 2.6 points: an impossibility.

"Ummm . . . Oh, that. Well, I'm glad you raised that, Captain, because—and you are going to laugh at this—I was never good at sums, so maybe I did get them a little . . . well, a little wrong there, sir," I replied sheepishly. "No. I was never a great lad for the sums."

"Your what? Sums? Sums! Whadda hell are 'sums'? Some sorta Irish secret code?" Capitano demanded, his frowns turning to furrows and his chin to Jay Leno's, as he looked to the men on his left and right in turn for clarification.

Murphy and Sullivan also had extraordinary expressions on their faces, and looked like deep-sea divers whose oxygen was running short.

"Moving on, we've got some other questions for you, Waters . . ." Murphy gasped, gulping air as he came to my aid, but Capitano wasn't giving the worm on his hook any wriggle room.

"No, no. I think this is important, you guys, we've gotta clear up this points issue," he insisted. "And none of you gentlemen have yet explained to this Italian what those—whadda ya call them?—sums are!"

Out of the corner of my eye I spotted an older plainclothes

policeman who had been hovering outside the office for the previous two minutes, and when he caught Captain Sullivan's attention, the captain mercifully invited him in to give us his opinion.

"We've got one of your countrymen here for an interview—as you know, Narcotics are recruiting. He's straight 'off the boat,' and his 'sums' don't seem to add up on his points. 'Scuse me, but maybe you can help?" Captain Murphy asked, recovering his composure as he talked to the newcomer, who was standing behind me.

Italian generals have a long reputation for pulling defeat from the jaws of victory, and now, seeing that this one was outnumbered by the Irish four to one, it occurred to me that perhaps their capitanos capitulate, too, so there was a chance I could get away with this. I was encouraged when the plainclothes guy started by throwing a few insults in the Irish language about my interrogator into the mix. This was becoming the oddest interview in police history.

"Ceart go leor, lads. Fear Éireannach, as Baile Átha Cliath, eh? Dia dhuit! Conas atá tú?" the newcomer said, somehow aware that not only was I Irish, but also from Dublin, before I had opened my mouth.

"Is mise Martín Ó Baoighill. Táim ag obair le na lads seo. Inis dom, a chara, an dtuigeann tú, nach bhfuil an captaen seo, an garsún, níl aon ach amadán? Sórt asal mór, indáiríre?" this cop, Martin O'Boyle, said, explaining that he worked with the boys and nodding towards the Italian, who, if I understood correctly, he reckoned was a gormless idiot and probably a big ass. The White Shirt in the middle chair didn't understand the language, but judging by the smirks on his colleagues' faces, he knew we weren't discussing his noble Roman profile. Still he just sat there. This old-timer was either a pal of his or had a real pair of balls.

71

O'Boyle cackled, and he and I chatted away in schoolyard Irish. As a West of Ireland man, he was a fluent speaker, but with a very heavy accent, and to be honest, I couldn't understand much more of what was being said than Capitano, but I knew when to nod and when to shake my head.

I reckoned that O'Boyle was a Narcotics sergeant, which, presumably, was where he became so pally with my interviewers, and he obviously knew them well, since he didn't use the term "sir" or "boss" once when addressing any of the trio, unusual for a sarge talking to his superiors. The familiarity didn't end there, either.

"Captain, now I know he's not Italian, but sure nobody's perfect. In my opinion—far be it from me to tell you your business—but in my opinion, for an Irishman, this is a stand-up guy," O'Boyle finally told Capitano, in English, clapping me on the back before walking out into the corridor to let us get on with the interview.

I went back to my side of the desk, figuring it wouldn't be long before I made an even more rapid return to the Pickpocket Squad, too, though by now the large-chinned one had finally given up on trying to figure out my sums and offered me the chance to ask my comedy question.

My joke of an interview over, I left the room and sauntered down the hall, where I spotted O'Boyle sitting in an easy chair beside a bound report in the office of the man in overall charge of Narcotics. The auld fella was sixty if he was a day, so he was entitled to take it easy.

"Martin, *conas atá tú*? What's the word, Sarge? Hey, nice to meet you earlier. I enjoyed that," I called out, cheekily sticking my head through the open doorway.

"Uh, Luke. How'd yer interview end up?" O'Boyle inquired

with a start, raising his head up from some report he was pretending to read. "That Italian still seemed to think it's okay to feed a Christian lad like you to the lions, I'd say. No craic at all, was he?"

"No, I suppose not. It didn't go good. I think I got those sums all wrong! Sure, I'll try again in a few years' time, Sarge . . ."

"Ah, don't be thinkin' like that, Luke Waters. It probably went better than you thought. How is Big Mike Collins these days, by the way? Been a bit busy lately and haven't seen him in a while," O'Boyle said casually.

As I stood there, it hit me. This must be the fella Collins reached out to, not one of the captains. At least he tried. Pity this old-timer had no juice.

Before I could make a further fool of myself, a civilian clerk click-clacked across the office.

"Excuse me, Chief," Ms. Heels said out of my eyeline, "there's a call for you. Line one."

Chief? Good grief! *Chief!* Oh, God.

"Thank you. I'll take the call in a moment," the chief replied, raising a hand in recognition to the secretary before turning around and shooting me a conspiratorial wink.

I was talking to Martin O'Boyle, no sergeant but chief of Narcotics.

"Actually, I made it past sergeant, Luke. They were stuck for a CO around here, and they're naggin' me to stay around a while longer. We're stuck for a bit of help up there in the Heights, too, so you might get a call to join us yourself soon enough, eh? Oh, it will depend on your interviewers, of course, but you never know."

Juice? O'Boyle had more of it than Tropicana. And I had my transfer, learning later that Collins and O'Boyle had been close friends since Big Mike was working his own way up the ladder years earlier.

The next morning I got a message—report to your new assignment, training as a Narcotics investigator, over at the Army Terminal in Brooklyn. I was several years closer to that coveted detective's gold shield in one giant step, or, to be more accurate, a single stumble.

CHAPTER EIGHT

KRUSTY

There were so many things that could save your life. One of them was listening to your sergeant.

"Here's an easy five hours, you guys," Krusty says with satisfaction as we cruise past the corner of Dyckman and Tenth Avenue one morning early in 2000.

Sergeant Keith Kollmer is known as "Krusty" to the eight of us on his Narcotics Field Team. He has the looks, locks, and peculiar rasping voice, and just like *The Simpsons'* cynical clown, he's no soft touch.

Outside one of the apartments our sarge has just spotted a man, age about twenty, sitting on a stoop smoking a blunt: a large hollowed-out cigar which users fill with everything from marijuana to heroin or even PCP (angel dust), meaning they can be meek and mellow or a primed grenade, ready to explode at the slightest provocation.

Usually when you approach a suspect taking drugs they make a run for it, but this mope is only interested in the dope between his lips, and to judge by the wheelchair a couple of feet away, he probably wouldn't get too far before we caught up.

We pull up to the sidewalk, our supervisor keen as ever for us to hit our overtime quota.

"Geddup," Krusty rasps.

"Can't . . . can't you see I's . . . par-paralyzed?" he gasps, drawing the fumes from the torpedo deep into his lungs and nodding to the chair, just visible behind the hallway door.

"Thaz ma wheels."

"Oh, yeah? How did you get from there to here, then?" I ask the guy, whose name, we learn, is Daniel Rodriguez.

"Crawled," Rodriguez replies, still gasping, eyes glazed over. "I like to . . . sit here, look like everyone else, man. Heps . . . heps me pretend . . . well, you know, Offica, pretend I's normal," he explains.

This guy isn't going to be much of a threat, and my partner George Weir and I relax a little, too. Life had dealt Rodriguez a tough break, and here we are, breaking his balls over a tiny amount of dope. Staring down at him sitting helplessly on the porch, I shift uncomfortably from one foot to the other.

"Jaysus, maybe we should turn a blind eye, just this once?" I suggest to my partner.

"Yeah, I think we will, buddy," Weir replies, tapping his cuffs against his belt and arching an eyebrow to our supervisor, waiting for the nod to go back to the car.

"Naw, forgetaboutit. Our numbers are low today. Guy is a user. Pick him up and cuff him up. Five hours is five hours, George."

What a heartless bastard Krusty is.

I carry Rodriguez to the car, and as I "toss" him—search him for contraband and weapons, standard procedure before we transport him back to our hub site in the 25th Precinct for processing—all thoughts that we're dealing with a con man or a gunman disappear as his legs flop uselessly from side to side.

"It's all good, Offica," says Rodriguez with a dopey, understanding smile, arms around me, as I place him carefully in the backseat. This guy might be a user, but clearly he's also a gentleman. "Don' worry 'bout it. The Man gotta do what the Man gotta do."

We're about to pull away when Sergeant Kollmer turns to George to remind him what to do. He'd forgotten our perp's wheelchair, though, strangely, Rodriguez seems happier to simply leave it behind.

"Hey! The kid's wheels—throw 'em in the trunk, you guys, will ya?"

Weir nods, stepping into the hallway and grabbing the wheelchair seat to lift it out over the stoop, causing the soft seat cushion to slide to the floor. It lands with a metallic clink.

"Jesus! Gun! I got a gun here!" George calls out, holding up the "Deuce Five."

These .25-caliber semiautomatic handguns were originally designed as "pocket pistols" about a hundred years ago and carried for personal protection. Useless from a distance, their small profile has one advantage: they are very easy to hide, which makes them the perfect choice for a surprise, close-up kill. Although the tiny-caliber bullet lacks any real stopping power, from a few feet away it will often bounce around inside a human head and break up as it dissipates energy, causing catastrophic brain damage.

Rodriguez is doped to his eyeballs, and if he had made it back to that chair to retrieve the gun when he saw us approaching, he could have easily shot me in the face when I leaned in to pick him up. Criminals don't risk packing a piece, preferring to stash larger weapons such as .38 revolvers, Glocks, and shotguns under dumpsters, where they run to if chased. Our gunman wasn't going anywhere, so he kept his shooter close at hand, a sharp reminder that there are no rules on the street. Even under the ever-vigilant Krusty we'd become ring-rusty, assuming we had nothing to fear from a kid in a wheelchair.

"You guys!" Kollmer rasps. "I keep telling you, stay focused.

NYPD GREEN

You can't trust these perps." Back at the station, we charge Rodriguez on the narcotics and the weapon—the latter is a serious felony in New York City—but our efforts are in vain. Soon after, a judge rules against the admissibility of the gun, which wasn't in plain sight. The NYPD should have applied for a search warrant before George Weir overstepped the line, and the stoop, as he reached for the chair. The judge doesn't elaborate on whether it was better to also leave the .25, which looks and feels like a toy, where a child could find it and shoot one of the other neighborhood kids. But the law is the law, even if it doesn't always make a lot of sense.

After my "fast-tracking" interview, I had arrived up at Northern Manhattan Initiative (NMI) in 1997, after a three-week crash course in narcotics in a prefab at the old Brooklyn Army Terminal in Sunset Park. Our instructors taught us how to identify different drugs and to operate B&Bs (buy and busts) and classic sting operations where drugs and dealers are swept up by undercover teams.

We also learned how to run snitches, an essential part of gathering intelligence on the street.

When I was promoted to Narcotics, my assumption was I'd gotten the promotion because the Brass were looking for bright, motivated young cops to fight on the front lines of the War on Drugs, and Washington Heights, where we would operate, would certainly live up to my expectations. What wouldn't was the day-to-day grind of the work. Millions of dollars of federal money had been poured into policing the drug problem, but, as I would discover, Narcotics was all about containment and all about the numbers and money, with set targets decided each day. Most arrests targeted pathetic habitual users carrying very small amounts of drugs, although that didn't make the perps

78

any less dangerous. We were firefighting, basically, caught in a revolving door that never stopped.

Our HQ was a low-rise at 107th Street and Lexington Avenue, bordered by a basketball court on one side and a busy thoroughfare on the other. As far as the locals were concerned, the most that was happening in this nondescript building was the processing of parking-fine notices. Keeping routine administration on the ground floor was a deliberate ploy by OCCB to stay below the radar, but if you pressed the correct code into the keypad on the door, an elevator took you to an upper story where the narrative dramatically changed.

On my first day I stepped from the lift into a fully operational squad room identical to that found in any regular borough precinct. The first person I met was Kollmer, who ran the Narcotics Field Team made up of about six or seven investigators in addition to myself and George Weir. It included, at various times, Mike Boyle, Eric Katinas, Greg McCarthy, Jose Ramos, Tony Agnelli, Juan Diaz, and two undercovers named Eddie Ramos and Rob Chang.

After the usual introductions Krusty called a TAC (tactical assignment) meeting, where we discussed the day's operation. Top of the agenda was not what we were doing on the streets or who we were about to arrest. The main concern was money. Our money.

"Okay, who needs overtime?" said our sarge, working out his calculations before deciding how many arrests he would need. Each perp is worth five hours per officer. It's a lesson right from the outset that drugs are all about "the green," no matter which side of the line you are on.

Washington Heights was a sea of dope and reeling in a catch was simple but dangerous. The neighborhood acted as

the distribution center for the South American cartels importing product, and literally millions of dollars were circulating
in the neighborhood twenty-four hours a day. It was impossible to know exactly how many dealers operated there: some
estimates put it at five thousand, with three hundred "outside
spots" where the dope was pushed—plus another hundred
crack houses where you could get high more discreetly. Stopping all of this was like trying to empty a bathtub with a tea-
spoon with the faucet running.

Federal money was freed up to help New York City try to
stem the tide, and many of the cops drafted in ended up in
Field Teams, just like mine, while the DEA (Drug Enforcement
Administration), the IRS (Internal Revenue Service), the FBI,
ATF (Bureau of Alcohol, Tobacco, Firearms and Explosives), the
Secret Service, U.S. Customs, and even Immigration sent agents
to work in their new Command HQ.

These agencies came together to form the El Dorado Task
Force, and innovative techniques were introduced whereby
federal laws rather than local statutes were used to put the dealers behind bars. Different indirect approaches combined effectively, such as on-the-spot checks for green cards or the more
elaborate Geographical Targeting Order (GTO) initiative, which
aimed to stop dealers from laundering money, a move which
drastically changed wire-transfer reporting procedures. The
law was altered to ensure money-transfer agents must report
transactions in excess of $750, not a huge ceiling but well above
the average $200 to $500 for legitimate transmissions. These
changes forced major dealers to go back to using couriers to
transfer money, so-called "drug mules," who were then placed
under surveillance by the feds. In some cases they uncovered

criminals far closer to home, as some of my NYPD colleagues were eventually caught in the same net.

While the FBI and other agencies dealt with the bigger picture, our day-to-day revolved around narcotics sweeps, and on my first day I was designated arresting officer. This meant I rode along with Krusty in the unmarked leader car to our RV—rendezvous point—about five miles away at 155th Street and Riverside Drive, a notorious Heights address.

The other members of our team were also given their assignments, and a few jumped into the P-van—a minivan handy for transporting prisoners back to the hub site, where we would process the perps we hooked—while others rode in the chase car, an unmarked Ford. The undercovers (UCs) had already arrived at the location in style, driving a luxury Mercedes with out-of-state tags which helped to sell the deception. They used the time to source suspects, which they tipped us off about over the radio in code, starting with "steers," usually drug addicts themselves, who don't sell but direct customers to crack houses or other less public areas in return for a baggie or two.

On my first day I got to grips with the KELL—a wire, basically—a receiver and recorder which picked up signals from the inbuilt heart monitors worn by our UCs: any sudden rise in levels would show us that the deal had turned sour, and part of my job was to flag this immediately to Kollmer, who would order us to either abort or move in, guns drawn. The KELL could be concealed in anything—a necklace, a pen, a ring. There was also a "booster," placed, say, in a decoy yellow cab parked outside the building where the deal was taking place, to boost the signal from the UCs.

Simpler signals were also used. For example, if the dealer

was armed, our guy might joke: "Hey, man—you packin' in yo' pants, or are you jus' happy to see me?" letting us know where he liked to hide his weapon.

On B&Bs we were lucky to have Chang and Ramos, since the Brass often used officers straight out of the police academy because they didn't yet walk, talk, or look too much like cops. But Washington Heights was no place for rookies to risk their lives and learn the ropes. One mistake could get them, and you, killed.

Working undercover is a stressful, thankless job, and experience counts. Thankfully my pasty Irish complexion and accent meant it was a role I'd never play. Chang fit right in and this day he was acting as the buyer—the Uncle—with Ramos acting as the Ghost, a job that required him not only to verbally guide us to the target, but also to shadow his partner and to act as primary backup if the shooting started. They would alternate these roles from time to time to remain focused.

Chang and Ramos would take as few chances as possible. They would have no contact whatsoever with us on the street, even using different entrances and exits in our building, because in the Heights a dealer would pick up on the slightest glance and make us all out in a second.

I was still fiddling with the KELL in our car park when Eddie Ramos's voice crackled through the speaker.

"Guys, I got a positive, 110th Street and Lex," he said. Succinct, to the point.

"Ten-four," Kollmer cooed into the radio. "Okay, you guys, suit up," he ordered the team. "We got a live one here!"

It only took a minute to drive to the location and about another thirty seconds to identify ourselves to the unhappy customer, who was cuffed and loaded in the P-van.

That day our Field Team needed five arrests to hit our overtime target. Not four, not six. Five.

"Easy pickings," our sarge chuckled, rubbing his hands together. "Four to go."

We made another arrest before spotting a woman smoking crack from a pipe, which we recovered and charged her with possession of a controlled substance.

Then it was back in the vehicles again and not long before another known junkie was spotted, stopped, and collared, then put in the P-van with the others. It was another routine, forgettable arrest, but one more body towards our quota.

The day was going well. Two to go.

We were back in the vehicles again and a few minutes later, as we rolled past the corner of St. Nicholas Avenue and 181st Street, my passenger spotted someone blowing his nose. Maybe this guy had a cold. Krusty believed it paid to be suspicious. And for his team, it did.

"Hey! You see that? What's this idiot got? Looks like coke to me," he said, pointing to the pedestrian. We jumped out and found a small box of cocaine, a simple misdemeanor arrest but good for our overtime target.

Mr. Sniffles was handcuffed and placed in the overcrowded P-van, as my attention returned to the KELL. Ramos was calling in another buy from a female Hispanic, this time at 204th Street and Post Avenue. He gave us a health warning before we arrived to arrest the suspect. Sure enough, as soon as we got there and tried to click the cuffs closed, the junkie started kicking, screaming, and cursing, just like the last time she was arrested. A couple of us wrestled her to the ground, where I struggled to hog-tie her ankles to her wrists. Now immobilized, Ms. Scuffles was patted down for weapons and placed in the van with the other mopes.

"Okay, that's number five. We've got our bodies, let's shut it down." Krusty sighed with satisfaction as I brushed the dust off my jeans. "Welcome to the exciting world of Narcotics, Waters."

My first day was nothing remarkable—we made twelve arrests on another particularly busy shift and we could make fifty if the manpower and overtime for it were sanctioned.

The actual arrests were only the start. The team members assigned to the P-van fingerprinted the collars and transported them to court, while the officers in the chase car vouchered the prisoners' property, either putting it into safekeeping or evidence, and helped me with the reams of paperwork which take up most of any cop's time and pay a lot of his mortgage.

This was the workplace, the marketplace—or for Chang and Ramos the stage—where we plied our trade.

Ricky Schroder, a child star from the movie *The Champ* and the eighties sitcom *Silver Spoons*, spent a day with us as a "ride-along" civilian observer, to help prepare for his new role in the hit show *NYPD Blue*. He was keenly aware that on-screen, just like on the street, small details matter, revealing that he often spent his downtime downtown, sitting in a sedan opposite a police station, making notes on the cops' mannerisms and behavior, and was taken with how one Mick patted himself.

"I like the way you do that. What's the reason?" he asked me, slapping his waist and groin as he demonstrated the move.

"Janey, I'd never thought about it, but, sure, I suppose I'm checking for my radio and my piece," I mused.

"You cops all do that, constantly. You ever notice?" Schroder enthused. "I like it. I think I'll borrow it for my character if you have no objection, Officer Waters."

"Feck it. Sure, why not?"

Sure enough, "Detective Sorenson" used the move through-out the next two and a half seasons on the show.

Chang and Ramos were the best actors I ever saw, walking the walk, talking the talk, wearing the right gold chains, flashing the correct tattoos, driving the proper sort of car, and most of all staying cool, all within a couple of feet of the harshest of critics: dealers who would put a bullet in their brain if they knew the truth; but success came at a price. Our UCs had been too close to too many arrested dealers, as they were occasionally reminded.

"You Five-O, homey! Ain't got nothin' for you!" was the slap-in-the-face response Chang got when he appeared on a corner one day, but he wasn't the sort of guy to turn the other cheek, and the dealer didn't get the chance to turn either of his before he was punched, full force, in the jaw, the blow sending him staggering backwards.

"Yeah? Well, I got that for you, motherfucker!" Chang snarled.

The short, sharp shock helped establish credibility, because on the street you never, ever show weakness. Stepping aside for somebody passing by on the sidewalk sends out a message that you are weak. Chang's usually got through.

"You callin' me a liar, you fat bastard? Gimme a bag! I be here for biznizz, not bullshit. Look like I give a crap 'bout you problems, homes?" the cop continued as the guy rubbed his face, figuring he must have made a mistake.

He was about to.

The deal was done. Another score for Chang. Cha-ching! Another five hours for us. The game went into overtime as the Ghost called in the good news from the shadows. A few blocks away we would pick up the pusher, still rubbing his bruised ego, the blue mark a reminder as he sat in the cells to always trust your instincts.

The B&B arrests were as strictly choreographed as any Broadway show, and after a few years they became boring and bullshit as far as I was concerned. The repetitive nature of our work meant it was easy to become depressed by the predictability of it all. Most users rely on crime to feed their habits, so they get up early and steal as much as possible, or prostitute themselves as often as necessary, to buy the junk their bodies crave, and as a result drugs play a large part in every cop's workload.

As part of a Field Team you have a good idea not only how many arrests you will make the following day, but what kind of dope you are going to find, too. If the statistics for seizures of a particular drug are below the expectations, your focus will change.

"How come it's all PCP and marijuana this month?" someone from the Brass will demand, waving a computer printout at one of his captains. "Where's all the goddam coke and heroin gone? Get me more coke and heroin!"

So for the following month we would concentrate on coke and heroin sales, and a month later it was back to PCP and marijuana again. No matter the orders, you always kept an eye out for crack, an ever-present scourge in the Heights, hooking users the first or second time they smoke it. Crackheads build up a tolerance to the drug within a few hits and begin to take more and more to try to reach that first great high, like a puppy chasing his tail. Ten years before I joined, the head of OCCB was clear about the threat it posed to society across all communities and tax brackets. "It doesn't matter if you're white, black, or Hispanic, or whether you have a white-collar job or are unemployed. Crack is the drug of choice," O'Boyle explained to a *New York Daily News* reporter.

The effects of crystallized cocaine are devastating on so many different levels, as a look through Tammy Black's arrest record showed. Tammy was tall, thin, and glamorous when we first hooked her up in the Heights, a woman who once literally had the world at her feet. Walking through our hub site, she turned heads, clearly out of place amongst the usual junkies and degenerates, but after a few more arrests she started to fit in. Within a year nobody could tell the former American Airlines air hostess from the part-time prostitutes, as her life collapsed, as her teeth fell out one by one, and as her worn-out clothes hung from her scrawny, scarecrow frame.

One morning Krusty and I were the only ones interested in overtime, so we partnered up and headed southbound on Riverside Drive, close to the corner of West 146th Street, where we spotted four Hispanic males walking in a beeline, single file, about ten feet apart.

"This looks wrong, Sarge," I said to my supervisor, who was at the wheel. "Turn around and we'll check these guys out."

We didn't hear any protests from our suspects, not that they had much choice, since we had them at gunpoint, and within seconds we recovered a loaded pistol, a 9mm this time, and a couple of "elbows" of cocaine, about two and a half pounds in weight, worth up to a hundred thousand dollars, depending on how it was cut. Amongst drug-dealing punks, quality control isn't such a priority, and product will always be heavily diluted with chalk, sugar, and any other bulking agents handy.

It was a great result and seemed like a slam dunk for us, but the assistant DA raised concerns as soon as I flopped the file on his desk.

"We may have a problem with this one, guys," our prosecutor said, poring over the details of the arrest.

"Officer Waters, you didn't have reasonable grounds to run a stop-and-search on these men. Their lawyers are going to say that you breached their constitutional rights by doing so. I can't pursue this."

We manfully argued our side, but the ADA had made his decision, and the Riverside boys walked back to their turf to help Tammy Black and her friends take one step closer to their long-drawn-out suicides. It wasn't the first time we felt frustrated with the laxity in the DA's office, and it wouldn't be the last.

After four years in OCCB I finally got my gold shield and soon found myself posted to a detective squad in Melle Mel's old stomping ground, the 42nd Precinct, in the heart of the South Bronx, the maddest, baddest place in NYC, before eventually moving up to Bronx Homicide. Tragically Kollmer wouldn't be joining me. Having a guy called Krusty based in a squad room at Simpson Street would be the ultimate gag.

I left Narcotics believing that we had made a difference in the War on Drugs, but it was only later that I discovered our efforts were undermined by fellow officers who were working just as hard to send the dope we seized out the back door into the arms, and lungs, of addicts. The motivator, as ever, was "the green."

As far as I was aware, Lieutenant John Maguire was a good cop and a fellow Irishman, and I was closer to him—literally—than I was to my own supervisor in many ways, because he spent more time sitting with the two investigators under his direct command, Thomas Rachko and Julio Vasquez, whose desks were near mine, than in his office, fretting about when he would make captain like any normal Lou (as lieutenants were universally known).

His hands-on approach made sense when it became clear

that a lot of the drugs and money they stole would end up feathering Maguire's retirement nest a couple of years later. Their racket only came to light when Rachko, by then retired himself on his departmental pension with seventeen years' service, and Vasquez, who had been promoted to detective second grade and transferred to the Firearms Investigation Unit, ran out of luck.

Rachko and Vasquez were stopped by members of the El Dorado Task Force after the two men had pulled over a courier carrying $169,000, totally unaware that the courier was a confidential informant under surveillance by the task force. The duo remained calm and the feds were at first taken in by the NYPD raid jackets and their appropriately contrite attitude, particularly when they dropped Maguire's name to help smooth things over, blaming the lack of notification of their "operation" on a communications mix-up back at the station.

El Dorado swallowed it, until one of their team picked up the phone and tried to hook up with the cops' supposed supervisor.

"I don't understand. Lieutenant Maguire is retired. Lucky SOB is over in Ireland. Least that was the last I heard," the puzzled police officer on the other end of the line explained. The phone was barely back in the handset before another call was made, this time to the Internal Affairs Bureau (IAB). IA is ruthless, particularly in Narcotics, where the temptation is clearly there. The NYPD conducts credit checks on all MOS, especially Narcotics, to make sure you don't give in to this temptation, but once IA is involved, all bets are off. You never know when you might be set up. You might take drugs from a perp's car, and if you don't voucher for the correct amount, you're in big trouble.

Rachko and Vasquez were quickly arrested, and their old colleague, who had indeed retired to Ireland, was also arrested as soon as he returned to New York. Now facing lengthy prison terms, the dirty cops soon became the "Three Tenors," singing like canaries to get reduced sentences.

John Maguire, who held a degree from Columbia University, admitted to his part in the scam, and to actively conspiring with several men under his command in dozens of other shakedowns, personally ripping off guys the rest of us were trying to catch. In one case he had stolen $100,000 a dealer had hidden in a cereal box. I could never look at a box of Lucky Charms the same way again. I'd never realized it could contain a real pot of gold, though I was a little more particular than Maguire about where my money came from. My view always was if your pension is worth a million dollars to you, it's not worth stealing a million.

The Three Tenors were in the spotlight, and so was I and every cop they worked with, as IAB brought attention to their arrests. Eventually nine other cops were arrested in the cleanup, including Detective Carlos Rodriguez and Detective Eric Wolfe, both of whom I had also worked alongside, never suspecting that all these men were far bigger perps than the miserable addicts I spent two years chasing down and shoving into the P-van.

That gold shield I rubbed for luck between my finger and thumb didn't bring any magical powers and didn't confer integrity on the man or woman carrying it, either, as I would be reminded throughout my years on the Job.

CHAPTER NINE

UNCHARTED WATERS

"...five...four...three...two...one..." The cop's countdown abruptly ends with the screech of a rocket, momentarily lighting up the windows of the precinct.

He braces himself against the wall, arms outstretched. To his left and right, two other detectives, one dressed in a SWAT ballistic helmet, another in a bright blue Kevlar vest, take similar cover, as a cacophony of explosions replaces the usual clatter of computer keys and rumble of conversation.

On December 31, 2001, Billy Brower isn't taking any chances. He's wearing both. So far we've had a quiet shift in the Detective Squad of the 42nd Precinct. Even criminals take a break to celebrate New Year's Eve.

Cue another loud crack from a nearby rooftop, followed by two more in quick succession. There's no way these are .44s, or .38s, either. They sound more like rifle rounds, and the next burst sends my ankles in the air and my backside crashing to the floor. I'd fallen for it after all.

"Jaysus Christ, they're shooting up the station!" I roar from the floor, cowering behind the nearest wastepaper basket as further bursts of fire light up a nearby window. My colleagues all seem remarkably calm despite the fact that we are probably about to be overrun by a bunch of gangbangers in a scene straight out of *Assault on Precinct 13*.

"Relax, buddy," George Chin reassures me, protected by the safety of a stairwell, well out of range of ricochets. "Locals ain't trying to break in. They celebratin'. Lettin' loose a few rounds from the rooftops, just for fun, as you do. They won't shoot into the station. Well . . . they probably won't shoot in here . . ."

This is how they like to party in the maddest square mile of New York City. The people in the academy forgot to put this sort of stuff in the *Patrol Guide*.

Six months earlier I'd stood outside the 42nd Precinct, surveying the place where I would spend my first posting as a newly promoted NYPD detective. Even then I couldn't help thinking there was something a little odd about this place. Turns out it was stark-raving bonkers, and half the people who hung around the place were the same, including most of those wearing badges.

Not that it mattered too much.

After I'd left Narcotics, Mike Collins explained that I would only be based in the 42 for a couple of weeks. The chief of detectives was under pressure to increase numbers here in the Bronx and over in Brooklyn, another high-crime area—both far different from the 25, where I had asked to be posted for family reasons. A few years ago I had yearned for the action of an A-house like this, but I was married now, living up in Brewster, an hour's drive north of the city, with Sue and our new baby daughter, Tara. While excitement was all very well, Manhattan was a borough both familiar and convenient. It was time to be practical. The hours would never change because we were always on overtime. On an average shift there would be five investigators, supervised by one sergeant; if your shift was from six a.m. to two p.m., five hours would automatically be added to that shift as overtime. At the time, Operation Condor was under way, and if we didn't use the federal money allocated to it we lost it, so if we arrested someone on a Friday and they were to appear in court on the Monday, we'd be "on the clock" for all of that time, making the most of it. But even if I still had to put in the long hours, at least in the 25 I'd have a quick train journey home.

From a distance my temporary home in the 42 looked exactly the same as any other precinct house in the ghetto, but as I stood in the chill morning staring at the facade, I couldn't help wondering why "36" was carved above the door in large numerals. The madness didn't end at that false front, either. Twenty years earlier *Fort Apache, The Bronx*, starring Paul Newman, had been filmed here, and every so often a tour bus halted outside the front door and a guide would step off and start a running commentary for the benefit of the movie buffs piling out.

Undercovers learn to keep their collars up and their heads down—by contrast, my problem was getting someone to notice me. I started with the sergeant behind the desk, who had more important things on his mind, like baseball.

"Hello, boss, Detective Luke Waters reporting for duty," I announced with a salute, tapping my gold shield with my index finger.

The sarge's nose remained in the sports section of the newspaper.

A tall, thin Hispanic man in a white suit and a crumpled trench coat with a detective shield pinned to the flared left lapel was paying more attention. He was eyeing me up from behind the security barrier separating public from police, flashing a toothless grin as I stood waiting for the guy behind the desk to finish checking the Yankees' batting game.

Another thirty seconds passed. I coughed politely. Nothing. I cleared my throat loudly.

Something. The sarge finally stared at me, before nodding to Columbo a few feet away.

"Detective Waters, eh? So, you're our new DT. Well, well. Bobby, I got a assignment for yah. Take Detective Waters here and show him up to the squad."

"Yes, sir!" replied my Hispanic colleague. "Follow me, DT," and he disappeared out the front door.

For a moment I looked after him. The man with the stripes on his sleeve let out a sarcastic laugh and resumed his reading.

Sarges could be sadists. Most were simply bastards, taking a personal delight in torturing detectives, particularly rookies like me.

"Er, great, boss. Thanks," I replied, walking out the door after Bobby, who stood waiting, his trench coat flapping wide open despite the cold weather.

"We gotta go to deh squat," he said, a single tooth defiantly protruding from behind his lower lip. The man had a speech impediment, rather odd for a detective dealing with the public on a daily basis, but it was probably from a shooting, I reasoned. The sarge had put me in the hands of a hero, the sort of guy so dedicated to the Job that he continued to fight the good fight.

My companion walked a few yards around the corner with me three steps behind, stopping at the door of the precinct's garage, pausing to press a button on the intercom. He missed. He tried again. Closer, but still no cigar.

Sticking his tongue out in concentration he gave it one more go, and this time finally landed thumb on plastic with a loud buzz. Clearly that shooting had damaged his coordination, too. What a guy.

"Detective Bobby Rivera. Got a . . . got a orda to go up to deh squat. Got deh new guy—Rivers—wimme. I jus' got . . . got grade, an' I caught annudah Hom-iss-side," he mumbled proudly into the box.

"Ten-four, Bobby!" the voice on the other end confirmed with a laugh, as the door creaked open.

We went in, took a right up the staircase, and climbed two flights of steps, reeking with the unforgettable scent of pine disinfectant, before reaching the open doorway to the 42 squad. I paused a moment to take it in.

My pause for posterity was lost on Bobby.

"Hey, whad'ya . . . whad'ya waitin' fuh?" he said, flashing me his toothy grin once more as he stared in fascination at the Smith & Wesson on my hip. I shifted uncomfortably. Maybe letting this guy return to duty so early wasn't such a good idea.

I stepped over the threshold and immediately spotted two men whose lives would intertwine with mine just about every day of the four years of my "temporary" posting, during which I would learn more about policing than a cop discovers in an entire career answering dog calls down in Manhattan.

To the left was my new "Lou," Lieutenant Frank Visconti, a middle-aged Italian who was, according to the grapevine, calm, mild-mannered, and a true leader, admired by all the men under his command.

"Luke Waters? Well, hello to you. Welcome to the 42, we're real glad to have you on board. We'll be seeing a lot of each other over the next while." My new CO beamed, shaking my hand.

To the right of Visconti stood another DT, about the same age, clumps of white curly hair sticking out from underneath his Yankees baseball cap. The boss introduced him as Billy Bruzack.

I extended my hand and got as far as my usual greeting: "H-e-y, buddy." For the second time that morning it was ignored. Billy had spotted Bobby, who'd been standing behind me during the initial introductions, his eyes now switched from my pistol to the other DT's holstered piece.

The guy was clearly a gun nut. It was also apparent that Detective Rivera and Detective Bruzack didn't quite get on.

"Rivera! You dipstick! Stop lookin' at my piece! Get outta this station right now, before I kick your ass!" Billy bellowed.

Visconti was frowning, hands on hips, looking around the squad room, which, buzzing with conversation earlier, had suddenly fallen silent.

"Rivera! Who buzzed him in? Do you guys hear me? Who's playin' around here?" Lou demanded, while over his shoulder Billy Bruzack was now chasing Bobby down the stairs, the hallways echoing with swear words.

"I'll leave you to settle in. Billy will show you the ropes. We'll talk later, Detective," Visconti said.

New York City raised the hyphen to cult status. Everyone here is African-American, Italian-American, or Irish-American, and now, having dashed after Bobby, Billy invoked the hyphen to new and impressive effect.

"That retard! Son-of-a-bitch-shit-for-brains-motherfuckin' asshole!" he fumed, finally flopping into a chair opposite me. "Sorry about that—Luke?—that Puerto Rican dimwit really yanks my chain. Hey, man. Nice to meet you. Did Lou tell ya? I'm your new partner."

The silence which followed was long and embarrassing. There was nothing else for it. I needed to ask him about the bad blood between him and the other detective, but the question was, how do I casually introduce it into our conversation?

"What's with the bad blood between you and the other detective, Billy?"

"Detective?" Billy replied, his eyes widening incredulously, his lip curling in contempt. "Detective! Rivera? That retard ain't no cop, Luke. He's a nut. Guy hung around so long that one of our assholes gave him a badge. You see any number on it, like ours? No, you didn't, 'cos all his says is 'DEA': 'Detective Endowment Association'!" Billy continued, warming to his theme. "Swapped it with the tooth fairy for all his teeth, if you ask me. Trouble is, the fairy took his brain, too. And believe me, that poor fuckin' fairy got ripped off!"

"Eh? Come on! What's he doing behind the barrier with the sarge?" I asked, my turn for eyes to widen.

"Hell knows! Some of these guys think it's funny to have Rivera around. He helps 'em with their reports. Fills in the paperwork, until he comes to the end of the line and writes the rest on the desk! You didn't spot his hearing aid, Luke? Deaf as well as dumb. Anyways, fuck him. Hey, let me introduce you to the other guys . . ."

It was a scene straight out of the fictional Fort Apache when Captain Duggan, tired of the madness, finally let it rip.

"What do you think of that son of a bitch, huh? That clown they dress up as a cop. That fuckin' banana. I mean, who does he think he's playin' with, some chickenshit?"

Bobby Rivera might be the oddest guy to hang around the station, but my new partner, Billy Bruzack, wasn't your typical street DT, either. Over the following weeks I learned that his nemesis, Rivera, was like Rain Man when it came to memorizing the New York Penal Code, which he could quote ad nauseum, but struggled with everyday tasks such as making a phone call. A hospital, or sheltered accommodation, was the proper place for Bobby, not inside the barrier of the local police station, where he would occasionally approach distraught complainants. Often they took him for a real cop, as he nodded sympathetically and scribbled meaninglessly in a notebook before finally rising to his feet and calling them a muddafucka as he remembered his real goal—getting back up to the squad and swiping someone's gun.

As far as I know he never achieved that ambition.

Bobby was more obsessed with finding guns than the ATF, and his search didn't end at the station. On one occasion coming into the Bronx courts I spotted him using the handheld wand, a metal detector designed to scan visitors for weapons, on the line of people, letting some through and pulling others aside for a chat. It was pretty clear that the Brass knew what was going on and simply played along with the gag, but bosses from outside the borough hadn't been let in on the joke, and when they first met our "challenged" detective the results were often hilarious, particularly when Bobby donned his NYPD sash every St. Patrick's Day and worked as a parade marshal.

You couldn't get rid of Bobby, because he summed up the 42 perfectly and, whatever his mental disability, our parade marshal picked up far more than he was letting on.

Nothing here was as it seemed. Even the station's nickname turned out to be a lie.

The 42 wasn't "Fort Apache" at all—at least not if you asked my buddy Sergeant Umlauft and his colleagues in Bronx Homicide over on Simpson Street, where much of the movie's other scenes were shot and where the cops insisted that it was their house. During the filming, many locals, tired of the constant portrayal of the community as a stereotypical crime-ridden, violent ghetto, mounted a protest. Unfortunately one of them also climbed up onto the roof and was so pissed off that he dropped the toilet which he happened to be carrying down on the moviemakers. The director liked the image of porcelain clashing with pavement so much, he added the shot to the movie.

In the South Bronx, fantasy and reality were always hard to separate.

Bobby and his presence around the house was also a bugbear of DT Billy Brower, the other Billy in the precinct, who was known as "Mighty Whitey" throughout the borough.

Brower's attitude toward life could be summed up by the picture pinned behind his computer. Most cops kept photos of wives, girlfriends, wives and girlfriends, their kids, pets, or the-boat-they-were-never-going-to-buy which they would take down and kiss when the going got tough. Mighty Whitey? A photo of himself—dressed in an old East German police uniform and WWII flying goggles. Carrying a rocket-propelled grenade.

He was a bigger nut than Bobby.

Brower and I would go through memorable times together, from the horrors of the 9/11 attack to chasing disabled gunmen along local streets. He had the uncanny ability to sum up the vagaries of life, and the Job, in a single sentence.

"Being 'shineboxed,' buddy?" our resident philosopher mused. "Means that you just got shitcanned. Being shitcanned? Hmmm. Well, lemme see . . . it's just a polite way of being told: 'Go screw yaself. Have a nice day, but have it somewhaz else!' "

Maybe the reason nobody in this joint ever bothered to take that "36" down from the front door of the precinct was that it was the ultimate scam. The more you confused the public, the more likely it was that they would take their uninteresting complaint somewhere else. Up to Brooklyn. Or to a talk radio phone-in. Or even to Boston.

That was where my first homicide in the station ended up. It would take three years to close and be overshadowed by the greatest mass killing ever on American soil—an investigation which I and every detective on the Job would be drawn into over the coming months.

I am asleep at home in Brewster when my wife wakes me.

"Wake up, Luke. Come on, wake up! You'll want to see this. There's been a plane crash in Manhattan."

Sue is six months pregnant with our son, Ryan; our one-year-old, Tara, is teething on the cot in the corner. Nobody gets much shut-eye around our house during my early days in the 42, but after today nobody in the USA would sleep soundly for a long time.

I am exhausted from work but I mumble back to conscious-ness, stumble to my feet, and stagger into the living room, where Sue is already standing in front of the television set, which is broadcasting pictures of an aircraft embedded in the side of one of the Twin Towers of the World Trade Center.

I let out a deep sigh as the station replays the strike, and I am just about to fall back to bed when a new image flashes across the screen.

"Is that a replay?" I ask Sue. "This plane looks different."

"It is different, that's another altogether. It looks like a jumbo jet," she says, her hand reaching to cover her mouth as the shock hits home.

"Jesus Christ!" I shout. "How could they let that happen?" The question would echo around the world over the next few hours, as the footage of two Boeing 767s, United Airlines Flight 175 and

100

American Airlines Flight 11, slamming into the Twin Towers is replayed time and again on a billion TV sets worldwide.

I get dressed hurriedly as our landline and cell phones start to ring. Family and friends, from Boston, Melbourne, Dublin, checking if we are okay, asking me what has just happened. Right now, they know as much as I do, and I know as much as the news anchors, which is not too much.

What is clear is that America is under attack. We have no idea from whom, and I don't need the experts on CNN, Fox, or CBS to tell us that the United States is now, effectively, at war.

Until this point, the U.S.'s greatest fear is of a chemical attack. Police officers are trained in chemical warfare—we know that one pound of anthrax can kill one million New Yorkers. I say to Susan, "I gotta go to work. If there's any sign that this is a chemical attack, take Tara and drive north to Canada, take water, diapers, phone chargers . . ." I never get a call from the Job to report for duty. Every cop in the city knows the seriousness of what has just taken place, though what to do about it is a different matter. The car radio keeps me up to date with breaking news in the hour it takes me to reach the 42. When I reach the house the place is quieter than I have ever seen a police precinct.

September 11, 2001, rewrote all the rules, the entire playbook.

I found out that everyone had been relocated to Bronx Homicide, where a tactical meeting was about to be called. Hundreds of cops from the nearby precincts had converged on the three-story building. By the time I arrived they were all crowded around TVs as the experts struggled for explanations and the Environmental Protection Agency checked the air to see if nuclear or biological agents had been released over the city.

From that day on we all carried gas masks, with spares for our family members at home.

Our first two days after the attack could be summed up in three words. Sit. Watch. Wait. Every set was tuned to a different channel as we tried to get a fresh insight into what had just happened, and it was pretty clear that the Brass had no idea what to do.

Eventually, succumbing to exhaustion, we grabbed some sleep wherever we could. Our waking hours were dominated by two emotions: anger and frustration.

Almost every one of the cops present, irrespective of sex, age, rank, or background, wanted to kill whoever was responsible. Not arrest them. Kill them. Many cops volunteered to fight, including one of our team, Ray Rosado, a National Guard reservist who would later serve with the U.S. Army in Iraq. For the first time the hyphen, the brackets, disappeared. There was no African-American, Italian-American, or Irish-American in our ranks, nor a single Republican or Democrat, either, as President Bush appeared on TV vowing to capture those responsible.

We were not even, for once, cops. Just citizens all united in one common cause.

The initial feeling was one of confusion, during those early, fraught days, but once rumor solidified into cold, hard fact, the mood morphed to anger, then despair, quickly followed by an overwhelming, vicious desire for revenge. Every New Yorker took the attacks personally, no matter where we had been raised. This was an attack on our city, an attempt to turn our wives into widows, our kids into orphans. Cops who normally advised victims' kin to remain calm, and not to take the law into their own hands, happily volunteered to put a bullet in the head of those responsible: judge, jury, and executioner rolled into one. I was no different. Mixed with the anger and tears was a feeling of utter helplessness.

For once, the cops couldn't cope. The NYPD was not in charge. Nobody was in charge for a while, and when the smoke started to clear, it was obvious that America, land of the free and home of the brave, where personal freedom is cherished above all, was close to a state of martial law. The streets of the Big Apple were now run by camo-clad soldiers and Marines carrying assault rifles, their Humvees topped with .50-caliber machine guns, rather than police officers in puny sedans armed with nothing more than puny pistols and cans of Mace.

Within a couple of days we were moved to a facility that was seldom mentioned but had been designated as an alternate to One Police Plaza as police headquarters in the event of just such an emergency. Two Police Plaza was located in a former Budweiser plant on the outskirts of the city, the conveyor belts and bottling equipment replaced by generators, powerful mainframe computers, communications equipment, a canteen, and an armory. Right then the main tactic employed by the Brass was to keep us out of Manhattan, in case there was another bombing. They didn't know if there would be follow-up attacks, and if there were, what would be their target, and what form would they take? Would it be chemical? Biological? Nuclear? Standard explosives? More suicide attacks? At this stage it was just guesswork. These were the questions the city grappled with, and our orders were simple.

Stand by, wait for further instructions.

"I'm sick of this, buddy. Let's grab a car and go down to the towers and see if we can do something," Rosado suggested eventually. Myself and Billy Bruzack readily agreed, and five minutes later we were driving through streets now controlled by soldiers, M16 rifles slung over their shoulders. They checked our IDs and waved us past parked Humvees and trucks armed with machine guns. For people used to manning any checkpoints with pistols, this came as a surprise. We were no longer in charge of our own city, much of which was utterly unrecognizable.

New York has been destroyed countless times by Hollywood, but to see it happen for real left all three of us stunned into silence as the scene of utter devastation surrounded us on all sides. It was about thirty hours since the attack, and rubble was piled up everywhere, half-collapsed buildings pancaked onto streets, and giant concrete beams, still barely attached to their superstructure by the metal cables added for extra strength, were slowly swinging from side to side—creaking and groaning high above our heads as heavy smoke continued to billow into the air, thick with dust.

As we got closer to the center of the attack we could just make out the body bags lying in the streets, while our cruiser crawled past destroyed patrol cars, crushed fire trucks, and abandoned civilian vehicles, all blanketed in debris. The Hi-Viz strips on the jackets of FDNY (Fire Department of New York) members glowed through the dusk as they picked their way through the destruction with powerful flashlights, which hovered like fireflies on doorways, as they called out, in vain, for survivors.

The city was now in near-darkness apart from giant arc lights set up by the military which cut a swath through air thick with particles of deadly dust that would hasten the deaths of many on duty that day. Asbestos in old buildings and benzene from jet fuel are both known carcinogens, and rates of leukemia, lymphoma, thyroid, prostate, and blood cancers amongst the first responders as the towers fell all soared high above the usual averages in the years which followed, meaning that the true list of victims from 9/11 may never be known.

We grabbed Maglites and ditched the car, heading on foot

to 5 World Trade Center—a low-rise office block in the shadow of Tower Two, which though badly damaged by the explosion was still standing—climbing over the rubble, stumbling as we made our way down to the basement level on precarious, hastily erected walkways to find a scene cut-and-pasted from a Pathé newsreel about the London Blitz.

We scrambled helplessly, hopelessly through the basement but had to accept that there was nothing we could do for anyone buried there, and with the danger of further collapses, the three of us reluctantly picked our way back to the Buick and returned in silence to Two Police Plaza. We were soon put into twelve-hour shifts, a roster rearrangement which would last for the next six months and hasten the retirement of many cops over the following year.

New York City is full of reminders that the Dutch, not the English, were the first Europeans to settle here, from the colors of the state flag to the images on the NYPD shields. The Bronx, Brooklyn, and Staten Island all owe their names to new arrivals from the Netherlands, but nobody working on the 9/11 cleanup failed to be struck by the fact that the 1.8 million tons of rubble taken out of Ground Zero was destined for another place named by those emigrants, the eerily appropriate "Fresh Kills."

Temporary buildings had been erected on the western corner of Staten Island almost overnight to facilitate personnel from twenty-five agencies, including the NYPD, FDNY, Port Authority Police (PAPD), State Police, FBI, U.S. Secret Service, U.S. Coast Guard, and the U.S. Army, the latter supplying generators, lights, refrigerated trucks, and kitchen equipment as well as cooks, mechanics, medics, and anything else required. The Red Cross and the Salvation Army worked together to staff the

"Hilltop Café," serving up hot food and drinks every day to fifteen hundred city, state, and federal employees, as well as producing stress management booklets to help people traumatized by what we had to face.

Outside, the grim task of sifting through the rubble from "the Pile," as rescue workers referred to the site, continued. The debris was first trucked down to the piers and dumped into giant 130-foot-long barges, which were then floated down to Staten Island. Upon arrival, it was trucked once more to our 175-acre rubbish tip, now filled with cops and federal agents armed with rakes and plastic buckets.

I stood in one corner of the vast site, while thirty yards on either side Bruzack, Rosado, George Chin, Billy Brower, and Johnny MacMillan, along with other detectives and bosses from the 42, stood expectantly as cops from other precincts and agents from diverse federal agencies scattered throughout our sector waited for the signal to start digging and scraping.

We were all in white one-piece Tyvek HazMat coveralls overlaid with Hi-Viz vests. Our lungs were protected by half-face respirators fitted with HEPA (high-efficiency particulate air) filters, and our shoes remained behind in the changing huts, swapped for bright yellow steel-toe-capped rubber boots. Everyone was issued goggles, a hard hat, gloves, and heavy-duty ear protectors, but nothing could dispel the smell from the ever-growing mountain of despair, so gut-wrenching that it is difficult to put into words.

You controlled the urge to hurl as you started to rake and put any item of interest in a plastic bucket, which was later taken to the Crime Scene Hut, where it was examined, photographed, labeled, and bagged for transport. Top of our priority list were the "black boxes"—which despite their name are bright orange—the all-important flight recorders. Each of the

Boeing 767s was fitted with two of the devices, which are the size and proportions of a small toolbox—a voice recorder in the cockpit and a data recorder embedded close to the tail. None of the four was ever found.

The U.S. Secret Service, which lost an agent in the attack, helped with our efforts and showed us pictures of a safe containing weapons, cash, and other sensitive material which was in one of their offices destroyed in the blast, but if it was ever recovered we heard nothing about it.

As time moved on, other methods were used on the larger lumps of compacted debris, such as a giant spinning cylindrical separator which broke the material down into fragments before they were placed on conveyor belts, where cops, federal agents, and firefighters struggled to stay focused as they sifted through the detritus.

K-9 cops and agents moved up and down past me with cadaver dogs, while the FBI had a forensic anthropologist on site for more detailed examinations. The Job later assigned Deputy Commissioner Maureen Casey to take charge of the attempts to identify the 4,257 pieces of human remains eventually recovered, comparing any DNA which survived against that found on personal items donated by the families of victims, such as combs, hairbrushes, and toothbrushes.

That was our work for the next six months, and for the first few weeks we did nothing else, our investigations suspended while we concentrated on raking through rubble. The search turned up other evidence, too. More than thirteen pounds of narcotics were uncovered from material taken from the Pile, along with thousands of rounds of ammunition and over $76,000 in cash. I personally found hundreds of dollars, along with a police radio and part of a seat belt from one of the aircraft.

Standing there, looking at that cop's radio, I couldn't help thinking of the last words he or she spoke into it. Did I know that officer? Had we ever met? Would we ever catch Osama bin Laden and the al-Qaeda planners responsible for killing them? Sixty seconds later the radio was in my plastic bucket, on its way to the hut, and I returned to raking the mound once more.

I suspect a large amount of the material we were sent to sift through was never properly searched and simply dumped into a landfill.

The attack on the Twin Towers also allowed a lot of criminals in New York to escape justice. Normally, when you returned after a week away, your desk would be piled high with new files, but there was no extra paperwork in my in-tray when I was told to resume more routine investigations, as little new crime was investigated, and while the work in Fresh Kills progressed I spent two days a week suited up on site and the rest of the week juggling old cases.

But this was just one aspect of the 9/11 attacks. As defense and security spending soared, New York's finest were amongst the first to benefit, and our wage bill went through the roof because of the new duty rosters. Just about every DT on the Job was getting twenty-four hours' overtime in what had been his or her two days off, to which you could add on four hours' overtime during normal workdays, too.

Many detectives retired in the following months, some for personal reasons, but for most the decision was purely financial. Half of your earnings are matched by the taxpayer in your pension, so the overtime surplus following the attacks resulted in a far more generous package for officers approaching their last months on the Job. They decided to put in their papers before the city started to return to something approaching normality, knowing they would never be in such a strong position again.

After a few weeks of sifting through death and destruction at Fresh Kills, I was happy to get back to what passed for normal violence in the 42. I was only back at my desk a couple of weeks when I caught the first homicide of my career. Strangely, 9/11 would play a crucial part in that investigation, too. If it wasn't for the terrible events of that morning, the killer would never have been able to escape our clutches.

CHAPTER TEN

IT AIN'T OVER TILL IT'S OVER

My first big case in the 42 turned out to be one of the most memorable of my career. It took a twist right from the start when the victim died in full view of an incoming Homicide detective.

October 13, 2001: the 911 operator logs a call that a man has been slashed in the leg on the corner of East 163rd Street and Third Avenue. I rush over with Billy Bruzack, George Chin, and Johnny MacMillan and we arrive to find our victim, a twenty-two-year-old black Hispanic male named William Mallard, sitting on a steep hill, his two hands clamped on his thigh, which is bleeding profusely.

Even as a rookie DT I know that we are looking at perhaps Assault One in the first degree. I'm keen to get stuck into the investigation, and squat down to talk to our victim, who, as it turns out, knows the man who has just stabbed him.

"Filipe did it," Mallard whispers as I lean in, notebook in hand, his voice weakening, his ashen face turning deathly pale.

I pay little attention to an unmarked car that has just pulled up to the curb. Billy Bruzack greets the first to alight, Joe Hourihan, a sergeant from the Bronx Homicide Task Force. My partner is insisting I come over and be introduced, despite my reluctance to leave the victim, who is with paramedics.

"Hey, Joe, whadda ya know, we've got one of your guys here—an 'off the boat' Irishman this time," Billy says with a grin as I walk, hesitatingly, back towards our car, nodding in my direction as Hourihan offers me his hand.

"Hi, howya doing—Luke, isn't it? Heard about you. So where you from?" the newcomer inquires cheerily, as the other Homicide guys shoot the breeze with George and Johnny.

"I'm out of the 42 Detective Squad, Sarge," I reply slowly, looking back over my shoulder as the pool of blood surrounding our victim—who is now out cold—grows ever larger and starts to trickle downhill.

Mallard is on the way out.

"No, you idiot," Hourihan replies. "I mean what part of Ireland are you from?" A silence descends.

"Dublin, Sarge," I say.

He extends a handshake once more. "Hey, nice to meet you. Looks like I'll be working with you for the night now, Luke," my fellow Emerald Society member replies.

"What do you mean? You're Homicide, and this is an assault..."

"Assault? Your boy is DOA. Take a look!" the sergeant invites matter-of-factly, amused by the shock on my face.

"Or he will be by the time that bus reaches the hospital." He points to the ambulance that is automatically called to all 911 incidents. "You couldn't tell he was likely, Luke? C'mon, man. Look at all the blood!"

"Holy shit! I . . . I was just talking to him. He told me, 'Filipe did it,'" I blurt out.

"Really? Hey!" Bruzack nods approvingly, clapping me on the back. "Good detective work, buddy! See, you guys? That's why the Irish make good cops, Joe! Proactive!"

To the casual observer it might look like the half dozen detec-

tives couldn't have cared less about the dead man being carted to the morgue or about catching the guy who killed him, but the reality was different. Death and destruction are our business.

It dawned on me that the cops who had just pulled up already knew that someone had been murdered, a child was dead, or a police officer had been shot.

They are New York City's Grim Reapers.

By now the street was a hive of activity, as Patrol marked off the crime scene and kept the onlookers back, allowing our techs to gather the forensics and photograph all around them while we started a canvass for witnesses, who told us that Mallard had a beef with a guy he knew from the neighborhood, Filipe Santana. Santana, who was slightly younger than Mallard, but half his size, had pulled a knife to even the odds, lashing out with the blade. Unluckily for both of them, he connected, slashing the bigger man across the femoral artery.

We had a name, but with the other man dead, Santana was elusive. Like many people living in the Bronx today, our suspect had links to the Dominican Republic and we suspected that he'd made it back there. Our theory was confirmed by his stepmother, who intensely disliked Filipe, for some reason. She told us that his brother, Ramone, and Filipe's girlfriend, Tania Walker, had driven our fugitive to the airport. Amid the confusion post-9/11 he had slipped away.

As a DT you succeed or fail largely on your ability to successfully juggle cases, keeping several files in the air at the same time. The 42 was responsible for policing a square mile of what politicians and census takers refer to as U.S. Congressional District 16, a place where a third of the residents—about a quarter of a million people—lived below the poverty line, making it the poorest part of the country, on a par with Puerto Rico.

Deprivation and depravity usually go hand-in-hand, and detectives in the precinct had to investigate about twenty murders a year, and perhaps three hundred other cases, too, meaning you had to review and reprioritize constantly during meetings with your CO several times every week to have any hope of keeping on top of things.

Juggling, like any skill, only comes with time. But right then this was a luxury the Job couldn't afford. Even when I did make progress on finding Filipe, within a couple of days I had to put the case folders away again and drive over to Fresh Kills to join the men in the white suits and sift through the rubble of the Twin Towers once more.

Extradition was an avenue we considered in our pursuit of Santana but it presented problems because sometimes the DR (Dominican Republic) authorities cooperate and other times they refuse. Refusal was the more likely option in our case because Filipe Santana would probably claim self-defense, which might result in a plea down to manslaughter. Although rendition could be used, it's not something a CO would sign off on lightly, though in the years after 9/11 it became far more common for all sorts of serious crimes, many with no connection whatsoever to terrorism.

The easiest method of bringing a suspect back to face trial is to get him to voluntarily surrender, and over the next few months I spoke on the phone with Filipe several times. I encouraged him to come back and get the whole thing cleared up, even sending him a plane ticket on two occasions, all to no avail.

This case was clearly manslaughter in the first degree, rather than murder. But, as always in cases like this, we charged

Santana under state law, in his absence, with murder in the second degree, leaving it up to the courts to decide if it should be a lesser charge. Our fugitive's attorney accepted an offer of seven years, though all our discussions were theoretical, since our perp was on the run and remained a free man over the next thirty months. Every day other files came across my desk which took precedence, but whenever a new lead turned up I returned to the paperwork and kept shaking the tree, hoping to dislodge our suspect.

Three years later, I picked up the telephone to hear Filipe's stepmother on the other end of the line, who told me that our fugitive was back, working construction in Boston. She even gave me his telephone number, señor.

As soon as she hung up I dialed the number of a fed who was good at finding guys who would rather stay lost. Bald, bearded, and burly, Manny Puri served as a special agent with the U.S. Coast Guard Investigative Service prior to joining the U.S. Marshals. Highly experienced, he just wanted to see every felon behind bars without letting interagency politics get in the way.

Although 9/11 proved a big help to Filipe in making his escape, it would also play a major role in bringing him to justice. Technological advancements which were fast-tracked in the wake of the al-Qaeda-led attack meant that all calls made after that date in the USA could be tracked via satellite. We used a "triggerfish," an ultrapowerful antenna and peripheral device which simulates a mobile phone mast site to trick your handset into automatically connecting into our equipment instead of the real mast used by the phone company.

Once the unit has registered with our phony phone site, the target's handset instantly transmits its mobile identification number (MIN) and other important information, such as the channel used, the MIN of every incoming call, and, crucially, the precise physical location of all the incoming and outgoing data. Simply put, it tells us where our fugitive is standing and is accurate to within a few yards.

High-tech techniques are fine, but they work even better with some old-school police pressure, so myself, U.S. Marshal Manny Puri, and Detective Tony Curtin were dispatched to bring Tania Walker and Ramone Santana into the precinct. Tony Curtin was a fellow Irishman and one of the toughest cops I ever worked with, providing security to Gerry Adams on his visits to New York. We didn't mention that Filipe's stepmother was our informant, but implied the police had caught them on video in Newark Airport harboring a fugitive: a serious felony which would cost Filipe's brother, who was applying for U.S. citizenship, his future.

As a former illegal alien myself, I could understand more than most what the threat of deportation means, but just to be sure, we put pressure on Tania, too. We didn't have to push too hard, because she knew that Filipe had been seeing other women while he was on the run. Any loyalty she felt evaporated with the news that the father of her child had been two-timing her.

Tania confirmed that Santana was working up in Boston and supplied us with an address in Dorchester, Boston's largest neighborhood. U.S. Marshal Manny Puri broke out the triggerfish data analyzer, which he connected to a speaker, showing us how it would beep louder the closer we got to our target's handset.

November 23, 2004, 10:30 a.m., was an unusually warm, sunny morning in Boston, and the guys renovating the outside of one of the houses were in T-shirts and jeans, their hammers bopping against the wall, as we emerged from a side street taking our cues from Manny, who was fixated on the triggerfish, which was beeping steadily.

All of a sudden he stopped, stared at the machine, took a couple of steps forward, and then back again.

"That's him, Luke, that's our boy!" he shouted, pointing in the direction of two of the construction workers.

"Hey, guys, how are you doing?" I said, breaking the silence, my hand already on my pistol, the Boston PD cops to my left, Tony and Manny to my right, all with handguns now drawn. It had been three years since Mallard was killed, but Santana hadn't changed much from the police photos we'd passed around earlier that morning.

"Don't move. Drop that hammer now, Filipe! Now!" I shouted as Tony Curtin reached for his handcuffs.

Santana was calm and didn't resist. Our fugitive knew right there it was over, and, without us asking any questions, confessed straightaway. This meant we could still use his statement, even though he hadn't yet been read his rights.

"I knew that guy from the neighborhood. He started the fight. How much time am I looking at?" Filipe said, asking if we could go by his apartment to collect his passport and other personal items. All fine by me, since we still needed to prove his identity for the state extradition warrant.

After a terrorist attack, a few thousand man-hours of work by cops in the Bronx, the U.S. Marshals, Boston PD, and lawyers in the DA's office, the cell phone in his jeans pocket was eventually what gave Filipe Santana away.

My one week in the Bronx would turn out to last a decade. Mike Collins, a gentleman as usual, was as good as his word and called me after my first couple of weeks to say my transfer over to the

25 had been approved. He didn't seem surprised when I asked to stay where I was, learning from the likes of Brower, who, for all his quirkiness, was an excellent DT, and Bruzack, who was just as talented if more than a little mad—which maybe was an asset in this precinct.

Any doubts I ever had about this vanished one morning early in 2002 when we pulled up at a red light at 138th and Cypress Avenue, a busy intersection a mile from the precinct, and a disabled gunman used our car hood as a rest to gun a guy down in the street.

Any kid in the Bronx could spot our Crown Vic as an unmarked cop car from fifty yards away, but this stocky, bald Hispanic man in a red Yankees shirt limped up, drew his "trey eight"—street slang for a .38-caliber revolver—and took careful aim at the barbershop across the street before squeezing the trigger.

"Holy Mother of Jaysus!" I shouted from behind the wheel, fumbling with the driver's door with one hand, the other reaching for my 9mm.

"Cocksucker!" snarled my passenger.

Unfortunately for his victim it seemed Baldy was a real marksman, because the guy outside the barbershop was down after the first round. To judge by the cane our shooter was carrying, history was once again being made: another first for the 42. We had witnessed the Big Apple's first ever "limp-by."

Mighty Whitey was unimpressed; he had his head under the dashboard and was reaching to grab my arm to pull me down, possibly saving my life. In his mind and in his attitude, Mighty was a tall, deep-voiced, heavily built black man; he listened to a lot of Barry White and knew the streets better than any cop in our squad. But this native New Yorker was doomed to go through life in a skinny white man's body, no matter his love of jive. It was like casting Matt Damon in a biopic about Biggie Smalls.

We paused for a quick tactical assessment of our options across the hand brake.

"Keep your ass down, buddy! You wanna catch crossfire? Chill, man," my partner hissed.

"Listen, Billy, we have to grab this lowlife before he shoots some other asshole."

Our chat was interrupted by a further loud bang, as the gunman popped off another round. Whitey peered over the passenger window and ducked down again to report that our 180-pound hood ornament had indeed shot an asshole, and the victim was now gripping his buttocks harder than Madonna.

My partner, right ear just inches from the floor mat, proposed an alternative to my idea.

"Okay, here's what we do. Nothing. We're gonna wait and see if the guy he's cappin' is packin' too, Luke."

We were so busy arguing that we didn't realize the shooting had stopped. When we looked up we saw our perp, still seemingly oblivious to our presence, stick his handgun into the waistband of his pants. He limped off up the block as quickly as his walking stick would allow.

Near the barbershop, his target lay moaning for help. A few yards away another man, unlucky to be in the wrong place at the wrong time but fortunate enough to stop a bullet with his hand, was also screaming in pain. We later discovered the intended victim was named Ronald Chestnut, who had unwisely chased our shooter with a screwdriver a couple of hours earlier.

Before I could even get on the radio to call in the shooting, the plot took another sidestep into the surreal when a fourth man stumbled out the door of the barber's, past the two injured victims, waving a pistol, a look of confusion on his face.

It was a uniformed cop, but we took no chances and tasted our floor mat again.

"Detectives Brower and Waters from the 42," Mighty shouted from the safety of the gas pedal. "Who you?"

"Antwane Reeve, out of the 44," the dreadlocked officer replied, pointing his piece at the gunman, who was moving slowly up Cypress Avenue. "Dude on the cane is the shooter, right, Detective?"

"Yeah," I said, leaning across Brower. "We're goin' to pull around the corner and see if we can cut him off, Reeve. Follow on after us."

We took off in lukewarm pursuit, as Reeve followed on foot, the flashing lights and sirens on the Crown Vic finally alerting our gunman that we wanted to have a chat with him. The scene was farcical, but no less deadly. Whitey grabbed his door and pushed it out at the waistband of the shooter's jeans, sending him sprawling to the sidewalk. Our perp, Eugenio Cortes, remained on the ground, too shocked to offer any resistance, and within seconds Reeve arrived on scene, handcuffs in one hand, handgun in the other, to place him under arrest.

We put the prisoner in the car and thanked Reeve for his assistance. Even though there were two of us on the scene we were glad of the help in collaring the guy.

Despite being convicted of attempted murder, for reasons best explained by a judge, Cortes would end up walking, or at least hobbling, out of court a free man, getting just five years' probation for his shooting spree.

Six years later Antwane Reeve stumbled upon another shooter with almost deadly consequences when out on a late-night stroll with his dog. It was early summer and Antwane ended up in an argument with a twenty-five-year-old mope named Michael Williams, who, unknown to the cop, had a dozen and a half previous arrests on his rap sheet and used a silver 9mm Taurus pistol to sort out his problems.

The cop wisely walked away, but on the way back home he bumped into Williams again, who produced the gun and pulled the trigger. The bullet hit Antwane in the head but instead of killing him it just left a small gash. Amazingly, he was able to pull out his off-duty gun, return fire, and call in the attack to 911. The perp was so shocked that he fled and was found hiding in his momma's house, where he was arrested and later charged with the attempted murder of a police officer.

Reeve spent an hour or two in the ER with little more than a splint on his little finger. It takes all kinds of craziness to make this city, and make it in this city, too. Just like in the NYPD.

CHAPTER ELEVEN

CURIOUS CASES OF U.S. CODE 18

"Luke. How you doing? The Lou asked me to reach out to you. How'd ya like to come over to us? If you can drag yourself away from the 42, of course . . ."

Joe Hourihan was part of the furniture around the Bronx, and there wasn't a young detective in the borough who hadn't hoped to someday get that call. In 1993, I had been just another probationary police officer in the academy, and one of the few amongst twenty-two hundred other green hopefuls who had never even fired a gun before. Less than a decade later I was being invited to join one of the most elite units on the Job by Homicide Joe, the man who had worked with me on the Santana assault-turned-murder case.

Although I had made plenty of mistakes along the way, Hourihan saw something in me he liked and had been impressed with my progress in the intervening three years. There was certainly no shortage of those with more skill and more time served than I had, all excellent detectives who never got the opportunity they deserved, but unfortunately for them their families hailed from Tijuana or Tampa, not Cork or Carlow. Life is not fair, but when the dice are loaded in your favor, you don't complain. Joe Hourihan had huge influence, and if he had put my name forward for Bronx Homicide, then the spot was as good as mine.

A week later I found myself sitting across from the smartest man I'd ever met in the NYPD. Lieutenant Sean O'Toole was yet another Irish-American cop and razor-sharp, understanding exactly what his superiors required of him as a key commander in the most crime-riddled borough in the city. O'Toole was all about results.

My new CO outlined my role in the squad, explaining that Homicide was about more than catching murderers: it was about stopping repeat offenders likely to end up in that category.

With that in mind, he revealed that he was not putting me in one of the usual Catching Teams investigating murders. O'Toole had something a little more delicate in mind for me.

"Luke, how would you feel about screwing people up for us? And I mean really screwing them up." The Lou beamed across his desk. What O'Toole had in mind was a program I would come to know well: Triggerlock.

Every cop knows the experts in this area are the federal agencies, so a couple of weeks later I joined another fifty or so police officers from departments all over New York State for a two-week-long program designed to teach us the real meaning of "making a federal case of it." In the process they turned us into experts on the 1968 Gun Control Act and subsequent amendments—or, as we came to know and love it, Code 18. Triggerlock is the program and Code 18 is the code under which felons are charged.

Under this federal statute anyone who is convicted of a felony, subject to a domestic violence protective order, or illegally resident in the country is not allowed to possess a gun. Depending on how many felony convictions you have, possession of a firearm could see you sent away for anything from three years to life. Career criminals with a history of violence need access to firearms to protect themselves and their interests, and Triggerlock has consistently been shown as the ideal method to put them behind bars for good.

The word "federal" is key here. In the States, each state sets its own laws and appoints its own police officers on a city, county, and state level. These work with local prosecutors to bring offenders before the courts on local warrants. If found guilty, they are sentenced to time in local jails, courtesy of local taxpayers. Federal laws are also enforced, and this parallel system is funded by national taxes and run by Washington, D.C.: these laws deal with individuals and gangs which pose a larger threat and which can't be contained by local law enforcement, as well as criminal enterprises that cross state lines. This division stems from the days of Prohibition, when gangsters would regularly cross state lines until the launch of the FBI put a stop to that. Today, the ATF, DEA, and many other agencies are funded better than many countries' armed forces!

In a federal case, federal agents and prosecutors target criminals under complex national laws, and the guilty go down for decades instead of years, moved to federal penitentiaries, often thousands of miles away, with no chance of parole. Of course, the feds need local support, and selected police officers are trained to liaise with federal programs. I was ultimately to be chosen for this specialized training and would gain expertise in a number of federal programs. Eventually, I would get the opportunity afforded to few cops on the city payroll: to work inside the most famous law agency in the world, the FBI.

Some of our targets would try to outwit us—and avoid a sentence of fifteen years to life—in Triggerlock by removing the legally required serial numbers from a weapon. This action, aimed at making a gun less traceable, is a felony, playing right into the hands of a federal prosecutor. Being in possession of a defaced gun means you are looking at probably twenty years to life. Your efforts are also often futile, since a number of techniques are now used to successfully restore deleted numbers, including chemical etching, which will render digits long erased readable once more. Such initiatives, like the ATF's Obliterated Serial Number Program, have the budget, staff, and expertise to tilt the balance in our favor.

In order for federal charges to stick, though, the arresting officer still needs to establish ownership of that firearm, and there are three usual methods. The first is through fingerprints—you might lift some good partials from flat areas. Second is DNA, if you are lucky enough to find a fleck of skin or a hair trapped in the slide or hammer.

The third, and most common in my experience, is through a confession, which often proves easier to get than you would imagine. You simply sit your suspect down in an interview room and ask him if the gun is his.

"So, do you realize that there are no serial numbers on that piece we found?" you say, staring your prisoner in the face.

"You foolin'? No way, man! I never knew that."

"No? Don't play me! You knew, because you erased them. That's five years, straight off, asshole. You're history."

"No way, I ain't goin' down for that!"

"So, let me get this clear: you're trying to tell me that when you bought the piece there were no numbers on it! You take me for a fool?"

"Yeah, that's it. That's how it went down. The guy who gave me the piece must have hacked 'em off."

There you have it. A confession that your suspect took possession of a gun which he believed had been illegally altered to avoid identification. The guy across the other side of the interview room has just given you a conviction, gift-wrapped.

Felons are, in reality, nonpersons in the USA. At best, from the moment the judge's gavel falls until the day they die they are second-class citizens, with none of the rights the rest of us take for granted, including grant aid, which is automatically denied to anyone convicted of a felony. That means that if you do try to turn your back on crime, there will be no money for college or business start-ups and no place for you in public housing. Felons are not allowed to vote, and at any point they can be stopped and questioned by members of law enforcement who have a reasonable suspicion they are up to no good.

A felony conviction ends your life as you know it. Ferdinand Nazario would learn that the hard way when he chose not to stash several rounds of ammunition before entering his apartment. It was a mistake that would see him sent to prison for fifteen years over a fistful of bullets discovered on a routine check.

When Ferdinand's parole officers had knocked at 4040 Bronx Boulevard for a routine check they were wearily invited inside. Contrary to the conditions of his parole, Nazario was out after the nine p.m. curfew, temporarily frustrating the duo's efforts to perform a drug check, a standard test for felons released back onto the streets, but when he eventually was brought back he dutifully filled the sample cup with urine. The result was gold. Ferdinand Nazario was positive for narcotics.

As the parole officers searched the apartment, Detective Joanne Hennessy from the Bronx Gang Unit stood in the background, doing her best to calm down the man's wife, who was upset at the prospect of another Christmas holiday ruined without her husband. Her agitation was understandable.

"Where did you get these, Ferdinand?" Parole Officer San-chez asked, pointing to the twenty rounds of 9mm ammunition, along with drug paraphernalia, sitting in open view on an ash-tray in a bedroom.

"The bullets? Some crackhead gave 'em me, man. Jus' a souvenir . . ." the parolee admitted, staring in helpless disbe-lief as Sanchez and his partner removed the projectiles, which were later passed over for examination by the Firearms Analy-sis Section. They questioned him about any guns present, but it appeared he was telling the truth. He had bullets, but without a gun they were useless. To him, perhaps, but not to us.

Across town, a day or two later, ADA Hannah Freilich glanced at her watch, picked up the phone, and punched in my number.

"Happy Holidays, Detective Waters! I'm hoping you can play Father Christmas and do me this tiny little favor . . ." she began hopefully.

"Merry Christmas to you, Hannah. Sure, ask away, can't do any harm," I replied.

"Great! Okay . . . just got a guy on possession of ammuni-tion. Name of Ferdinand Nazario. Habitual offender and a drug addict. Same old story. The maximum I can hold him for is nine days, but if we can get him to plead guilty in the meantime . . . well, then we can nail him for a parole violation. Question is, can you Triggerlock him?"

Peace and goodwill towards all men stops at the door of the Bronx district attorney, and for us, too. Christmas is all about the green, hanging out the holly, digging out the tree from the garage, and insulating your wallet against the chill winds of New Year's bills. Right then I would take all the overtime I could get, and I told Hannah to drop the paperwork over. I reckoned the Nazario case should be good for maybe twenty hours, which was another thousand dollars towards the nasty credit card bill which would drop in my mailbox in a month's time.

The case seemed like just a simple narcotics collar. Ferdinand was a New York native with multiple felony convictions, mostly for drug dealing, and a history of weapons possession. He was another parolee who, under the state system, would probably be released and spend the New Year with his family. He wasn't learning any lessons from his time inside, and it was the DA's intention to send him away for a much longer period of reflection at a federal facility.

I needed a second opinion, however, and knocked on the lieutenant's door. Sean O'Toole was a family man himself, with a wife and kids.

"I just got this dropped in my lap by Hannah Freilich over in the DA's office, boss," I explained to O'Toole. "Five-time loser named Nazario. She wants me to Triggerlock the guy. What do you think?"

O'Toole paused for a moment. His reply was short and succinct.

"Fry him."

Ferdinand's file appeared utterly unremarkable, but the way this case goes marks it out for special mention. He was a three-strike career criminal, with a wife and a young son. Now he would have to serve whatever time he had left on his sentence before he was paroled—being caught in possession of bullets was an automatic revocation of that parole. Although he was not found with a piece, federal law draws no real distinction between a firearm, a silencer, or ammunition. Checks had shown that four or more of the rounds found at his apartment contained tiny manufacturers' marks which indicated that they were made outside the state, leaving Nazario open to federal prosecution under 18 U.S.C. § 922(g)/924(e): "Felon in possession of ammunition."

The curse of Code 18 had struck once more because, as far as a federal prosecutor would be concerned, our subject might as well have been arrested taking a bazooka through the Jersey Tunnel, since it amounted to that same automatic fifteen-year minimum term in prison, with no prospect of early release.

This guy was perfect for Triggerlock.

My views changed when we took a closer look at his known associates. We quickly realized that Nazario might be of far more use in our ongoing efforts to put a suspected killer, named David "Whiteboy" Marrero on the streets, behind bars for life.

Marrero had been peddling drugs for years and Homicide suspected him of a few killings. The DA had managed to put him before the grand jury facing a murder charge a number of times, but on each occasion the witnesses either developed amnesia or suddenly disappeared. Marrero was far too smart to get caught with guns or ammo in his possession, so Nazario's possession charge might be the best chance we had to take him off the streets.

As well as being a real lowlife, Whiteboy was also our felon's uncle.

Reading through the arrest reports it was clear that these facts potentially gave us great leverage with our parolee. Added to that, Nazario's mother-in-law and his wife were sick and tired of the life. So we offered him a simple, stark choice: your wife and child or your uncle. Give him up or the assistant U.S. attorney throws away the key. You decide.

Initially this drug addict had meant nothing more than a few hours' overtime to me and a drop in the crime statistics for

O'Toole, but he was now an important pawn in the game to take down his uncle—or would be, if he didn't steadfastly refuse to cooperate and give him up.

In reality I had some sympathy for the man I was working to put away. A moderately successful pusher, several steps below Marrero, could make a couple of thousand dollars a day, in contrast to a couple of hundred bucks a week in a minimum-wage job.

Ultimately his silence, and sacrifice, were in vain. Whiteboy was later collared in Brooklyn holding a large quantity of coke, which for him meant a lengthy sentence. For our parolee blood did indeed prove thicker than water and although we couldn't prove that his uncle put a bullet in the head of anyone who crossed him, the system used a few unfired rounds to take Nazario's remaining productive years from him.

On balance this man probably didn't deserve what happened to him because his sin was that he'd made bad choices, but it didn't help that he was unlucky enough to be related to a criminal whom the cops really wanted. Few people get a reprieve under Triggerlock, or deserve one. Nazario might just be the exception, on both counts. He was convicted but appealed because he was only in possession of ammunition and was sentenced to seven to ten years.

Over the next two years I worked with several other detectives, excellent cops like Scott Patterson, Michael Rodriguez, Robin Womack, and Al Hickey, working as a team to put, on average, fifteen to twenty people a week back in the pen and keep them there with nothing more deadly than a Bic Biro and a cell phone. After a while it prompted a standing joke around Homicide with the guys in Catching Teams.

"Hey, Luke, chase any good perps today?" Sergeant Kenny Umlauft would call out as I signed out in the ledger.

"Yep. I chased one right back into his orange jumpsuit this morning, Kenny," was my stock reply.

Most Code 18s were routine, but one which took place less than a year after Nazario stood out, particularly as it involved the worst stickup artist I ever came across in all my years as a police officer: Latie Whitley.

Bodegas are a common sight in the South Bronx, serving the community everything from groceries and lottery tickets to beer and cigarettes. The name in Spanish means "wine cellar," but Whitley, who had felony convictions for drug dealing and armed robbery dating back as far as 1986, treated them like banks. Whenever he needed twenty dollars to get high (which was several times every week), he walked into a shop and used a combination of pester-power and low-level threats to make a cash withdrawal. Detectives out of the 40 and Bronx Narcotics knew him well, but local merchants realized that by calling the cops on a guy like him they would risk further attacks on staff and the store, so they paid up just to make him go away.

On this night, Whitley walked into the tiny shop at 362 Willis Avenue and as usual began by begging the two clerks, Ali Mohammed and Ali Aluorami, for some loose cigarettes, but for once he struck out. Our one-man crime wave stormed out on Willis Avenue and returned, moments later, with an accomplice and a loaded .38 Saturday Night Special.

Highly agitated, he wildly waved the cheap, nasty revolver at the two immigrants, demanding not a couple of bucks, but the entire takings. When the terrified clerk closest to the counter didn't move quickly enough, Latie suddenly pulled the trigger, to speed things along, shooting one of those present in the head. Himself.

Any normal armed robber who had just taken a bullet at point-blank range would scram before the cops arrived. But this addict was dim and grim in his determination and, though bleeding profusely, he staggered behind the counter and grabbed about $1,400, mostly in coins. Whitley stumbled out the door and across several lanes of traffic, disappearing into the lobby of a nearby apartment building. His partner escaped at speed in the opposite direction as several detectives arrived on scene, guns drawn.

After questioning the two clerks, the cops, backed up by colleagues from the 40, followed the trail of spilled coins across the road into an apartment building, checking floor by floor. They picked up the line of bloody coins dropped by their new owner, which disappeared behind a resident's door. Inside they found a number of people, including Whitley's girlfriend, and hiding in a closet one lame perp with a towel jammed against his bloody head. The NYPD had caught the shooter literally red-handed, and the takings as well as his gun were also soon recovered.

Latie was lucky. Really, really lucky. The .38 bullet had only taken a lump of his jaw and by the time we came to trial, almost two years later to the day, he had made a full recovery.

Latie Whitley's trial was a perfect example of how well Triggerlock worked. Under state law our perp would be out and terrorizing the neighbors within a couple of years. But since his holdup took place on a commercial premises, I liaised with the DA and we pushed to charge him under the Hobbs Act—a felon discharging a firearm while committing another violent felony—catching a break when the Honorable Richard Conway Casey was assigned to our trial.

From convicting Cold War Russian spies as a prosecutor to presiding over the trial of Peter Gotti, a leader of the Gambino crime family, Judge Casey had enjoyed a successful career on the bench while still finding time to attend Yankees games wearing a three-piece suit and a straw hat, and was the sort of judge unlikely to swallow any sob story from our perp's lawyer.

The judge had heard it all over the previous thirty years. In his case justice was literally blind, as Casey relied on his constant companion, Barney, a black Labrador "seeing eye" guide dog who dozed off during the boring bits.

The trial lasted four days, and just after Christmas 2005 Casey and Barney emerged from chambers with the verdict as an expectant hush fell over the courtroom.

Prosecuted under state law, with good behavior, the accused could have been back cheerfully terrorizing the stores of Willis Avenue in thirty-six months, but the judge sentenced him to concurrent terms of 282 months for the Hobbs Act robbery and firearms possession violation, plus a consecutive mandatory minimum term of 120 months for discharging the gun.

Thirty-three years for the robbery. And ten years for shooting himself in the head while doing it.

In just over a decade as a cop I'd seen every imaginable reaction to a sentence—anger, denial, tears, recrimination, stunned silence, relief—but that day I added another to the list. A dead faint.

Latie was another tick in the win column. For O'Toole, the case was a small drop in his future crime stats. For me, it was another fifteen hours' overtime.

Triggerlock was one of the most effective tools I ever used—feared and hated by repeat offenders, who would often readily confess to serious crimes and beg the DA to send them to state prison because, no matter how unpleasant that system was, it offered hope and the chance of a parole hearing in a few years.

After I'd spent two years in this work, O'Toole called me into his office and told me that I was now ready to catch cases, assigning me to the B-Team. I still used Triggerlock from time to time because, despite its brutality and flaws, it was still the most effective tool we had to protect the public from those determined to prey on them.

CHAPTER TWELVE

ARTHUR'S THEME

Sometimes one case is like a box full of other boxes, like a Russian nesting doll. It turns out to have many more aspects and intersections—and crimes—than the one you think you are investigating. That thought is somewhere in the back of my increasingly addled mind as I stand in the shelter. From the other side of the room the thirty-seven-year-old woman moves slowly, mechanically towards the cage as I murmur a silent prayer to Saint Anthony, patron saint of lost causes, that the bundle curled up on a blanket behind the metal bars is indeed her missing beloved.

We have already spent half the morning here at the American Society for the Prevention of Cruelty to Animals shelter in Manhattan, and when it comes to finding Coca the truant tomcat, I've been useless.

"Ain't my baby. Nothin' like Coca!" Nikki mumbles listlessly, her eyes filling with tears. I've known Nikki Wiley for several years, long enough to see her pregnant many times, but on each occasion she's lost the life she was carrying. This cat, along with her other moggies, Gizmo and Pinky, are the closest she ever will have to babies. Nikki loves Coca, but her real romance is with coke, particularly crack.

I keep helping her search because an elderly man was bludgeoned to death in his apartment and the case remains open months later. I suspect that Nikki Wiley can put two of her fellow addicts at the scene and ultimately behind bars. The deal is simple: if I want her to rat, then I have to help find that darned cat.

It had all started a year earlier, on November 7, 2006, the same day New York went to the polls to elect a new senator and governor. The 911 operator logged an emergency call from a distraught woman at 1558 Bryant Avenue in the Bronx, and when patrol arrived they found seventy-year-old Arthur Jackson with his head cleaved open in a vicious attack which left parts of his skull embedded in the ceiling of his apartment.

Next door the caller, Bernice Poindexter, a former girlfriend of the victim, was still in shock, being comforted by neighbors. She had discovered the body when she'd dropped off a meal to the man at ten a.m. The person who calls in a homicide is often the perp, but we soon dismissed this woman as a suspect.

During the autopsy the ME later discovered trauma to the body indicating that a hammer had been used to hit him repeatedly around the head, shoulders, and stomach. This all fit with what had been found: the wall beside the body covered in a line of blood spatter which continued from floor to ceiling. The weapon was found in the grounds of the local public school on Vyse Avenue, an hour after the murder.

"Media case for sure, buddy," Pete Tarsnane said with a sigh as we took in the chaos.

The appearance of a female detective from the 42 momentarily lifted our gloom.

"Hey, Maria. What's the word?"

Pete's greeting was to Maria Hoy, a tall, thin brunette who'd only recently received her gold shield but seemed to be surviving Bobby Rivera and all the craziness at the 42 pretty well.

"Hey, you guys. Looks like we have a media case, eh?" Hoy said, hands on hips, as she surveyed the blood and gore.

We sat down with Bernice Poindexter and the other neighbors who possibly witnessed or heard something to put us on the track of the killer—or killers—of Arthur Jackson, or "Mr. Arthur," as our victim was affectionately known on the block. The motive seemed pretty clear right from the get-go. Arthur Jackson had just won the lottery, in a fashion.

"The Numbers"—run by black hoodlums in Harlem and other African-American neighborhoods, and the Mob almost everywhere else in the early days—survived the crackdown on organized crime in the eighties and nineties, mainly because this lottery paid out regularly and allowed regular moms and pops to bet a couple of dollars.

Jackson had collected his thousand-dollar win and everyone had heard of his good fortune, particularly the local crackheads like Nikki, who congregated on the stairs at his building most days. But Mr. Arthur's popularity went beyond the block's drug users. He was equally well liked by many local alcoholics, one of whom told us of how she would ask the old guy to hold a few dollars for her each week to help her avoid the temptation of spending all her grocery money on booze. Turned out Mr. Arthur also sold drugs on a regular basis, which probably accounted for his popularity with the local skells. The man lying on the bloody carpet also had a conviction for rape, dating back many years.

The Numbers which the deceased played at the local store didn't interest us. I was far more concerned with the illegally defaced .22-caliber handgun which our victim had hidden under his mattress and the ammunition the Crime Scene Unit (CSU) found close by the body. Although he was older than our typical mopes, Jackson was still a pistol-packing, drug-dealing convicted felon.

We rang Narcotics, the NYPD Gang Unit, Crime Stoppers, and anyone else we could think of to turn up the heat, because the more pressure we exerted the more likely it was that some dealer unable to move his product, or some pimp unable to work his girls, would give us a name just to make us go away. We started to arrest anyone with outstanding warrants, and almost straightaway several people nominated Nicole Wiley as a Person of Interest.

I knew Nikki from my years in the 42 and it was quickly clear to us that she had nothing to do with the homicide herself. Her prior arrests were for possession and steering other addicts to dealers in return for a free bag of crack, a pathetic addict rather than a killer who smashes someone's head in with a hammer to get money for drugs.

But I was certain that she knew who did it. Conversations with crackheads infuriate, and the frustrations of my years in Washington Heights came back as Nikki made statements which she later contradicted—with no memory of our earlier conversation.

She was known to hang out with two other zombies, crackheads with a history of violence. One of them was immediately identified as a suspect and was already facing an Assault One charge after stabbing Jose Rivera, the super of his old apartment building.

Normally Assault One is of little interest to Homicide, but the DT who caught the case did nothing with it, so when I learned that one of the crackheads had left the super needing twenty-one stitches, it gave me the ideal excuse to arrest this powerfully built six-foot-three, 240-pound black male and question him on the last time he saw our victim.

When I picked the suspect up I told him he was being held on a murder charge, rather than the recent assault, just to see if I could rattle his cage, but he kept cool. He ultimately got two years for stabbing the super, good news for us, since we now knew exactly where he was—if only Nikki could get her head together and place him in the apartment with our victim.

It was clear that Nikki Wiley felt something for the dead man, whose grandson she claimed to have once dated and who apparently gave her money whenever she asked. So, in her own drug-hazed way, she tried to tell us who killed her friend.

In her most coherent statement our witness claimed she woke up at three a.m. with the sudden urge for a pizza, calling to her mother's to borrow the money, and that she saw her old pals enter Jackson's building at about six a.m. Nikki followed the two junkies inside and made her way up to the deceased's apartment on the second floor to see if he had any baking soda, used to turn powdered cocaine into rocks of crack.

Our witness later refused to sign this statement and left me banging my head against the wall in frustration, so we did whatever we could to keep her onside—even if that meant spending my morning in the cattery and the inevitable off-color jokes.

Then Nikki missed a court date and reached out to me to see if I could help, so I spoke to the ADA working the case, Sarah Jacobson, and suggested that we put her in a prison rehab program for twelve months to see if she could get clean. At that moment Nikki was useless as a witness. Three-day binges are not uncommon amongst crack addicts, resulting in memory loss and even full-blown paranoid psychosis, as they occasionally throw their arms over their heads to protect themselves against the giant bugs scurrying to attack them. The prosecutor agreed, and we took the case before a judge. If Nikki could get her head together—even temporarily—and return to the land of the living, she might be able to take the stand against her two crackhead friends, who had disappeared off the face of the earth since the day of the murder.

Even when you can't find a suspect, you keep going; you make life uncomfortable for innocent people who care about that person you are trying to chase down. We used pester power, knocking at the door at the most inappropriate times. Birthdays, family BBQs, and parties are good. Christmases and Thanksgiving dinners? Even better.

"My boy is innocent! Why are you harassing him and disturbing this family?" the mother of one of the crackheads demanded when she answered our ring at the family home on Seabury Avenue, a quiet and respectable corner of the Bronx.

"That's fine, ma'am. But like we said last time, you haven't seen him, and we can't find him at any of his usual haunts," I replied. "Don't you find it strange that he's on the run if he's done nothing wrong?"

"He was scared, Detective!" his mother retorted, defensively. "Scared of you cops harassing him. Why can't you go after real criminals?"

I thanked her for her time and left a business card, reminding her that we'd be checking back regularly just in case he dropped by, and I paid a similar visit to the mother of our suspect's five-year-old daughter, whose reply was the same as his mom's.

Our efforts soon paid off. The fugitive called me to explain his innocence.

"Why you bothering my family with this bull, man? Back off and leave them be! I ain't comin' in to see any cops because I ain't done nothing wrong!" he insisted before hanging up.

Over the next few months we paid return visits to his family and reached out to the U.S. Postal Inspectors, the Department of Probation, the New York/New Jersey High Intensity Drug Trafficking Area (HIDTA), a multi-agency Fugitive Task Force, and U.S. Marshal Manny Puri to check on addresses in Richmond, Virginia, where we'd been tipped off that our suspect might be lying low, but once again we could find no trace of our suspect, and the investigation continued with little real progress being made.

It was a week before Christmas and the sidewalks of Manhattan were full of ho-ho-ho-ing as we handed out "Help Us Help You" posters to the old man's friends and neighbors near Arthur Jackson's building. We had little choice. But we caught a break, a bit of seasonal good cheer.

I got a call informing me that one of Mr. Arthur's crackhead neighbors had just been arrested with about forty grams of cocaine. His lawyer had contacted the DA to tell him that he had information which he was willing to trade.

The man who potentially could help us put our chief suspect away was a former U.S. Marine, Tyrone Little. But when we produced our would-be informant at the Bronx DA's office our drama took an utterly unpredictable twist.

"Mr. Little, as you're aware you are here today because we wish to question you on the murder of Arthur Jackson—'Mr. Arthur'—at his home last November," Sarah Jacobson said across the table to our interviewee.

Little was represented by an attorney named John Mangialardi, and his opening comment amazed us.

"My client is happy to talk to you, on just one condition. He is willing to make a statement that every morning he goes to buy drugs and comes back to the building beside where the deceased, whom he knew as 'Mr. Arthur,' lived.

"On the morning of this man's death, my client sat down at approximately five-thirty a.m. with [and here he mentioned the names of Nikki's two pals] and a crack user he knows as 'Nikki,' and he has information pertinent to your investigation."

"We're listening, Mr. Mangialardi," Jacobson responded, tapping her pen on her desk. "What does he want in return?"

"It's quite simple, Ms. Jacobson. My client wants Detective Waters here to take care of this matter on his behalf," the attorney replied, sliding a small file across the table towards the increasingly intrigued ADA, who bent back the flap of the foolscap envelope and eased out a xerox of a burial record and a copy of an old newspaper report.

The piece, dated February 29, 1988, reported how a little girl and her mother were discovered hog-tied with articles of clothing. They had been raped, before being manually strangled in the mother's apartment just down the block from where Arthur Jackson lived, at 1007 East 174th Street.

Eighteen months before the horrific crime, the offices of Special Services for Children had ruled that the child's drug-addicted mother, Selina Cooper, was no longer a fit parent and handed custody to her paternal grandmother, Phyllis Little, whom the girl lived with next door.

The dead child, whose picture smiled happily at me from the newspaper article, was the daughter of our prisoner, Tyrone Little, and Selina Cooper, his dysfunctional common-law wife. She was a regular in a group who took drugs in apartments and motels with various men who supplied them with narcotics in return for sexual favors.

Nobody had ever been charged with the rapes and homicides, in spite of compelling evidence against one of the men who'd partied with Selina Cooper, Robert Fleming, currently in prison and with a long record which included sex offenses.

Little's offer left me openmouthed with amazement, while the usually articulate ADA looked equally surprised by the "solve one for me, and I'll solve one for you" proposal. It was an offer we couldn't refuse.

I made a few calls and discovered that the investigation was now assigned to another detective, Wendell Stradford, in the Manhattan Cold Case Squad (MCCS), which was based in Brooklyn, and Nancy Barko, a senior assistant district attorney and one of the most experienced lawyers in the Bronx prosecutor's office.

I got a copy of Stradford's report, which mentioned that victims' swabs from the 1988 double rape-homicide had gone missing. The cold case DT held numerous meetings with forensics experts to try to locate the missing evidence and eventually discovered it in an evidence locker. On May 14, 2003, Stradford had joined Dr. Marie Sample, assistant director of forensic biology, and Helen Rafaniello, forensic scientist, at the ME's office, where tests were carried out which showed a positive DNA match for Robert Fleming, twenty-five years old at the time of the attacks, whose semen was found in the body cavities of both mother and daughter.

Without a doubt he was the rapist, and almost certainly, either by himself or with others, was also the killer. The problem was that while the lawyers agreed he might have killed our victims, the DA believed time had washed his record clean.

Fleming was a real piece of work. At one point he had been living in Brooklyn, when his girlfriend was arrested by officers from the 71 for arson after trying to burn down their apartment with him inside. The unfortunate woman had discovered that he had infected her with HIV, an accusation other women had also leveled at our suspect.

Fleming and the woman had then disappeared, but it was believed he had returned to live with his mother at 1160 Colgate Avenue in the Bronx, his address for many of the arrests earlier in his criminal career, which included sex offenses in California, as well as larceny, drug dealing, and possession. As so often happens, he had ended up back in the system anyway when he was picked up on other charges. But, despite his incarceration, no charges were brought on the rapes and homicides.

I dropped by the DA's office at 198 East 161st Street to see ADA Nancy Barko and to find out the reason for the delay. She seemed to be intimately acquainted with the facts of the twenty-year-old case, but to my astonishment had no intention of acting on them.

"Robert Fleming? Oh, yes, I know all about the guy, Detective. Certainly, he is a match for the rapes, but the problem is we can't pin the homicides on him, so we won't be pursuing a prosecution," Barko said with a shrug.

"Are you kidding me, Nancy?" I said incredulously. "We have a career criminal who infects his girlfriends with HIV, and whose semen is found in the bodies of a skell mother and her poor little daughter, who are strangled after being assaulted, but the DA won't go after the guy?"

"Look, Detective, I know where you are coming from, but we simply can't arrest him on this," Barko said wearily. "We can prove he raped her, but we cannot prove he killed her, and as you know, the ten-year statute of limitations for the rape has expired, so he gets a pass on that. There may be no statute of limitations on murder, but who is to say that he didn't just rape her and someone else strangled her?"

"Who? Me, for one, Counselor. And any member of any jury. Do you really think they won't convict this bastard? Give me a break!"

Barko's patience was lasting far longer than mine.

"Luke, we would go to trial and get a conviction on the murder, but the same day the Court of Appeals would overturn it based on the doubt that someone else might have killed the child—"

"Do it, then. Do it! Lock this mope up for murder. Are you crazy, Nancy? You're letting him get away with this for the last five years?"

Barko and I continued to argue, and I eventually stormed out, utterly frustrated. Since Robert Fleming had HIV he would probably be dead soon enough, and I couldn't understand why the DA wouldn't prosecute. Even if the case was overturned, it would be of some comfort to Little, and his mother, to see the man responsible for destroying their loved ones' lives having to answer for his crimes.

Plus, it would help me clear the Arthur Jackson homicide.

I reached out to the cold case investigator, Wendell Stradford, a heavyset six-footer with over twenty years on the Job, who I heard was a worker. He did things at his own pace and resented interference, which was exactly how he viewed my questions.

To make it worse, Stradford's office was located in Brooklyn in a building once used by the now-defunct NYC Transit Authority Police Department and was now home to both the Manhattan and Brooklyn Cold Case Squads under the Fugitive Enforcement Division. I was far from home and far from welcome.

Wendell and I did not get off to a good start.

147

"Who do you think you are, to walk in here and ask me how I do my job, Waters?" the other detective demanded. "This is my case, and I've put a lot of time into it, so back off!"

"That's the problem, buddy," I said. "You and Nancy Barko have already put lots of time into this, and you've got nowhere. I have an unsolved homicide resting on this, and I need to know if you're going to sit on the case for another four or five years. Go and talk to Fleming," I urged.

"Don't give me orders!" Stradford replied, pointing his finger at me.

"Okay. Sit on your ass, then. I'll go and talk to the guy, if you don't want to," I shot back.

"You know what? Get back to your skells in the Bronx, Waters. You don't know shit about this," the other DT replied, rising to his feet.

I had other conversations with my cold case counterpart over the telephone, even less pleasant than our first face-to-face, so it was with some surprise that I heard Wendell had gone out to Rikers Island prison for another chat with Robert Fleming. In his latest mug shot, Fleming was going rapidly downhill, the skin on his head, down as far as his eyebrows, peeled off to reveal a white layer underneath.

The next news I got from Wendell saw me grabbing Kenny Umlauft and dancing a jig around Bronx Homicide.

Wendell Stradford had just delivered a confession from our suspect that he'd raped and killed both Selina Cooper and little Joi. Justice for her father and his woman and child after all these years. And it should ensure his cooperation in the Jackson murder.

A couple of days later I bumped into Nancy Barko at the Bronx DA's office while I was over on another matter, and from the smile on her face I could see there were no hard feelings on her part.

"Congratulations, Luke. We're going to authorize the arrest of Fleming for the rape and the homicide."

On June 23, 2009, Case 564/2009 Pt. 40 came before the jury. Almost twenty-one years after he had raped and killed a mother and daughter, Robert Fleming was charged with two counts of intentionally causing the deaths of the victims and nine additional counts of felony murder during the alleged commission of rape, sodomy, and other sexual offenses.

Nancy and I were delighted to see the case finally make court, but it did little to restore what small credibility the DA had with me or the cops I worked with. The Bronx district DA's office was hit-or-miss. Some DAs were great, others poor. It was the luck of the draw who you got on any particular case. According to statistics, in 2013 the Bronx had a 31 percent success rate in jailing offenders for gun crimes, compared to 76 percent in Queens. Additionally, the Bronx had a 47 percent release rate of violent offenders, compared to 20 percent in Manhattan, and the confidential report indicated a substantial backlog in prosecuting felony cases—six months in some cases.

The *New York Post* got an interview with Fleming in prison, and he told the reporter that as he was brought to court he felt his victims' pain.

"I told the detectives my cuffs were too tight. I thought of Selina and how she couldn't ask anyone for help. I could ask. I felt bad she couldn't ask for anyone."

After two decades, and facing his own death, it seemed Robert Fleming's conscience had finally kicked in, but had he kept his mouth shut he would never have been charged with these crimes and it would have remained another dark stain on the Bronx district attorney's record.

"The Wild West": Finglas, where I grew up.

My grandfather Thomas Kiely, one of the first members of An Garda Síochána in Ireland.

Me and my pals in our back garden in Finglas. I'm on the far right.

Me in uniform as Probationary
Police Officer Luke Waters,
Company 93-13, 1993.

My graduation, Company 93-13, 1994.

On graduation day with my proud family (from left to right): my brother Thomas, me, my
father, and my brother Vincent.

(From left to right) PO Mike Edwards, PO Thomas Byrnes, me, and Sergeant Brian O'Leary, the Pickpocket Squad, at the St. Patrick's Day Parade, 1996.

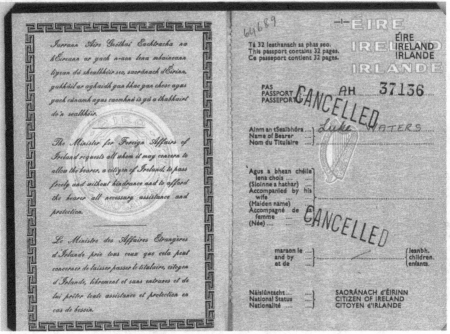

My canceled Irish passport. I'm a US citizen at last.

On the cover of *Garda Review* magazine: "From Finglas to Forty Second Street," March 2001.

© GARDA REVIEW

"We are the best": Bronx Homicide baseball team, undefeated, summer 2009.

Sept. 12, 2001, the day after. Billy Bruzack, Ray Rosado, and I went down to Ground Zero to see the devastation for ourselves.

The side of the World Trade Center on Church Street, with 5 World Trade Center in the background.

My official thank-you from the
United States Attorney's Office
for assistance in connection
with the prosecution of Latie
Whitley, April 2006.

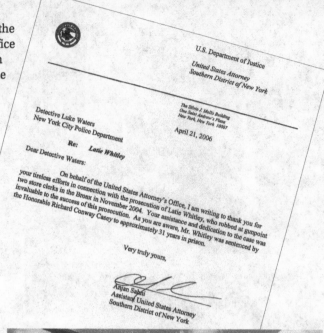

Sean Murray and me
at the Aviation Unit,
getting ready for an
aerial view of a
target location.

Sean Murray and me
at my second home,
Rao's restaurant.

(From left to right) Detective Barry Sullivan, me, and Detective James Conneely on Pope Benedict's detail, Yankee Stadium, April 2008.

On a covert operation in 2012.

U.S. Department of Justice
The Federal Bureau of Investigation
is proud to recognize
Detective Luke Waters
of the New York City Police Department, Bronx Homicide Squad

for your many years of distinguished service in law enforcement and your selfless efforts to protect and serve the American public. You have always recognized that a key to combating crime is unstinting cooperation among law enforcement agencies at all levels of government. The FBI and the American people have been the beneficiaries of your professionalism and dedication to duty, and we congratulate you on a remarkable career.

June 2012
Date

Robert S. Mueller, III
Director

Citation/certificate from the FBI recognizing my many years of distinguished service, June 2012.

A proud moment, standing in Croke Park with my wife, Susan, and children, Tara, Ryan, and David, at a Gaelic football match between An Garda Síochána, the Metropolitan Police, the PSNI, and the NYPD, 2013.

CHAPTER THIRTEEN

END OF INNOCENCE

Life changes you, new life particularly. When you become a parent, your whole way of looking at the world changes, along with your priorities. It was December 12, 2006, and with Christmas Day less than a fortnight away, all our six-year-old, Tara, and her younger brother, Ryan, could talk about were toys and the speed of Santa Claus's sleigh, worrying, at bedtime, about whether they'd been good enough for Santa to come. Our youngest son, David, was just nine months old and slept contentedly in his cot. Over the next few hours, I would be sharply reminded that other children in this city wouldn't be lucky enough to have such childish concerns.

Life is not fair, and we learn to accept it, but the day we accept the premature death of a child is the day we lose our humanity. Today would be the day Baby Binns was born, and would die, at the hands of the person she would have expected to protect her.

"Okay, guys, who's up? Sounds like maybe some crackhead threw a kid off a roof. C'mon, Pete, time is money, buddy."

"Nice," mutters Detective Peter Tarsnane. Always one to see the glass half empty, Miserable Pete slips his arms through a

151

sweater, the first thing he'd laid his hands on when exiting the family home an hour earlier.

It's 8:20 in the morning, December 12, 2006, just two weeks till Christmas. In any other office across the five boroughs my announcement would be met with a deathly silence, but the other members of the B-Team at the Bronx Homicide Task Force—Miserable, Bobby Grant, Mike De Paolis, and Joe O'Neill—are half a career past appalled. But for all our hard-bitten practicality, the Job is about to show us all a side of human behavior we will find hard to believe.

The Eastchester Houses on Burke Avenue are some of the better housing projects in this part of the Bronx. Bracing themselves for the media scrutiny which always surrounds child killings, police management have allocated all available resources to the address, starting with squad DTs from the 49, who are already on the scene.

NYPD Unusual Occurrence forms have a section reserved for the age of the victim. In this case it reads "zero." It's only half an hour since our Jane Doe was discovered, facedown, naked, covered in bruises, cuts, and garden debris, by a couple of city housing employees inside a low fence by the grassy verges to the rear of the block of ten five-story-high buildings.

The original call was that the body of a child had been found, possibly thrown from a roof. The full picture is a little different, and we soon confirm that our dead child is actually a seven-pound, full-term female newborn infant of black/Hispanic descent, only minutes old when dropped to her death, and currently awaiting autopsy at Jacobi Medical Center.

Andy Hernandez and Jorge Chico out of the 49 brief us on arrival, and a Level One Mobilization is in operation, which means a frozen crime scene, as uniformed cops from the local precinct struggle to keep not just reporters but also curious bystanders and residents twenty yards from the front entrance.

"What do you think, buddy?" I ask Bobby Grant as we examine a bloodstained towel found close to the spot where the body landed. My partner stands in the early morning December sunshine scanning the building from top to bottom, while Mike De Paolis chats to Maulicci and Short, two CSU detectives who have just arrived to swab and are making use of the good light to photograph all around them.

"You know what, Luke? I'm thinking whoever tossed the kid was above the first floor, or the body wouldn't be marked, and was probably up higher, considering the injuries," Bobby, the sharpest DT in our office, continues thoughtfully.

My partner is not only New York's finest, he's also New York's furthest. The NYPD has strict rules on how far we can live from the city limits, making New Jersey and Pennsylvania out of bounds for MOS, but Grant's wife and family live two hours away—two hours by Delta jet, that is—in Atlanta, Georgia, a city famous for Coca-Cola, the Olympics, and Gone with the Wind, *which is precisely where you will find him as soon as he has worked his overtime, though our high flier keeps an apartment in New York for the times when he unexpectedly has to catch a case, instead of the next red-eye out of JFK.*

If the bosses down at the Puzzle Palace ever find out what he's been doing, Bobby will probably be facing a little chat with the chief, but he's winged it for a few years now, and, so far, his luck has held.

From the top of the building we get a different perspective on our tiny victim's first, and last, moments of life, though my own tentative glances over the edge of the roof barrier offer no further insight into the mind, or identity, of a person who tosses a new-born to her death.

Crackheads and those who supply them will stop at nothing to feed their habit and extract money owed. Between the public revulsion at this crime and the manpower at our disposal, we're confident that we will persuade someone to come forward and finger the perp.

Teams of DTs knock on the doors of the apartments in the building, working their way through the list one floor at a time in the usual canvass for witnesses, but two hours later we've got nothing to show for our efforts.

All local precincts provide a couple of detectives for an investigation like this, and any officers available are called in to help out in some way. The Emergency Services Unit also assists in searching through garbage incinerators, swapping submachine guns for rakes and yard brooms as they sift through the garbage from the incinerator.

Overhead, one of the department's helicopters hovers above the rooftops, providing intelligence to the mobile command post, a catchall term which describes a range of vehicles, from Mercedes vans to articulated trucks, in which the Brass coordinate the efforts on the ground with the help of a bank of computers and technicians.

Clothing, a towel, and tissues near where the body was found are individually marked with numbered yellow plastic "flags," each of which is photographed and bagged for transport back to the crime lab at headquarters, but right now I am more concerned with the expressions on the faces in the crowd than DNA samples. Sometimes your perp is amongst curious onlookers who throng the crime scene, so I watch for anyone who stands out, with another eye for anyone who deliberately signals us from the crowd.

My eyes crisscross the faces several times before I realize that a number of different people are pointing in the same direction, which seems to be the window of an apartment on the fifth floor, so I walk towards the entrance only to find my progress halted by uniformed cops and noisy, frustrated residents packed into the small lobby, while on the stairs a middle-aged black woman sits, sobbing, head in hands.

I go down on one knee to introduce myself and ask her name.

"I'm Michelle Williams, Apartment 5F. I think . . . I think my daughter might be the one," the woman sobs.

"'The one'?" I echo.

"The one who . . . you know . . . who had that baby, Detective. I think it was my Latisha. I just phone her, and she crying. My God, until now I don't even know she is pregnant."

"So, where can we find—Latisha? Where can we find your Latisha right now?"

"She told me she in class. She's only fourteen years old." The radio, still in my left hand, drops slowly towards my waist as Bobby's eyes roll towards the ceiling.

"No way, buddy!" he whispers, with a scornful scowl. "A four-teen-year-old carried a child full term and then gave birth, all without the mother knowing anything? And not one of the neighbors we spoke to noticed, either? Gimme a break! We're wasting our time here."

At this stage Michelle Williams is the only lead we have, so although I agree with Bobby's assessment we escort her to our car, leaving Tarsnane, De Paolis, O'Neill, and the local DTs to continue the canvass for witnesses while we take the woman up to MS 144, Michelangelo Middle School. Their motto is admira-

ble, "Where today's children prepare for tomorrow's world," but we are totally unprepared for the scenes which will unfold in front of us in the headmistress's office in a few minutes.

"I'm certain you are on the wrong track with this, Detectives," Principal Katian Lotakis says confidently, while a social worker is sent to take the child from class. "I know the student, and she certainly does not look pregnant. She's good in class—she got an A for her essay yesterday—and she took gym this morning— hardly likely if she'd just given birth," she says with the stare school principals reserve for pupils—or police officers—who waste their time. The atmosphere in that office changes from skepticism to incredulity ten seconds after Latisha Binns appears at the door.

Although only three months past her fourteenth birthday the teenager stands at almost six feet tall and is over 160 pounds in weight, but as her mother rises to greet the teen, her daughter's response is that of a frightened child, a tearful reply that leaves us all utterly stunned.

"Latisha, are you the one?"

The youngster looks at her mother, turns to look at us, and simply replies, "Yes."

"You had a baby, beside my room?" the older woman asks, wiping bitter tears from her eyes with the sleeve of her blouse.

"Last night. When it was born, I . . . I was afraid you'd hear it, Mom. I didn't . . . I just didn't know whadda do," Binns blurts out. "So I . . . I pulled away the cord, picked it up, and I threw the baby out the window to stop it crying."

Bobby Grant, as sharp a cop as I ever worked with, looks at the teenager in openmouthed amazement. He utters just one word. "Jesus!"

I am so taken aback that I'm frozen in my seat, unable to respond to Binns's confession. I have three kids and have wit-

nessed the pain of childbirth and the time it takes for a woman to recover with the help of nurses, midwives, and pediatricians. Here is a junior high school student who has just come from gym, claiming to have had a baby twenty-four hours earlier, without so much as a paracetamol.

Time seemed to stand still in the room, and I had no idea of how much of it passed, seconds or a minute, before Bobby and I led our suspect back to the car accompanied by her mother. We took her to Jacobi for medical attention, the same hospital where the baby lay cold on a slab in the mortuary. Our drive to the hospital was short, fast, and upsetting, as both mother and daughter were crying in the backseat of our Buick, Latisha's shrieks growing louder as the full realization of what she had done hit her.

"I'm going to jail now. I'm sorry, I'm so sorry," she moaned, adding that she became pregnant after being raped on her way to school.

"Bullshit," muttered Bobby as we weaved through the traffic.

As the doctors tended to our prisoner we got permission from her mother to have the apartment at Burke Avenue searched. Once the doctors had taken care of Latisha we tactfully questioned the fourteen-year-old on the details of her pregnancy, the birth of her child, and the reasons why she threw her baby out an upstairs window. Next Pete Tarsnane and I drove back to MS 144 to speak to Principal Lotakis once again, who gave us a copy of the school yearbook, which we took back to the hospital to see if our prisoner could identify the father of the baby from class photographs.

It emerged that Michelle Williams was a religious woman who, concerned for her daughter's future, had stopped her from playing with many of the other kids in her neighborhood. Her mother made sure that she concentrated on her studies and sports. A year earlier Latisha, unknown to her mother, had developed a crush on a Hispanic boy at school, and back in Jacobi she immediately picked his picture from the yearbook and named him as the father of the dead child.

Grant and I followed up on the earlier claims of rape, only to discover that the youngsters had had consensual sex after all. The boy, age fourteen at the time of conception, told us they had only had intercourse once, which proved enough to get the then-thirteen-year-old Latisha pregnant.

Our suspect told us how, having given birth, she cut the child's umbilical cord herself and placed the severed material, along with her pajamas and other bloodied clothing, in a plastic bag. After killing the baby, the teen cleaned herself up, dressed, and left for school as usual, passing by the Gun Hill Road McDonald's en route. She told us that she dumped the bag in the trash can and, sure enough, later that day a police dog uncovered the piece of cord and bloodstained clothes in the rubbish at the fast-food outlet. The evidence was photographed and placed in a special biohazard bag before CSU then moved on to the family apartment, in which they found bloodied bedclothes, carpet, and other material which tested positive for the girl's DNA.

Emotions can run high in cases like this, but we were very aware that we were dealing with a child and were tactful and professional while still focused on solving the crime. Every DT on the case was shocked by the news, and also amazed that Latisha Binns managed to hide a full-term pregnancy, and give birth, without her mother, classmates, or schoolteachers suspecting the truth.

You could argue that a teenage mother, exhausted after giving birth in silence and emotionally distraught, panicked and tried to rid herself of her unwanted infant by the quickest means possible, giving no thought to the consequences. On the other hand, Binns could be depicted as a coldhearted killer, who not only treated her helpless daughter like garbage but tried to cover her tracks by dumping evidence far from the scene of the crime—and was so unmoved by her actions that she sat through class just hours later as if nothing had happened.

The next day, the Medical Examiner's Office called Detective Andy Hernandez confirming that the baby was alive when she hit the ground and telling him that the case was now to be reclassified as a homicide.

Our prisoner was charged with one count of manslaughter and one count of murder in the second degree, which for a crime like this would normally result in decades in prison upon conviction.

The case was heard in family court, away from the glare of the media and the public, and as we gave evidence, one by one, the reaction of all present in the courtroom was identical to that in the principal's office at MS 144 a month earlier, as even the judge struggled to understand how the defendant hid her pregnancy so well, sitting exams and taking gym class right up to and after the birth.

Despite the understandable sympathy towards Latisha, the accused was found guilty on both counts, but her earlier predictions that she would go to jail proved incorrect. The accused girl sidestepped imprisonment and instead was paroled, walking free from the courthouse, as she would remain as long as she kept on the right side of the law.

Although the death of Baby Binns left all in Bronx Homicide

deeply shocked, the sad reality was that cases like this were all too frequent, and long before Principal Lotakis's personal letter to NYPD Commissioner Ray Kelly, commending us personally for our sensitive handling of the case, the details had already started to fade.

Less than a week after the death of Baby Binns, an infant was found by a passerby near the crossroads at Crotona Park in the Bronx, still alive, thankfully, with his umbilical cord attached. A day later another newborn was found dead, deposited like just another piece of commuters' rubbish, at a Long Island train station.

Eventually it became clear he was smothered to death by his mother—a thirty-four-year-old nanny—his body placed in a shoe box.

As a cop you become desensitized, detached from death. If not, you won't be able to do your job as a link in the chain from cradle to grave. Detective work isn't about emotion, it's about facts, but cases involving children test your objectivity and dispassion no matter how long you have been a cop.

The worst case of all is where you attend the autopsy of an infant.

A few months after we closed the Baby Binns investigation, I caught a case that will stay with me for the rest of my life: a potential multiple homicide as a result of a catastrophic fire at 1022 Woodycrest Avenue in the Bronx, an area popular with new immigrants trying to get a first foothold in the USA.

On March 7, 2007, FDNY responded to a three-alarm emergency call in the building, and although it took their trucks less than three and a half minutes to get to the address, they arrived to a scene of utter devastation. Two families, both new arrivals from Mali, shared an apartment in which a fire had broken out.

The victims were rushed to various hospitals locally for emergency treatment, along with four injured firefighters and a paramedic who came to the immigrants' aid.

Some of these victims had been badly burned in the blaze and others had internal injuries from jumping out of upstairs windows to escape the flames and fumes. We later discovered what occurred was a result of a heater being turned over on a mattress at about eleven p.m., while the children inside were fast asleep.

One by one the victims were being transferred from local hospitals to Jacobi Medical, a level one trauma center and the best-equipped facility to deal with major emergencies. I decided to take a look at the scene, but there was nothing much we could do, so we left it to the fire marshals and drove over to Jacobi to set up a command post for our investigation.

The medical staff were some of the most experienced in the country and a lot of gunshot victims in the Bronx owed their lives to the men and women who worked there. We were still getting organized when the bodies of the kids, aged from just one year up to eleven years, started to arrive in a fleet of ambulances.

With each one, the supervising physician caught my eye and shook his head, and I silently whispered a little prayer. By this stage one of the mothers had arrived at the hospital to receive the news that her four sons, one-year-old Bilaly, Abudubucary aged five, eight-year-old Mahamadou, and Bandiougou, who at eleven was the oldest victim, had all died of smoke inhalation.

The woman stood in the corner, doing a deal with God to spare her daughter, Diaba, aged just three, who at that moment was in the back of an ambulance racing through traffic to the ER, but as soon as the bus carrying her arrived it was pretty clear that all our prayers were in vain.

"This little one looks bad, Doc," one of the paramedics said as the gurney was rolled in, its three-year-old occupant foaming at the mouth as blood rushed from her ears.

For all the professionalism and the detachment, when it came down to it, neither the doctor nor I had the heart to break the news to the child's mother as her last child was pronounced DOA.

As dawn broke on another day, we had eight dead children, as well as several adult victims. Fatamata Foumare, forty-five, lost her life in the blaze, along with her children Djibril, aged three, and seven-month-old twins, Sisi and Harouma. One child, their seven-year-old sister Hassimy, survived.

Facing the bodies of eight dead adults, you don't even flinch—it's just another routine day in the Bronx—but this case, and any with a child, was different. The names and faces of these tender children who died will stay with me always.

CHAPTER FOURTEEN

THE SLEEP OF THE JUST

Detective William Fisher is not happy. In fact, right now he is totally fed up with life in general, and the Job in particular. He's missing sleep, shut down on overtime, and to make matters worse the double stabbing case which has just landed on his desk is looking like another routine homicide.

Or, as Willie puts it, a bag of shit. A detective needs stimulation.

"You know what this is, buddy?" he asks, arms folded, feet propped up on his desk in that corner of the 49 Detective Squad he calls home.

"A bag of shit, Willie?"

I nod approvingly, my chin dropping onto my chest, as my eyes blink, then slowly close involuntarily. Twenty hours without sleep will do that to you.

"Any start on the DD5s, buddy?" I ask, trying to pretend I don't know the answer.

When it comes to paperwork Willie believes in outsourcing the workload.

"Just having a quick nap, then I'll make a start. Hey, any word of a spot opening up at Homicide, Luke? You know I'm trying to join you guys and get away from this 49 squad."

I shrug my shoulders, reach for a Detective Unusual form,

and slide it into the printer, as my partner slips into uncon-
sciousness once again.

An hour earlier I'd arrived with the rest of my team at Bronx
Homicide for the start of my eight a.m. shift and checked with
the overnight detail, only to learn that we were starting into a
possible double homicide, with one victim DOA, lying on a slab
at Jacobi Medical, and the other hanging on grimly to life in the
intensive care upstairs.

"The second guy, Frank Cuevas, is likely, Luke," said Scott
Patterson, yawning as he reached for yet another coffee. His
shift was over, but his day and mine were only beginning.

"Who's up on this one?" Kenny Umlauft called from his
office door as one of the other cops picked up a pen to log the
case into the ledger. "I'm catching, Kenny," I replied, looking up
from the newspaper the night-watch guys had left on my desk.
"Anybody seen Barry?"

We were still one short and Umlauft was grinning, well
aware that Detective Barry Sullivan was not known for his love
of early starts, as our sergeant reminded him when he walked
in, immaculately dressed as ever but "lookin' a bit shook," as me
ma would say.

"Hiya, Barry. Bit early for you, eh?" said Umlauft, looking at
his watch in mock horror.

"God, not today, Kenny. Please, not today," Sullivan whispered with a groan.

"Okay, so what we got?" I asked DT Brendan Mallon, who
was cursing his coffee as it burned his tongue while he started
printing from the nearest computer. We wallpapered the folders with paperwork, following the basic twelve-step investigation process, every step of which had to be documented and
accounted for, from our first response to the scene, to the posi-

tion of the body, to the canvass of witnesses, the interviewing of 911 callers, and the victimology, as we called it, which is a complete and detailed biography of our victim.

"Not much. DOA is a Hispanic male named Christopher Velez. 'Bout three a.m. this morning he and his homey, this Frank Cuevas, are playing pool up at Park Billiards—you know, that big sports bar on White Plains Road? Anyway, they go outside, and some guy drives up on the sidewalk, clips one of 'em, and a fight breaks out. Usual BS argument. He-said-you-said, yada-yada-yada. Driver ends up stabbing both of them. Willie Fisher is catching it out of the 49. He has two witnesses down there now, Luke."

We worked as a team, without ego, each taking a task, with the ultimate aim of wading through the case and getting another one squared away. It's the nature of detective work.

Sean Murray knew more than most about getting results, and although he hadn't moved from his seat, his mind was already working through the details. If Bronx Homicide had a baseball team, Sean would be the safe pair of hands, the player you'd call up to the base when you needed a home run. No matter how high the case files were piled on his desk, he never complained when the CO handed him another, which he did whenever he needed a result.

Murray was an Irish emigrant like myself, but he was raised far from Dublin, in the rural west of the country, and was married to a girl from the Aran Islands. Reaching Galway from the islands meant crossing choppy open water in a ferry, or, a generation earlier, a currach rowboat, so the spirit of meitheal— lending a helping hand to a neighbor—was vital, and it had migrated with him from farmland to the city street, ensuring that Sean would never let you, or the victim, down.

"Just thinking out loud, Luke . . . the witnesses said that the driver was from St. Andrews, up in Yonkers, right? And the guy drove a weird-looking little box-shaped blue car—ten-to-one that's a Scion. Can't be that many of 'em around the streets. Maybe Brendan and I will take a little drive over there and have a gander to see if we can spot the yoke. C'mon, Mallon! I'll let you drive if it makes you happier."

Ten minutes after Murray and Mallon drove over to Yonkers, I was listening to Willie's woes over in the 49, nodding sympathetically as he whinged about his lot in life, before we sat down to take statements from the two distraught witnesses, James Equiziaco and Oneal Smith, who explained the lead-up to the events of a few hours earlier.

The two men, along with the deceased Velez and critical Cuevas, were all in their midtwenties. They were regulars at the Park Billiards Café and Sports Bar, where they played a few frames of pool and chatted up the women on Ladies' Night, a scene played out in every town and city across the country. At the next table that night, Eddie Rodriguez was doing much the same thing with his friends, and when the club DJ asked if anyone was from Yonkers both groups were quick to declare their allegiances.

"Hey—you guys from Yonkers as well?" Rodriguez said.

"Yeah. You, too? Where'bouts?" someone replied from the other table.

"St. Andrews, man. How ya doin'?" Rodriguez responded, saluting his neighbors.

"For real. Small world," Velez said with a smile.

The players went back to their game, and after a few minutes Rodriguez went outside to sit in his car and light a cigarette, paying little attention to the man who had followed him to the back door and, likewise, was lighting up. Rodriguez started up the car. It was time for him and his friends to head home, so he pulled up on the sidewalk to get closer to the door, in the process narrowly missing the other smoker, who took exception to almost being snookered by the blue Scion.

"Yo! What's your problem, man? You nearly hit me!" the pedestrian's voice called angrily from the darkness.

It was Christopher Velez, the neighbor he had chatted to earlier. Rodriguez rolled down the window, and the insults flew.

Someone stepped inside to tell the other players that a fight was about to break out, and soon the space was filled with people—most of them were drunk, or close—who egged on both parties. At this stage the whole incident was barely worthy of the cops' attention, but then one of Velez's group stepped forward and kicked Rodriguez's car—he angrily objected and was punched through the open window as he tried to get out.

A knife was produced—we never could establish by whom—and in the struggle which ensued, Rodriguez swung at both Velez, who dropped to the ground, fatally wounded, and Cuevas, who was seriously injured.

Rodriguez was also cut in the fracas and had already left the scene by the time cops out of the 49th Precinct responded to the 911 call to find Frankie Cuevas screaming with his hand against his bleeding chest. Outside a nearby Laundromat, Christopher Velez sat in his car dying from a fatal wound to his heart. Cuevas was lucky. EMS stabilized their patient before rushing him to Jacobi, where the staff have dealt with hundreds of stabbings. Cuevas was tough and pulled through, but fortune is finite, as he would soon find out.

Once we took the statements from the witnesses we left Equiziaco and Smith in the hospital awaiting news on their injured friend and we headed back to the squad room. I had just started to type up their account when my cell phone rang, the sound momentarily rousing my partner, who was soon fast asleep across the desk again, snoring deeply, a smile etched onto his face.

Willie was grabbing forty winks, and pocketing eighty-five dollars an hour overtime, too. If we had been in Bronx Homicide right then, Kenny would be drawing little dollar signs on his eyelids with a dark green Magic Marker, because by the time we'd clock out, we would be up about a thousand dollars on the day apiece.

"Luke, it's Sean. Myself and Mallon are up in Yonkers, outside an apartment at nineteen Grey Place. I think we have our guy's car."

Sean explained that he'd run the plates on the dark blue Scion, and it came to a Joanna Cruz, so he'd rung Yonkers PD to see if they had any information on her.

"Funny that you should ask," Detective Trainer had said over the phone, after Sean introduced himself. "Her name came up this morning. She has a boyfriend. Let me see . . . Ramirez? Where did I put that report? . . . No, scratch that, it's Rodriguez, Detective Murray. Eddie Rodriguez. We interviewed him a few hours ago down at St. Joseph's ER. Guy was stabbed. Told us someone tried to stick him up at a gas station."

It was a real break, and I sent a couple of cops over to relieve Murray at the address. I accessed Eddie Rodriguez's photograph from our files, copying details of his height, weight, color, and other information into the department's Force Field software, which produces several dozen pictures of similar-looking individuals. From these I selected five, plus our suspect's image, so we could show them to our witnesses waiting to see Cuevas, who was still in intensive care.

Right then Willie was doing a pretty fair impression of a corpse, too, but his loud snores were a dead giveaway that he hadn't clocked out just yet.

"Huh? Wh-a-a-t?" said Fisher, blinking as I stood over his chair, in which he had been flopped for the last couple of hours, shaking his shoulder.

"Time to go, buddy. We have to interview our witnesses. Looks like Sean Murray has found our perp."

"Ugh, great. Right behind you, a-a-a-g-g-g-h-h-h!" said Fisher.

We headed across the car park to Jacobi, and took great care to separately show James Equiziaco and Oneal Smith a different version of the printout, making it harder for them to tip each other off about whom to pick out. Each of them immediately identified Rodriguez on their copy as the man who'd stabbed Velez and Cuevas.

On the drive over to Yonkers I briefed sleeping beauty Willie on what had been happening for the last few hours so we were both up to speed when we arrived at Joanna Cruz's apartment. We had backup from several cops from Yonkers PD and a couple of guys from the 49.

Our knock at the door was answered immediately, and when we identified ourselves, Joanna Cruz ushered us in to meet her boyfriend, who was sitting on his bed having a Chinese takeaway meal. The atmosphere was cordial and relaxed and he readily agreed to come in to the station with us and explain how he got injured. No mention was made of the double stabbing, the seriously injured man in Jacobi, or our homicide victim chilling in the morgue. There would be plenty of time for that later.

Rodriguez wasn't too pleased when he realized we were

on our way to the Bronx and not Yonkers and was even less impressed when he realized we were not buying the story he'd concocted to explain his cut hand to the other detectives who were called by the ER staff—standard procedure when someone comes in off the streets nursing an injury.

I have never investigated a serious stabbing where the attacker has not cut himself in some way in the melee. Even if your target is unarmed he will try to grab the weapon, and in the struggle the blade will often cut both the perpetrator and the victim. Rodriguez's injuries were consistent with the statements of Equiziaco and Smith.

Our suspect eventually decided to be cooperative, and at about one a.m. admitted that he'd stabbed both men. He agreed to make a written statement of his involvement, explaining that he'd had no choice, clearly intending to claim self-defense should the case come to court. If this had been a simple assault his stance might have made sense. With a good lawyer and a sympathetic judge and jury he might even have walked on probation, but he was not aware yet that one of the men he'd attacked was dead. He was looking at a possible charge of homicide and a lifetime in prison.

I called Larry Piergrossi at the Bronx DA's office and explained what we had, and he agreed to come over with a technician and set up a video recording of Rodriguez's statement, for the record, authorizing me to formally place our suspect under arrest for murder in the second degree and another charge of attempted murder. We explained this to Rodriguez and broke the news to him that Velez was dead.

At first he seemed unable to take it in, but his incredulity soon turned to rage, and he started ranting and raving that he had been tricked and cursed me, Fisher, the DA, and the system in general as the seriousness of his situation started to dawn on him.

The crucial points were that he'd made a statement of his own free will, and that he did stab both men, but in his position I would probably have felt the same. Our prisoner's lawyer, Howard Levine, arrived at the 49, and we left them alone to confer while we grabbed a couple of hours of sleep.

My eyes closed as soon as my head hit the couch in the TV room; three hours later, still wearing the same clothes, I was back in the game. I drove over to an address in Crotona Park to speak to the nearest thing the Bronx had to a casting agent. Robert Weston was the sort of guy who was always on the clock, which was one of the reasons so many detectives reached out to him when they, like me, needed five "fillers."

"And this time, try to get me some guys who actually look like our suspect, will you, Robert?" I said, giving him a detailed description.

"Whatcha mean? I ahways do, Detective," he grumbled. Years earlier Weston had been having lunch when a cop walked up and asked him if he wanted to make a few dollars sitting alongside some other citizens, and their suspect, in a lineup for a witness. It had been the start of a new career. Soon he was not only appearing himself but rounding up bodies who would get ten dollars apiece, with twenty going to Weston for setting it up. Lineups are a pain to put together, and Robert's number was soon on the speed dial of half of the investigators in the department.

A few hours later, in the presence of Rodriguez's lawyer, both our witnesses positively picked our prisoner out from the other five as the man who'd stabbed both our victims. This identification, added to his statement, should have been enough to convict him.

Still, somehow there were a couple of further twists and turns in the case. The first one occurred almost six months later when the GMC Envoy in which Frank Cuevas was traveling at speed along East Tremont in the Bronx clipped the curbside, sending the SUV sailing through the air, where it met a thick steel pole in a traffic island. The post opened the two-and-a-half-ton truck like a key on a sardine can, decapitating one of the passengers and cutting several others in two.

Then it seemed that our homicide case might be pleaded down to a lesser charge, particularly when the ADA in charge of the case, Cynthia Lindblum, got a call from Rodriguez's lawyer, Howard Levine. He said that he had new information about another man whom his client claimed was responsible for killing Christopher Velez—a Latin Kings gang member named Rafael Alvarez.

Eddie told Levine that Alvarez, a longtime friend, had admitted to him that it was he who had finished off Velez while Eddie drove himself to St. Joseph's. Alvarez had visited him in Rikers to apologize for how it had turned out, offering to pay his family five thousand dollars.

The claim was intriguing, if it was true, so when Cynthia passed on the information I followed up. I started by obtaining a copy of the prison visitors' log from the Department of Corrections, which lists the name and date of birth for all visitors to Rikers, including a unique ID number which is used every time someone comes by to see one of the prisoners. Sure enough, Rafael Alvarez was listed in the log, and when I ran his details through our computer system I discovered that he was currently on probation. Alvarez had already been arrested a number of times for charges including threatening people with weapons, and he was listed as a member of the Latin Kings. The Kings had originally started as a sort of benevolent society in the 1940s to protect Hispanics living in Chicago; by the 1990s they had spread as far as New York City and were now just another violent street gang heavily involved in drugs.

I prepared a "wanted" card for Alvarez, so if he was stopped by any local cops a note would appear telling the officer that Detective Waters in Bronx Homicide wanted to speak to the man he or she had pulled over. It would be of little use out of state, and we had no idea where Alvarez was at this stage.

I paid half a dozen visits to his apartment and his girlfriend's place, but to no avail. I reached out to his probation officer, Ronald Levy, who offered what help he could, but the guy was nowhere to be found, which fitted with Eddie's claims that Alvarez had something to hide.

Bronx DA Robert Johnson was anxious to pursue a conviction against Rodriguez and we still had two eyewitnesses as well as our suspect's signed and recorded confession, so we proceeded with the prosecution, and on June 14, 2009, two years after the fight in the pool hall car park, the People of the State of New York vs. Eddie Rodriguez, Indictment Number 1553-07, came before Honorable Judge Barbara Newman.

From the very start the accused seemed confident of beating the rap, a demeanor shared by his attorney, who shouted and displayed flashes of anger in the opening days which did little to endear him to the jury, or the judge, who told him on several occasions to calm down.

I was called to the stand to testify and was questioned by ADA Lisa Davis, for the People, with whom I had run through the questions in detail in the lead-up to the trial.

Next it was Howard Levine's turn to cross-examine me, and he adopted an aggressive stance, becoming fixated on, above all things, my pronunciation of his surname.

He said to-may-to, I said to-mah-to, but as I kept slipping up his face slowly started to resemble one.

"It's Lev-een, not Le-vine, Detective!" he said in exasperation, as I mispronounced his name again. I apologized once more and explained that growing up in Ireland it was pronounced the way I kept saying it. "Fine, Detective Watt-airs . . ." he responded, sending the jury into hysterics.

I remained completely impassive, because whether Eddie Rodriguez was innocent or guilty was not up to me: it was up to a jury of his peers. And despite his confidence, the way this was going there was a very real possibility that he would end up being taken away to start what amounted at his age to a life sentence behind bars, which was no laughing matter.

Judge Newman smashed her gavel, calling for order, and glared at the defense attorney before lecturing him. All of this was doing little for the accused, a fact confirmed when, a couple of days later, after a short adjournment, the verdict was finally handed down.

Eddie Rodriguez got twenty-five years for the homicide and fifteen for the attempted murder, to run consecutively. He went berserk, insisting he was innocent and demanding to know why I had not found Alvarez.

"He knows! That Irish detective knows I didn't do it!" he screamed, swearing loudly as he was taken away by the courts' officers.

We went over to Cynthia's office, where the mood could not be more different, and she congratulated all of us on a job well done, as much amazed as delighted by the verdict.

"Great result," she cooed. "Forty years! Forty years, you guys! I can't believe it!"

It was an impressive conviction for any prosecutor but left

me feeling far from wanting to celebrate. The system did not screw Eddie Rodriguez. He stabbed two men, and one of them died shortly afterward, a fact he admitted to in a written statement, but to this day I would feel far happier had I had a chance to grill Alvarez and establish if there was any truth to the allegations that he had also attacked the victim, as our convict claimed.

Eddie Rodriguez did not adjust well to life behind bars, and by the time I retired he had not begun to cooperate with the system, making any chance of parole highly unlikely. Even if he does come to terms with his new reality, he will be in his sixties when— sometime around 2040—he walks the streets a free man again.

CHAPTER FIFTEEN

JUSTICE DELAYED

Sometimes a cold case can be revived by a phone call, sometimes by a confession. On rare occasions it's through a combination of both, but as I learned on one investigation the enthusiasm of the most motivated witness can cool when faced with the dysfunctional state justice system.

Sean O'Toole invites me to take a seat in his office and tells an intriguing story.

Two states away a woman called Catherine has just telephoned the NYPD and told the officer at the end of the line that a man whom she has been dating confessed, after their Bible study class, to a murder. According to the caller, her boyfriend, whom I'll call Jayson Smith, told her he had shot the victim dead in revenge for killing his brother in the Bronx, back in the day. Revenge hits like this were pretty common in New York in the eighties and nineties when the city recorded about three thousand homicides a year, but Catherine, a hardworking legal aide and single mother of two, is appalled.

Our caller is originally from the South but now lives in Wilmington, Delaware, and she has details of the crime which were withheld from the media. Getting this kind of information is customary in investigations so as to weed out the usual attention-seekers

177

and serial confessors. While Catherine's claims spark our interest, on the face of it the alleged confessor seems an unlikely murderer.

Jayson has carved out a successful career in Wilmington in IT support with a huge international law firm that would have vetted its employees carefully.

Still we feel there is merit to the woman's claims and I partner with Detective Billy Simeon from the 42 and travel to Delaware to interview Catherine. She impresses us both with her clarity, candor, and straightforward manner. We report back to the Bronx ADA assigned to the case, Larry Piergrossi, that he has a very credible witness regarding a homicide.

Simeon and I turn to the unsolved murder of Jayson's brother, which Jayson has allegedly avenged. That crime took place in a different county, meaning a different jurisdiction, different detective squads, and different courts. Once we manage to cut through all the red tape, we establish that Jayson's brother may have been killed in a dispute over a woman named Monique. We set off to interview her but within a minute of the introductions she tells us that she has hired a lawyer to whom we must now direct our questions. This is a most unusual move for a witness in a homicide dating back a decade and a half.

We try another approach, and clock up more air miles, flying across six states to Winston-Salem, North Carolina, to interview another witness who was in the car the night Jayson's brother was shot—our trip was a futile endeavor, as he could not or would not cooperate.

With only Catherine's testimony to support our case, we and the ADA decide we should speak to Jayson in Delaware. Apart from confirming the known fact that his brother had been murdered in Manhattan back in 1992, he keeps his mouth shut. A confession is always welcome, particularly in cold cases like this, which present all kinds of technical and legal problems. Witnesses get older and forget details, others move away and leave no forwarding address, while some, by now, are deceased.

After our conversation with Jayson I get a call from the huge international law firm that employs our suspect. Their director of security is Peter Tuffey, a forty-year-old former inspector in the NYPD, where he headed the 71st Precinct. He has been told that the feds like one of his technicians for a homicide and wants to arrange a meeting to discuss the case. The relief in his voice when he realizes he is talking to a cop, and not the FBI, is palpable. It also means we can avoid a lot of paperwork even before we meet at the company's office, in a tower of blue glass and steel which soars over the heart of Times Square.

Tuffey tells me that he is flying to Switzerland for a face-to-face meeting with the company's CEO, whom he predicts will immediately sack our suspect, and who is understandably worried about the likely fallout from the banner headlines sure to follow.

The firm does a lot of work providing political law advice on campaign finance, conflicts of interest, and other related issues for politicians at every level, right up to presidential campaigns. Murder trials are not part of this picture. Tuffey knows that the tabloid press will have a field day covering a homicide even loosely linked to the company and the simplest way to protect the firm's reputation is to fire Jayson.

It transpires he already has a conviction for armed robbery back in 1991, which he did not mention on his application. Our suspect has also been arrested for domestic violence involving money since moving to Delaware. That is another red flag, because any issues relating to financial irregularities leave legal firm employees open to blackmail or bribery, which can compromise clients' cases. I am worried if our suspect loses his job *he will disappear, so I ask the former cop to hold off until I can build my case.*

"Look, Peter, you can't let him go," I plead. "Think about it. He can start a lawsuit against you, which is your problem, but it will make my life a lot harder."

"Oh, yeah? Let him try. We're not exactly short of attorneys, Luke," Tuffey replies.

"Okay, but my problem is that I don't need to start a manhunt on the guy, if he decides to go on the run. I need you to go back to your CEO and do me a favor. Give me two months to build a case and indict this guy. Why not wait to sack him when he's convicted?"

Tuffey agrees. Following the meeting in Switzerland he calls me to say that I've got my eight weeks—after that the firm will tell Jayson to clear out his desk and take their chances with any future lawsuit.

Weeks pass and we exhaust all avenues and leads open to us, so it is agreed with some trepidation—as probable cause is weak—that Piergrossi will present our case to a grand jury. They come back with an indictment and when we approach Jayson for the second time in Delaware with an arrest warrant, I can see almost a sense of relief in his face. His new cooperative attitude is highly beneficial, as we do not have to fight for his extradition across state lines back to New York. Once Jayson waives his rights in that extradition process, we hand the case over to the district attorney and Jayson is arraigned before a judge in New York, who sets his bail at half a million dollars.

While this makes front-page news back in Wilmington, the journalists don't realize that the Bronx DA may ultimately accept a soft plea bargain from our suspect, as the evidence is not so strong. Jayson, in the eighteen months he spends on remand, refuses to comment about his involvement in the killing.

"Plead guilty, Jayson, maybe you'll get two years in prison and maybe five years' probation," I tell him during one of our interviews. "You've already done a year and a half. Another eight months and you could be out of there, a free man, able to get on with your life and start again."

"And what if I don't take a plea?"

"Then you roll the dice and go to trial, but don't forget, you're playing with your life," I respond.

In Manhattan this would have been a slam-dunk case, but in the Bronx nothing was ever straightforward, and Larry Piergrossi started having second thoughts on his prosecution, and initially I agreed with his concerns.

"Detective, the more I read over this case, the more I think we might have made a mistake. Three witnesses said it was a male Hispanic who shot the victim. Jayson is black," he mused.

This identity issue raised serious questions, so I contacted the witnesses again and they revealed that in their statements to the cops in 1992 they thought the shooter was either Hispanic or black. They couldn't be sure. This uncertainty was good news, since it meant the detectives back then either misunderstood or were as overwhelmed with cases as we were. Some of my worries over a potential miscarriage of justice had been eased, and I returned to the squad thinking that was the end of the matter. Until I got another call from Catherine. Our complainant had just seen Jayson, the man she'd said had confessed to murder, walking past her down the street.

"Why didn't you tell me he had been released?" she demanded. "And how come he's not in jail waiting for his trial?"

"I think you're mistaken," I replied, trying my best to soothe the understandably agitated woman. "There is no way Jayson has been released, believe me. Perhaps it's someone who looks like—"

"Don't patronize me, Detective Waters. I know what I was told, and I know who I saw," she responded firmly.

I was straight back on the phone again to Piergrossi, who, to my amazement, confirmed the suspect's release on a bond of just five thousand dollars, a fraction of the original bail. I was furious.

"The grand jury indicted this killer—how come you see fit to release him on such a low bond?" I demanded.

"Yes, actually I wanted to talk to you about that, Detective. You know what, I'm thinking maybe we should dismiss the case altogether. I've learned a little more about this witness, Catherine. There are some prior issues there which lead me to doubt her statements," the ADA replied.

"Well, you screwed up on this one, Counselor. I hope you're right, because if you're not, you have a killer walking around the same town as the one woman who could put him in jail for decades," I replied, slamming down the phone.

A month later I got a call from Piergrossi again to tell me he'd had a change of heart. Jayson was, he now believed, guilty, so we took another field trip to Wilmington, Delaware, this time to meet with a lawyer who I suspected was about to effectively kill off our entire case.

Catherine, who originally picked up the phone to ring us, was now totally disillusioned with the process, so much so that she had hired a former federal prosecutor named Dan Lyons to represent her.

Speaking on his client's behalf, Lyons told me that it was Piergrossi whose call to our complainant convinced her that she no longer wanted to testify. Although I tried to put our case to him, I couldn't blame his client for her change of attitude. The whole thing was now an unmitigated disaster.

"Look, your ADA rang Catherine and told her she might be putting an innocent man in jail, Detective," Lyons explained. "That's when my client realized that she must protect herself in this matter."

"All I can do is apologize," I said to the woman sitting beside me. "This was the DA's decision. On behalf of the NYPD I want you to know that we believed what you told us, right from the start, and we still do."

I was in a rage when I left the meeting, and my mood improved little on the flight back to New York. Larry Piergrossi was a nice guy, but without Catherine's testimony the case was shot.

Jayson never faced trial, and the charges against him were dismissed.

The whole episode was another reminder of the screw-ups that passed for a week's work in the DA's office, my jaded view of the system reinforced with every passing year.

To most of New York, the Bronx, not Manhattan, was the Place-Where-People-Shoot-People, and the Job would do what it could to ensure that this was the narrative presented to the reader even when the facts told a different story.

On one occasion I responded to a call that a perp had just shot and killed a number of people on the Willis Avenue Bridge, 350 feet of concrete and steel which turned on a pivot to link the Bronx with First Avenue, nicknamed "the Wall" by competitors in the New York City Marathon, as it marks the make-or-break twenty-mile marker in the event which literally unites the entire city.

Our killer sprinted past astonished cyclists and pedestrians towards Spanish Harlem, with an NYPD captain, who'd witnessed the shooting, in hot pursuit.

The perp made it to the other side, racing up East 128th Street and disappearing down Harlem River Drive, while back on the bridge we called Manhattan North Homicide to let them know about their DOAs. A few minutes later word came from the Brass that our victims were killed in the Bronx, no matter what we or the map said to the contrary.

Nobody was going to notice another homicide in our borough. And none of us was to question Mayoral Infallibility. The stiffs were our problem.

Back in the South Boogie you knew the killings would keep on coming—you just didn't reckon that the bodies could slide several hundred feet from one borough into ours. But we shouldn't have been surprised: hit men regularly dumped bodies on us which had been killed elsewhere, knowing their victims would be less conspicuous in a long line of cases.

Within a few days another murder landed in my lap—it, too, barely made the inside pages. A couple of detectives following a lead on an unrelated investigation literally stumbled across the dead body of Thomas Jones lying on the rooftop at 1500 Popham Avenue in Morris Heights. The man had been shot to death, his pockets still stuffed with cash and his red Lamborghini parked on the street fifty feet below.

The notifications were made. Initially there was some media coverage, since the body had been missed by cops on a sweep the previous night. Tales of mix-ups, Internal Affairs investigations, and red sports cars sold papers, but nobody cared much about our victim, so just the usual two-man-strong team was assigned. I found myself partnering up with Detective Tim Donovan from the 46 as we started a canvass for witnesses, and learned little except that our victim's death followed an alleged violent altercation linked to gambling.

A week later I found myself in the 41, pouring a cup of coffee for Detective Rene Cabazas as we discussed the details of the Jones shooting. Not Thomas Jones, you understand. No, that investigation was already consigned to a distant back burner and might never be solved. On our hot plate right now was the murder of Ollie Jones, committed four and a half miles away from Morris Heights, and as usual there was little to explain why a gunman broke into the apartment our victim shared with his wife at 1010 Longfellow Avenue.

Jones was initially wounded in the attack, so the Wheel, the central office which liaises with all Bronx detectives, sent an ECT—Evidence Collection Team—made up of plainclothes cops as opposed to the Crime Scene Unit, part of the borough's never-ending struggle to save money. In Manhattan the CSU is dispatched as a matter of course to almost every incident, and I know that if any member of my family was seriously assaulted I would want experts on the investigation from the very start.

When Ollie Jones died of his wounds the ECT stepped aside to let the Crime Scene people take over, and I sat down and compared notes with my latest partner.

"Okay, Rene, let's see what we have here . . . 'A Ford Explorer was spotted leaving the scene after the shooting with several males inside,'" I said sarcastically. "Great, eh?"

"Yeah, not much, Luke. This ain't gonna be no easy ground ball. Just gotta work it. What about mistaken identity? More I think about it, more I figure our shooter maybe mistook Jones for one of his neighbors," my pal replied, rearranging the silk handkerchief in his top pocket before easing himself into the chair behind his desk.

Ollie Jones had no criminal history, so with no other leads we got a subpoena of his neighbor's phone records, which quickly arrived on my desk, hopefully holding the key to unlocking the case. Whether they do is still a mystery, though, because there they remain, unopened, to this day, and will probably stay that way unless someone else is murdered and it crosses that investigation or a Cold Case team reheats the investigation.

For all our progress with new technology, a lack of manpower means that justice is delayed at best and often denied for our victims and those who mourn them. I remember being up in Homicide one afternoon and blowing the dust off one unsolved murder dating back to my first days in the city in the early eighties. I tracked down the detective, now retired, who had caught it to ask why he hadn't done anything with the case. His answer was honest, but unnerving.

"I take your word about what's in the file, Waters. I don't recall anything about it, to be honest. I ain't gonna lie. And you know what? I don't really give a crap, either." It's easy to be critical, but he summed up the attitude of the generation which followed him, and ours, too, after a few years on the Job.

"Priorities in Homicide" was a short list:

1. Cop shooting.
2. Dead kid.
3. Case some boss wants solved.
4. Some vic. He can wait.

Before you retire, the relentless workload takes its toll on every investigator, myself included.

If one partner was on vacation, the other had to catch every investigation for the duration of the holiday. All this would change with a media case, when, whether warranted or not, twenty detectives would suddenly and mysteriously descend to ease the duo's workload. The system was clearly dysfunctional, but there was no appetite to change it.

A human being has only so much empathy, and after a while you had to check yourself or you simply stopped caring. We all had different ways to relieve stress when the workload got too much, and we got tired and emotional after thirty hours with little or no sleep. DT Tarsnane? He simply went insane.

"Why the hell should I even care anymore, you guys?" Pete would suddenly demand of nobody in particular, launching into a monologue which, though comical on one level, also summed up exactly how we all felt.

"Nobody cares! None of you guys care. Cops are the worst! The Job doesn't care. And we know that our mayor don't care! Bastards! You know what? I am tired of caring, too. To hell with all you assholes, and fuck this bag of shit!" Pete would snarl, storming out the door, returning a few minutes later to reopen the file he had just thrown in the trash can.

Pete had a point. Police work is not your nine-to-five job, and there's not much room for teary-eyed sentiment. It's easy to become hard, embittered, and cynical when you see people at their worst, humanity at its most depraved—and that's just in the squad room! In seriousness, one morning, if you're lucky, you wake up and decide you've had enough, and a few hours later you are "pulling the pin" and turning in your retirement papers. Next week, some other guy will be sitting in your seat. If you are unlucky, you stick with it and stop caring about the oath you took and the people who turn to you for help in a crisis.

The NYPD is not like *Cheers*, the TV program. Here, nobody knows your name and if they do, guess what? They don't care.

We are all expendable and we all move on. I called everyone "buddy," and I showed respect for every person I worked with, but the reality was few became friends. The rest were just guys I used to work with, same as any job. Same as life, I suppose. But with more corpses.

Departures from Homicide normally didn't leave much room for long goodbyes. Claude O'Shea, a fellow detective, spent his last five hours as a cop wringing another five hundred dollars in overtime out of the Job, and when he finally did decide to go he simply picked up his riot helmet as a souvenir for his son, debated whether he should take it or not, decided he would, and gave me a hug with tears in his eyes. I walked him to the door, watching as he lit his first cigar as a free man on the steps, then he went out onto Simpson Street and disappeared into the darkness.

It happened in our office on a regular basis. A member of the team would suddenly stand up, say he'd had enough, and be retired by the end of the day.

Kenny Umlauft went one better, managing to screw the boss, whom he'd never had much time for, choosing to sail off into one sunset as O'Toole prepared to fly into another. Kenny freely admitted that the only thing that stopped him from pushing our CO out one of our third-floor windows was the width of his arse, but he did drop the boss in it on the morning that O'Toole was preparing to leave for the Dominican Republic with his wife, who was from the island, on a long-anticipated family holiday. Kenny went home on Friday knowing that he was in charge of the squad for the next two weeks, but waited until Monday to ring the boss, who was at home packing, with the news that he was pulling the pin after more than twenty-five years in about twenty-five minutes.

O'Toole spent half his holiday on the phone with us, trying to put out fires, making it a truly unforgettable vacation.

At the end of my career I was running empty on empathy, just like the rest.

"What have you got, Luke? Any Unusuals?" asked the sergeant or DT who picked up at the other end after I called in another murder.

"Just a drug dealer, multiple convictions. Shot eight times in one of the low-rises. He's at Lincoln, but he's likely."

"Shot in the low-rises, eh? It really stings when you catch a bullet up there! Couldn't happen to a nicer guy." Nobody would write about it in a newspaper, because none of us, out there in the real world, had any interest in this victim.

Maybe Tarsnane was right. Maybe nobody cared.

CHAPTER SIXTEEN

EYES WIDE OPEN

Nobody pays much attention to the tall man pushing the shopping cart along the quiet city streets on November 18, 2007. He had rattled along the one-mile route several times this evening, disappearing into the darkness, crossing the bridge over Interstate 87, and turning towards Roberto Clemente Park. Months earlier the local families would have flocked here in the summer sunshine, picnicking, playing baseball, and killing time in canoes along the Harlem River.

Tonight, with the city already in winter's embrace, the waterfront serves a different purpose and the pedestrian struggles with the heavily loaded cart—grimly pushing across the mud and grass until he reaches the riverbank. He unloads more plastic sacks, then a suitcase, and slides them into the water below, watching as they bubble briefly, then sink into the freezing water. He turns and clatters back across the bridge once more. It was his final trip, but his night's work is only beginning.

A week later, and forty million Americans packed up and got back on the roads, piling into planes, trains, and automobiles, their annual Thanksgiving exodus over for another year. In that number was a sixty-five-year-old Jamaican immigrant named Elveda Wright, who was braving a five-hour journey along the most congested roadway in the country. Elveda was setting out, not returning, to check in with her daughter, Marlene Platt, who lived 240 miles down the I-95 corridor, which links D.C. with NYC.

The women were close and talked on the phone every day, but Elveda had not heard from the younger woman in almost a week. Marlene was a nurse's aide who lived in the Bronx with her adult sons—Nashan, a twenty-two-year-old hospital worker, and his brother Lamar, a twenty-four-year-old barber. When Marlene's birthday and Thanksgiving both passed with no word, an increasingly worried Elveda set off to find out what had happened. She finally arrived at the family's apartment at 1610 University Avenue at about three p.m.

Her knocks on the door, like most of her phone calls over the past seven days, went unanswered. She decided to walk to the barbershop where her older grandson worked to check that everything was okay. Lamar Platt had been unhelpful and vague with his grandma over the phone, offering no clue as to where the rest of the family were staying. He was equally uncooperative face-to-face and refused to hand over the key to the apartment.

Elveda called the police and the responding officers learned from neighbors that they hadn't seen Marlene or her younger son Nashan in several days. Only Lamar had been spotted, coming and going to work, and now he stood outside his home, staring as one of the cops climbed inside through a window.

The officer was hit with an almost overpowering smell of bleach, which pervaded the apartment, and he coughed as he called out the names of the missing residents. His cries echoed through the empty rooms, unanswered.

When Elveda Wright stepped inside with the other patrolman she confirmed that the purse and ID the officers had just found belonged to her daughter.

The call went out that Patrol might have a homicide and Detective Stephen Geary caught the case out of the 46, while I responded from Simpson Street. Though the circumstances were suspicious, all we had at that stage were two missing persons but no real evidence that foul play had been committed.

We ran a search on the new "Real Time" computer and we learned that a week earlier Marlene Platt had called 911 to report that she was being threatened at her home, possibly with a gun. Patrol had responded but had difficulty in speaking to her, and when they eventually did make contact she assured them that she was safe. The call had been a mistake, so the job was logged as a 10-90Y, or "Unnecessary."

Relations between Lamar and Marlene had been strained, and he explained to his distraught grandmother that they'd had a fight and Marlene got cut. He'd had to clean up a stain with a bottle of bleach and the kitchen mop. Elveda was furious and disbelieving; she reacted angrily and demanded he tell her what had become of her family. We decided to take Platt down to the 46 where we could question him further and he was fully cooperative as we made our way to the car. Patrol remained to control the crime scene and soothe our complainant as CSU took the usual samples and photographs.

"Listen, Lamar," Geary said, "it's clear that something went down at the apartment. That's okay, but we need to know the details. We have to find your mother and brother to make sure they are safe, so come on, pal, help us out here.

"So, where are they now? Tell us so we can help them," Geary, a small, soft-spoken former schoolteacher, urged.

That's when our conversation veered way off the beaten track. Or rather, into the park.

"They're in the river," Platt replied.

I glanced at Geary, took a breath, and turned back to the other man.

"The river, Lamar?" I said, trying to match his casual tone.

Platt nodded and was about to tell us more when suddenly his voice trailed off.

"Don't really want to talk 'bout it now," he said, his mood darkening.

We cajoled him to continue and explained that once CSI got there they'd give us the details anyway.

It actually worked.

"I shot 'em both, in their sleep. Mom was in the living room. I shot Nashan in the bedroom, in the back of his head. Then I chopped 'em up, man, and I put some bits in bags, and some in luggage, and put 'em in a cart with weights. When I got to the park, I dumped 'em in the river," he continued, adding that it took several trips to get rid of all the body parts.

Lamar Platt later gave us a detailed written confession at the 46. He outlined how he'd used a serrated knife and a machete to dismember his victims, even telling us where to find the tools in the apartment. We returned to the crime scene and immediately found them, before checking out Nashan's bed. It was clean, just as we suspected.

Geary and I grabbed the mattress and turned it back over to its original position. Sure enough, it was covered in dark stains. After shooting his brother in the head and butchering his corpse, he'd simply flipped the mattress over and slept on the reverse side for the next week, getting up and going in to work as if nothing had happened. Rooting through a cabinet drawer, we soon found the shells for his .38-caliber revolver, which ATF later confirmed was stolen in Birmingham, Alabama, ten years earlier. We located the shopping cart nearby with mud from the park embedded in the wheels. Our forensics technicians were busy spraying almost every surface area in our crime scene with Luminol, which reveals even cleaned blood with a bluish green hue under a special lamp.

Detective Sam Gilford blocked off the windows and moved his light in a slow arc.

"There's your blood, guys," he declared.

You didn't need a degree in chemistry to see what had happened here—1610 University Avenue was more than a slaughterhouse: it was a house of horrors straight out of a slasher movie. Close to where we stood, the ceilings, walls, floor covers, and kitchen sink were covered with splashes of blue, and the glow from the stains continued on just about every other surface in the apartment. Even the knobs on the TV screen, the remote control, and the sofa cushions glowed under Gilford's lamp as Forensics got to work, taking several swabs, each carefully sealed in an evidence bag.

Back in the kitchen one of the other Crime Scene techs was grimly cutting through the pipe underneath the sink, which was also dropped entirely into a plastic bag and tagged with a bar-coded sticker. Meanwhile, a K-9 handler led Pal, a specially trained cadaver dog, from room to room, just in case Lamar had tired of the two-mile round trips to Roberto Clemente Park and stuffed some of his relations' remains under the floorboards.

We let them get on with the science bit and headed back to the 46 for another chat with our suspect, who sat drawing a picture of dark, brooding faces and a ticking clock. He was still cooperative and revealed more details of where to find the remains of his mother and brother, before he recorded his confession on videotape with the assistant district attorney present.

Geary and I drove back to the Harlem River as the sun rapidly set, casting long shadows over our second crime scene. The waterfront was full of feverish activity. The NYPD Aviation Unit was hovering in a helicopter above. They had already made several sweeps of the river as the spotter tried to distinguish any distinctive shapes in the freezing water below. Divers from the Water Unit, clad in wet suits and sub-aqua gear, repeatedly submerged and resurfaced empty-handed. The senior command called a halt to the search for the night but the next morning one of the divers rose from the murky depths holding a plastic sack. Back on dry land we opened it to examine a lump of what, tests would later show, was Nashan Platt's buttock—remnants of the shorts he wore in bed still clinging to the decomposing flesh.

Other remains were uncovered as the divers continued their grim search, and one came up holding the most gruesome discovery of the entire investigation: a waterlogged piece of luggage which was dragged onto the bank. An officer pulled the zipper back to reveal a dreadlocked human head, one eye still wide open, the other drooping, half shut, the mouth slightly ajar. The features were those of the missing woman.

Lamar had been straight with us from the start. Marlene Platt was indeed in the river, just as he'd said.

We never recovered his dead brother's head, just some small parts of his watery remains. The swirling current had most likely carried them away. Nature has her own methods of recycling and renewal, but the remains we did find, along with the evidence and signed confessions, were enough to charge our killer with one count of first-degree murder and two counts of second-degree murder.

Lamar Platt came to trial before the Bronx State Supreme Court on March 11, 2010, nearly three years later. He sat impassively in an orange Department of Corrections jumpsuit listening to the evidence, and we learned that he was psychotic and his mental illness was made worse by his marijuana habit. Lamar agreed to a deal worked out between his defense counsel and ADA David Birnbaum. He was sentenced to twenty years in prison for each murder, to be served consecutively.

He opted for prison rather than an indefinite stay in a psychiatric hospital—not much of a choice, really.

CHAPTER SEVENTEEN

COP OUT

The scene plays out in slow motion. The teenager stands over his victim, a Tech-9 pointed at the back of the store owner's head.

The weapon the gunman grips between his fingers is beloved of drug lords for the ease with which it can be illegally converted into a fully automatic submachine gun. All of this matters little to the man lying with his face pressed against the floor of Cap Urban, the small, narrow shop which he owns—selling ball caps and T-shirts to passersby on the Grand Concourse.

The armed teen pulls the charging handle of his weapon, loading a round into the chamber, and pulls the trigger, killing the store owner instantly, the blood seeping slowly out the entry hole and spreading from under his prone body in a dark pool across the wooden floor.

Four police officers stand with arms folded, pistols holstered, staring impassively at the scene. One calmly drinks coffee, another scribbles in a spiral-bound notebook, while two others seem to be doing little more than propping up a wall a few feet away. They are calm, unemotional, and unhurried. Attention, rather than action, is what is required now.

"Hey, Rick, can we see the perp's face? Rewind the tape and get pictures, will ya?" asked Barry Sullivan, a well-dressed detective in his early forties.

Rick Garcia stepped forward—he had a way with technology. All of us brought something different to the game, and we were a rather oddly matched team—at this stage, I'd been moved from the B-Team, with the guys I'd worked with for a while, to this new team, and we were just getting used to each other.

Barry Sullivan was a stylish, articulate black man who'd grown up in the Bronx and knew more than any of us how the locals thought and behaved. Rick Garcia was Puerto Rican, a computer genius known as "Gigabyte Garcia," and a native Spanish speaker, ensuring that Hispanic witnesses who felt uncomfortable making a statement to me would open up to him without hesitation.

Jimmy McSloy served in Warrants prior to joining us in the Bronx Homicide A-Team and was good at tracking down people who didn't want to be found. He was the son of an NYPD inspector, raised in Long Island.

Patrol and EMS were on scene when we arrived, but it was too late for the owner of Cap Urban. Amou Fall was a thirty-two-year-old Senegalese immigrant, a devout Muslim, and a keen amateur soccer player. He left behind four grieving brothers, one of whom worked in their other store—Amou's other brothers were still living with their parents back home in Africa.

CSU technicians arrived and got to work while we continued to review the store tape and recordings from external cameras overlooking the entrance, which had been installed by the city in an attempt to deter attacks such as this.

We compared these recordings to the pictures off the store's security system and immediately picked up the youths leaving Cap Urban. They looked like any other trio of teens as they ran out onto East 167th Street and towards the nearby subway. One carried a basketball under his arm; all of them sported backpacks slung across shoulders. I was so intent taking notes that I barely noticed the uniformed cop standing beside me who let out a shout as Rick froze the pictures and started to replay the images, frame by frame.

"Jesus, Detective! I jus' stopped that kid a few minutes ago!" the cop said excitedly. "Plus, I got his information," he continued, fumbling in his pocket for his memo book.

"Where did you stop him?" I asked, unable to believe our good luck.

"In the subway, 'bout two blocks away," the Transit cop, whose name was Jorge Arbaje-Diaz, replied. "I heard the radio run on the suspects, when I spot this kid holdin' a basketball, just like the perp, and he's, you know, sweating, man, really sweating. Gave me some bull 'bout how he's shooting hoops in the park, but I search him anyways. Didn't find no gun or hats or nothing, so I let him go."

Having just committed murder, most people wouldn't be foolish enough to give a police officer their real name, but in stressful situations we all do things we later regret. I headed out to the curb to enter the name into the computer system through the terminal we carry in our cars.

The details appeared on-screen within seconds. Terrell Lamar, seventeen, had an arrest for marijuana possession, and there was little doubt in our minds that this was one of the gang. Thanks to Arbaje-Diaz stopping our perp in the subway, within hours we had him and his nineteen-year-old accomplice, Joshua Hughes, in custody. Neither of them would give up the third youth, who both claimed was the one who pulled the trigger. Snitching could get you killed in this neighborhood, either by the perp or by one of his family.

Our suspects blamed the victim for his own death.

"We jus' robbin' hats, man. Why'd da dude try to stop us?" one claimed in frustration. "We didn't want to shoot nobody."

Amou Fall's brother later told me that there was tension between many African-American youths and local African immigrants. Some of the kids resented the success and hard work of these businessmen, most of whom wouldn't employ the local kids because they didn't trust them. In turn the kids ripped off the merchants, which ultimately could get out of hand, like the tragedy we were now investigating.

For the Fall family the killing was devastating, but for us it was yet another case, a straightforward enough case, too, and it represented a key moment in what would be a short career for Officer Jorge Arbaje-Diaz. Helping to close a homicide only a couple of years out of the academy was the sort of thing his boss would take notice of. A month later he would catch the attention of his boss again, and a couple million other people.

I was sitting in the squad room one morning flicking through a copy of the *New York Daily News* when I spotted a vaguely familiar face under the headline "Cop in Drug Disgrace" and a picture of a thirty-year-old officer holding a fistful of dollars.

"City officer busted for robbing and selling millions in cocaine," the piece continued.

It turned out that the man who'd helped us put Amou Fall's killers behind bars had a very lucrative moonlighting gig. According to the DEA, Arbaje-Diaz was garbage, and he had played a crucial role as part of a gang of stickup artists who stole money and drugs from pushers which were then resold to other dealers.

"This is a despicable action on the part of this individual," Commissioner Ray Kelly told the paper. "It is the highest form of betrayal."

The Transit cop used not only his uniform and badge, but also a car with lights and sirens, to pull dealers off the streets and confiscate their cargo, classic tactics for a narcotics sweep. In all, the feds estimated that Arbaje-Diaz and his accomplices netted 750 kilos of cocaine and four million in cash in robberies in the Bronx, Queens, and upper Manhattan, while they also targeted dealers as far away as Florida and Pennsylvania.

Earlier that year another Transit cop, not long out of the academy, named Christian Torres, was arrested after using his service pistol to hold up a Sovereign Bank in Muhlenberg, Pennsylvania, from which he stole $113,000. This was just months after he had robbed another branch, closer to home in the East Village—twice—during which he'd made off with a similar sum.

Even if you paid every cop a million dollars a year, corruption would still exist, and it can never be excused. However, you don't need to have done your master's thesis at John Jay College of Criminal Justice to realize that low pay and corruption go hand in hand. All you have to do is look at a few other police departments.

Mexico teeters on the brink of failure as a result of drugs, and police there regularly arrest hit men who turn out to be fellow cops, taking on contract killings as a way to meet their mortgages. Puerto Rico, a U.S. state in all but name, has similar problems, as does New Orleans, where corruption has long been a harsh reality of life, and here, too, the FBI refuse to work with all but a few carefully selected local officers.

When I entered the academy in 1993 the base pay for a rookie, with overtime, was something like fifty thousand dollars per annum, hardly a fortune but enough to get by on without turning to kidnapping, murder, or extortion. A decade and a half later, it hadn't fallen, it had plummeted, hovering at just over twenty thousand, and as one cop who was arrested for pulling stickups told IAB, "You just can't live in the city on twenty grand a year."

The idea that the next time I bumped into the two kids we collared for the Amou Fall shooting they might be wearing their Police Academy dress blues seemed ludicrous, but it wasn't far off the mark: if they got lucky on their day in court and cut a deal with a soft DA who was happy to accept a lesser charge, it meant that they would have a sheet clean enough to clear the NYPD selection process. Pretty soon rumors started to surface that a lot of our new recruits had criminal records, whereas when I came on the Job an unpaid parking ticket would see your application in the trash can at One Police Plaza.

Internal Affairs soon had their hands full with the graduates of the classes of 2005, 2006, and 2007. Home invaders and armed robbers who had managed to plead down to a misdemeanor were now carrying badges and guns, many carrying on with their old lifestyles while the Job turned a blind eye, the department desperate to fill spaces in an academy funded by federal money. We all turned a blind eye, in our own way, and if we did talk about it, we figured that Internal Affairs—the Rat Squad—would take care of the latest infestation, which was at best a cop-out on our behalf.

"Luke, you have no idea of the shit we're dealing with from these cops hired a few years ago," one of the IAB guys confided with a sigh as we sat watching the NYPD Gaelic Football Team trade punches with a Boston PD selection. "There are a shitload of criminals carrying badges in this city."

Naturally the media used the unions' outrage as a stick to beat Mayor Bloomberg over the head with, selling lots more newspapers in the process, so our publicity-savvy mayor did what any good politician would do in the same situation and increased the starting salaries to the old levels, knowing the problems would fade away, along with the coverage, once the press became distracted by another story.

By the time I retired, a uniformed cop with only a year or two of service was earning over $90,000 per annum before taxes, and clearing $100,000 gross even with only occasional overtime. Experienced guys brought home significantly more than that: I worked with several detectives earning $170,000 in a good year. Bloomberg's attention now switched to the retirees, who were living longer and longer, typically drawing down maybe $2 million in total pension payouts per person before they passed away—which was a real worry to the accountants and actuaries because cops were a lot more health-conscious than when I came on the Job. The fast food, smoking, and hard drinking were giving way to gym membership and healthy eating.

Such a change in habits never really caught hold in the projects, and in certain neighborhoods dying for a cigarette had a more immediate meaning, as one nineteen-year-old woman found out at one a.m. on September 28, 2008, just a few weeks after the Amou Fall murder.

"Hey, where you goin', girl? Fun's just startin'!" one of the partygoers said to Julie Bryant as she headed out the door of one of the apartments at the sprawling Patterson Houses tower blocks at 315 East 143rd Street, just off Third Avenue.

One of the first projects in the borough, Patterson had offered decent families good-quality housing. But in the 1960s it declined like much of the South Bronx and now they were a regular stop for EMS and cops from the 40.

"Just stepping out, I'll be back," Julie Bryant replied with a smile, raising the cigarette between her fingers and slipping out into the hallway, where several other guests were gathered, the tips of their Newports and Marlboro Lights glowing through the thick smoke.

Earlier that evening Jonathan "Bebo" Rodriguez and some of his crew from the neighborhood had tried to gate-crash the private party, but left without much fuss when the hosts protested, and Julie was relaxed as she lit up and slowly breathed in the fumes, barely spotting the black male who had walked up towards the knot of people. It was Rodriguez. He suddenly raised his hand to reveal a black 9mm pistol, adding the smell of cordite to the narrow, smoke-filled hallway as he fired two shots into the chest of a man called Brandon Howard, a revenge attack for the victim's alleged involvement in a previous murder.

Howard's friends shrieked in panic as the bullets pounded through the young man's body, and he collapsed and instinctively rolled over to protect himself. A 9mm round carries a lot of kinetic energy, but it travels at high speed, and there are many cases of people surviving a close-range hit when the shots pass right through. But our killer left nothing to chance, and stood over his helpless victim, pumping another four bullets into his torso, before turning to look Julie Bryant in the eyes. He disappeared back down the hallway before Patrol responded to the neighbors' 911 calls.

Street justice in the Bronx was always being served, so Rodriguez's stare was a warning to Bryant, and its meaning was not lost on the teenager, who was about to become a pawn in the justice system.

Witnesses are invariably traumatized by a shooting like this. People in shock will often tell you something which they regret later on, and several partygoers were so upset at the brutality of this murder that they nominated Rodriguez as our triggerman. I acted quickly with Detective Mark Davis, a fifteen-year veteran out of the 40, and tied them to their statements. Revenge shootings are regarded by most of the population in the projects in the same way as honor killings are in countries like Afghanistan or Pakistan: an inevitability which is no business of the police, so when it happens, just keep out of it—and if you get picked up, keep your mouth shut.

I ain't seen nothin'. I don't know nothin'.

While pinning the charge on Rodriguez would prove difficult, finding him proved simple. All I had to do was pick up the phone ringing on my desk.

"Detective Waters? Agent Sean Mullin, FBI New York Field Office. How you doin'? Hey, I hear you like this Jonathan Rodriguez for a shooting in the projects off Third Avenue? Yeah, I saw the notification. That's why I'm calling. One of my CIs tells me he's hiding out with his girlfriend, Jessica, at her apartment on Grand Concourse, near the Bronx Courts? Yeah, that's the address my boy gimme, too. Thought you'd like to know . . ."

I told Mullin to thank his confidential informant and we made tracks to talk to Bebo's girlfriend, who seemed more interested in the two-thousand-dollar reward money on his head from Crime Stoppers than her beau's continued freedom. It took about five minutes for her to give up her man, who was then lying low just around the corner.

At five a.m. on December 2, just five weeks after the shooting, we took Bebo down. It was still pitch-black outside as we put our perpetrator in the back of a Crown Vic and drove to Central Booking. I let the girlfriend know that he was in custody and that we'd be in touch to arrange payment of the reward.

Half an hour later the phone on my desk rang again. It was

an attorney named Dawn M. Florio—with an early morning wake-up call on prisoner protocol.

"Detective Waters, I believe you have a client of mine in custody?" said Dawn M. Florio rhetorically. Lawyers usually only ask questions to which they already know the answer.

I recognized Florio's voice immediately. A former ADA in Bronx County, who was in her mid-forties, she'd spent a decade on the prosecutor's side of the courtroom. She was now a gamekeeper-turned-poacher, building up a successful practice.

"Good morning, Counselor. What's the name again? We have a lot of guys down here," I replied, though I had a good idea of the next two words out of her mouth.

"Jonathan Rodriguez," Florio responded.

"Who? Oh, him. Yeah, certainly we have a Mr. Rodriguez here. I only just arrested the guy an hour ago, so I'm surprised that—"

"Fine. Please ensure that he's not interrogated until he can consult with me. You know the rules, Detective," she interrupted. "I'll be over shortly." I got off the phone and let out a long, slow whistle as the air in the squad room turned blue with curses. We couldn't figure out how Florio had gotten wind of our arrest and stalled our interrogation within thirty minutes of bringing Rodriguez in. We figured his girlfriend, who'd given him up in a heartbeat, maybe had second thoughts about snitching on a guy who thought nothing of shooting someone half a dozen times in cold blood.

Florio turned up an hour or so later and I escorted her into the interview room. I turned towards the door to let her confer with her client, who was so confident of his imminent release that he was telling his lawyer to relax.

"Don't worry, ain't nobody gonna testify 'gainst me," he predicted with a smirk.

"Don't talk to anybody, stay cool, and you'll be okay, Mr. Rodriguez," Florio cautioned. I closed the door and walked away. Attorney–client privilege isn't only sacrosanct, it's completely inadmissible in a court of law.

The fact remained that we had a silent suspect and no physical evidence. In fact, we had nothing apart from a few eyewitnesses, the most promising of which were Julie Bryant and another young woman, Keysha Hughes, and we had to play it out by the rules.

I could make an arrest on my own initiative on just about any charge—burglary, assault, robbery, even rape—anywhere in the city, but for a murder charge cops must first clear it with the DA. So before I drew up my arrest report I went over to talk to Ed Talty, a veteran lawyer who knew Florio well from her time as a prosecutor.

A gas station down the block served the best coffee in the city, and I knew how fond Ed was of a good cup of joe, which I presented to him on arrival. "Detective Luke Waters—he always remembers. And what do you guys give me? Nothing!"

He sat across the conference table, sipping his coffee, and listened intently as I outlined exactly what I had for him. He tapped the braces he always seemed to wear as I explained our lack of any real evidence.

Talty didn't believe in trusting cops' guts, but I made our argument and got the authorization I needed to make the arrest, right away running into a little problem—the 180/80 Clause, which in simple terms says in New York your case must be presented to a grand jury within five business days of the arrest. If you fail to do so, no matter how overwhelming the evidence is, your suspect must be released. They cannot be rearrested and charged again with this offense.

Keysha Hughes and Julie Bryant were already on the run, figuring it was better to disappear and be charged with contempt of court than risk being toe-tagged, but we followed up on another lead and drove over to 2645 Third Avenue—the home of Antonnette Boone, a cousin of our victim, who was also present at the shooting. As we scooted into the lobby we watched out, as ever, for airmail.

Going into the projects you got all kinds of stuff dropped on you from high above, ranging from the downright unpleasant to the absolutely lethal. A few years earlier a cop had been killed instantly in the Bronx when some local crushed his skull by dropping a bucketful of concrete on him. The worst I ever got hit with was a bowl of chicken soup, though at first I had assumed the yellow slime slowly trickling down my neck was something far worse.

The walls were full of holes, and the halls had the nasty tang of stale urine. Upstairs wasn't much better. Our witness, Antonnette Boone, told us in no uncertain terms to piss off. She explained that when she testified seventeen years ago to the grand jury in a homicide case, the police left her to protect herself. She left me in no doubt that she had no faith in the system anymore or in its ability to protect her. I went to report back to Talty but the case had been assigned to one of his assistants, an attorney with whom I had not worked before.

The nameplate on her door, which, unusually for an office in Talty's building, was shut, read "Shareema Gadson-Shaw." Underneath another note read "Please knock."

"Come on in," a voice floated from inside as my knuckles tapped lightly on the paintwork.

"Sorry, Detective Waters, I was meditating," Gadson-Shaw volunteered, sweeping the paperwork on her desk to one side.

My new colleague was a thirty-something black woman, and maybe this would help in persuading our black and Hispanic witnesses to come forward. I headed back to the projects and asked them to come down with me to the prosecutor's office. The ADA got no further with Boone than I did.

"Look—it's like I told this cop here. Don't give a shit, even if it was my cousin got his dumb ass shot. Ain't seen nothin'. Ain't heard nothin'!" was our witness's short and succinct response to the attorney's questions.

We moved to the next witness, Keysha Hughes, who lived at 340 Alexander Avenue. Her mother, Linda, answered the door and told us she hadn't seen her daughter in several days, had no idea where she was, and even if she did, she would tell her not to testify.

"My brother was shot dead. Ain't nobody helped him, so why should we help anybody?" she revealed. Though I hated to admit it, she had a point, and in her position I would probably feel the same. I was part of the system which had utterly failed these people, but I still had a job to do, and the five-day countdown was ticking in our suspect's favor.

Mark and I dropped by the Monroe Academy for Visual Arts and Design at 1300 Boynton Avenue, passing armed security guards and metal detectors before being ushered into the office of the principal, a well-dressed forty-something white man named Richard Masser.

Far from being upset that we were there to question one of his students, Masser was actually relieved that we were seeking one of them as a witness, rather than as a suspect.

The teachers who spoke to Hughes's classmates were told the teen had disappeared since the shooting. With the minutes continuing to tick by on the 180/80 clause, we were back on West

143rd Street to seek Julie Bryant. We spoke to her mother, Carmen, who seemed to take her role as a parent more seriously.

"My Julie only comes home when she gets hungry, and I don't know where she lies up. I lost my daughter to the streets," she explained, with a sad shake of her head. We were farther than ever from finding our witnesses.

Over at Bronx Regional High School, Principal Colin Thomas, a young black man, offered us further insight into the warped morality of the projects.

"Actually, Detectives, Julie came to me after this shooting and told me she saw the victim die right there in front of her, before asking me for a transfer. We haven't seen our student since. She told me she was forced to come forward to you by the family of the victim. It seems they wanted justice and somebody else could take the risks."

Old-fashioned police work hadn't gotten us anywhere, so Jimmy McSloy suggested we apply for a warrant for a Pen Register Trap and Trace, which would allow us to triangulate Julie Bryant's phone's location. We quickly found our reluctant witness hiding, pathetically, under a pile of dirty laundry in a friend's apartment at Gerard Avenue. She burst into tears as she was Mirandized and handcuffed before being taken back to speak with ADA Gadson-Shaw.

Our prisoner was presented with an impossible choice: testify and put her life—and the lives of her loved ones—in danger from a man she knew would kill her without hesitation, or refuse to testify and face charges herself, perhaps ending up in the same prison as the perp's associates, who may decide to kill her anyway.

I've arrested over a thousand suspects in my time and most of them got less than they deserved, but I never felt lower than

I did leading this teenager back to our car. Julie Bryant found herself as the rope in a tug-of-war among the police, the DA, the perpetrator's family, and the relations of the victim. That was life on the streets. Like anywhere else, being in the wrong place at the wrong time could have serious implications for your health.

Trouble was, in the South Bronx the wrong place could be any hallway, or any store, on any day.

CHAPTER EIGHTEEN

YOU CAN'T STAY OFF THE GRID

"Sarge, what's the word? Sign me in or show me at the five-two or whatever, will you? If you need me I can be there in an hour."

I put the phone down and my feet up, looking forward to a nice lunch with my old Cavan friend Martin Fay and his family, up from Philadelphia, knowing I'll be signed in and, at least officially, I'm at work as opposed to fifty miles upstate. An hour later my cell phone rings again. It's the sarge with bad news.

"Sorry, buddy. We got two people shot and one stabbed. One of them is DOA—1496 Vyse Avenue, down at West Farms."

"Okay, Sarge. I'm just sitting down to dinner. I'll be there as soon as I can. Gimme two hours."

The first rule I learned as a squad DT back in the 42 was the dead might not look pretty, but they are always pretty patient. One hour, two courses, and a change of clothes later, I descend the stairs wearing a navy pinstripe from Brooks Brothers and a shirt and tie which I got on sale at Kohl's. Martin is waiting at the last step with my share of the ice cream.

"Nice look, Luke. Bit late in the afternoon to go to a wedding, though, isn't it?" Philly Fay mumbles through a gobful of Ben & Jerry's.

"Very funny. It's for a funeral, Martin. I'd tell you the name of the deceased if I knew it myself."

An hour's drive later, and I pull up to the curb near the crime scene.

It was January 19, 2009, and through the early evening gloom I could just about make out the foyer outside which the attack took place. It was the usual hive of police activity as Patrol marked off the area with tape and Forensics took pictures of a broken broom handle, smudged with blood, on the slowly melting snow. It was carefully placed with other evidence in small plastic bags, their locations marked with bright numbered flags.

I walked over to the back of our Real Time Crime Center (RTCC) van and stuck my head in with a cheery hello—only to be met with a stream of curses. The "ice-cream truck," as it was popularly known, had recently been purchased by the department and retrofitted with computers, printers, scanners, routers, and a satellite dish. It provided an invaluable link back to the RTCC at police headquarters. Most importantly for the half a dozen cops packed inside, it also boasted a heater on that freezing January evening. Gigabyte Garcia was working away, sitting with a laptop in the back, going through the list of numbers which the 911 operator had received after the fight and subsequent shooting had taken place.

"Buddy, shut the door, will ya? Hasn't Kenny told you—us Puerto Ricans can't take the cold!" he said dryly.

"Stop moaning, Ricardo. What have we got?"

"One male DOA. Some other guy shot him after an argument in the street. Victim is a member of the Bloods. Don't know about the shooter yet. Might have some gang affiliation, but we're not sure if it's a hit or not," said Garcia, handing me a list of complainants to interview.

Even if a 911 caller doesn't leave their name or number,

the Emergency Services system automatically records their phone ID, and my colleague pointed to one number which looked promising.

This 911 caller lived in one of the apartments overlooking the crime scene, so when she picked up I asked her to stay on the line and I stepped out of the van. I raised my free hand above my head to identify myself, while the woman who thought she saw the shooter directed me to a smart three-story apartment block. It was fronted by high metal gates a few yards from where I stood.

Billy Simeon, who was catching out of the 42 Detective Squad, had left the warmth of his car and we rang the bell and introduced ourselves to the owner of the building, a middle-aged Puerto Rican woman named Maria Rivera who lived on the ground floor. She appeared upset at the recent events but directed us to people on the top floor, suggesting that they may be our perpetrators. We climbed the steps to interview the couple concerned, Christopher Maxwell and his common-law wife, Laqunanta Carter, whose mother was Rivera's tenant.

Christopher and Laqunanta often visited and stayed over with her mom, so they were on first-name terms with the landlady. They knew that Rivera's thirty-year-old son had been released recently on parole after serving ten years on drug offenses. They fingered him as our shooter, adding that the landlady, and possibly her adult daughter, were also present throughout the attack.

Back in the van, Rick ran Maria Rivera's name through Real Time and discovered that two days previously she had had an altercation with a handful of Blood street-gang members who were harassing her by banging the gates of her building. They had shouted abuse and threats when she told them to get lost.

Rivera had her life invested in her building and, like any responsible citizen, called in that incident, but when Patrol arrived on scene they told her that, since no crime had been committed, there was nothing they could do.

"Be careful, keep your doors and gates locked, and watch your back with these gang kids, ma'am," one of the uniforms had advised as they turned to leave.

Rivera's son, Carlos Valentin, had seen it differently.

"No way. I'm gonna kill these motherfuckers," the felon vowed to the departing cops.

He proved to be as good as his word.

Maria Rivera had taken the officers' advice and started to lock the security gates, which made the apartments more secure, but ironically only placed her in even more danger, as it denied the teen gangsters access to the apartments above hers, where they liked to hang out with one of the local kids.

Rivera was now genuinely afraid and did what people do when the police fail to address a threat against them: she looked for a weapon, settling on a long kitchen knife, which she carried when she stepped out a few hours later to visit Willy's Grocery and Meat Market next door.

The Bloods weren't deterred by the blade, and inevitably a confrontation developed in the street, during which threats and insults flew once more and weapons were flashed by both sides, as Rivera waved her kitchen knife and one of the Bloods picked up a splintered mop handle.

Valentin heard the commotion and rushed to his mother's defense, ignoring her pleas to him to return inside, since any violent incident would almost certainly see his parole revoked, but her son followed through on his promise to even the score and instead of pulling out a knife he suddenly produced a .22 semiautomatic pistol and pulled the trigger, hitting an eighteen-year-old Blood named Edward Hogan in the arm.

The Bloods are one of about sixty gangs of various types active in the Bronx, and they all have one thing in common: weakness is despised. Standing your ground and backing up your homeboys is the code you live by or, as Justin McWillis was about to prove, you die by. He ran at the shooter and tried to wrestle the pistol from his hand. In the struggle which followed, Valentin pulled the trigger again, this time shooting his victim in the chest at point-blank range.

Another Blood, Javiel Ramos, then joined in the fight, jumping on Valentin's back, and was struck from behind with the knife by Rivera, who stepped in to protect her son.

Valentin shook himself free, told his mother not to worry, and ran down the street just as the first cops responding to the 911 calls appeared in the distance, while McWillis lay dying, bleeding heavily into the snow, and the other Bloods, including Ramos and Hogan, melted away at the first sign of a blue uniform.

EMS arrived on scene and desperately set to work on the teenager, but the bullet had penetrated his heart. The paramedics' efforts proved futile as they struggled to keep their patient alive in the back of the ambulance, now racing to the hospital some two miles away. Dr. Suzana Bogdanovska pronounced her patient dead on arrival at the emergency room in St. Barnabas at 5:02 p.m. Justin McWillis was just eighteen years old.

Maria Rivera was a hardworking mother of four adult children, but her son was not the only one we were now investigating. Hogan also put her adult daughter at the scene, so I picked up the phone and outlined what we had to the Brass in another command. Within minutes Lieutenant Zevon from Internal

Affairs' Group 33 was on the other end of the line, keenly interested in the fact that Police Officer Abisay Rivera, who worked as a member of the Citywide Vandals Task Force (CVTF), had been placed at the scene of the murder. Zevon pulled Abisay Rivera's personnel file—and arrived over at the 42 to confer with Simeon and myself about establishing her involvement. IAB always assumes any officer they investigate is guilty.

Reading through her paperwork, it was clear that Rivera had declared on her application form that her brother was Carlos Valentin, that he was gang-affiliated, and that he was serving a long prison sentence, which was in her favor, since a failure to disclose these facts would probably have seen her fired even if she had no knowledge of our homicide.

We continued to work the case through the night, and the next morning a call came from Dr. Carolyn Kappen, the medical examiner, that the autopsy was scheduled for ten a.m. I drove down to the morgue to see what additional information it might reveal. The autopsy would allow us to brief Kappen on the details of our case, and the results might corroborate any statements made by our witnesses, victims, or suspects. When you are attacked with a knife you instinctively use your hands to block the stabs and slashes, leaving defensive wounds to the hands and arms, and being knocked to the ground will result in bruises and scrapes, so if these marks were not present on the victim we'd know a witness was trying to hide the truth.

Kappen was already busy dissecting the organs, which were weighed before she sliced them into half-inch-thick pieces with a one-foot-long sharp blade known as a "bread knife."

"Well, there's your bullet, Luke," the ME said, picking up the tiny .22 round from a piece of lung with a pair of tweezers.

The ME then moved on to the heart, noting the small entry

hole, before she cut it open with a pair of surgical scissors. But we had what we needed, so I thanked Kappen for her time, and she smiled in acknowledgment. There is little or no emotion during an autopsy, no time to reflect or mourn on a life cut short. The ME's job is clinical in every sense of the word, and it was her responsibility to find out what had caused McWillis to die; it was ours to find out who was responsible.

Simeon and I picked up Javiel Ramos, the Blood who'd jumped on Valentin after he shot McWillis, and took him down to the 42 for questioning. He was still seeping blood from a puncture wound to his back, so EMS were called to patch him up. Not very gratefully, he confirmed only his name, the fact that he and the others were Bloods, and that he and his fellow gangsters didn't talk to the police. Ramos was released, and we picked up a female gang member who was also present and asked her to help us. Demaris Rodriguez was skinny, as foulmouthed as any of the males, and tough as a bag of rocks, telling us to go screw ourselves.

"Fuckin' Five-O! Bloods don't talk, and we don't snitch," she replied pleasantly, as I asked a few routine questions. I broke the bad news to her gently.

"Yeah? Listen, sister. I have some information for you. Your Blood gangsta pal—Justin? He's DOA, Demaris. Shot to death. Don't you want to help put the person who did it in jail?"

"So? Still don't care. Yeah, he a brother Blood. Now? He dead," she said, pursing her lips.

Rodriguez was released.

We went over to the hospital to talk to Edward Hogan, the gang member who was shot in the arm by Valentin. He at least was willing to talk to us, though his disdain for the police was just as strong as his friends.'

"Yo, I got what I deserved, man," Hogan said, wincing with pain as he lay on the gurney, a drip connected to his injured arm. He confessed that he'd brandished a sharp, pointed pole at Rivera and her son raised the stakes by pulling out a pistol. He confirmed that Javiel Ramos had been stabbed by Rivera when he ran at Valentin, which explained why our recent uncooperative witness was covered in blood when we picked him up.

"Her son, he the one who shot me. Know him from the hood. I ain't got no complaints, but, yeah, he capped me an' Justin."

On the way back to the 42 to review what we had, we got a call from Billy's boss, Lieutenant Kevin Moroney, who told us that a Detective Jason McWillis out of the 28th Precinct was waiting to speak with us about the murder of his nephew. Unusually, there were direct links between the Job and the family of both victim and perpetrator alike—something I had never encountered in a case before.

The Harlem-based cop's agitation, and upset, when we met was understandable. He was keen to get a heads-up on our progress and we were sympathetic, polite, and tactful in our chat with our colleague. But we were tight-lipped in terms of details regarding the information we had gathered. As soon as we shook hands and said goodbye to McWillis Senior we locked down the files related to the case in the NYPD computer system, which could be accessed by any detective under normal circumstances. We did this as much for his protection as for the integrity of the investigation, realizing the temptation any of us would feel to intervene in the same position.

Simeon and I sat down with Zevon from Internal Affairs to see whether Officer Abisay Rivera had anything to do with our homicide. We put together a mug shot lineup to show to our eyewitnesses who may be able to place her in the street the previous evening.

Cooperating with IAB isn't pleasant, but it isn't optional, either, no matter how most cops feel about members of the Rat Squad. There is an acceptance of rank-and-file officers who serve there for a couple of years, but most of us have a thinly disguised contempt for the senior officers there because their bottom line, like ours, is about numbers: hitting targets and making arrests, and IAB never seem too fussy about how they close their cases. It seemed that they were hell-bent on hanging Rivera, insisting that she drove her brother that night. We were able to prove that she didn't.

When we showed the spread of images, our witnesses shook their heads one by one, independently confirming that the woman on the scene looked nothing like Officer Rivera— she was out of the picture in every sense of the word, and Zevon from IAB soon followed.

"Good luck with the case, Detectives. Let me know how it turns out," he said with a wave, donning his hat and coat as Simeon and I nodded in acknowledgment and got back to doing the sort of police work we'd signed on for.

Our attention turned to Carlos Valentin, who was in the wind, but it's extremely difficult, under pressure and alone, not to pop up on somebody's radar somewhere.

Valentin had $68.50 remaining on his Electronic Benefit Transfer (EBT) card, a government-issued piece of magnetically encoded plastic which operates in much the same way as a preloaded credit card, allowing recipients to buy food and other necessities by swiping it through a reader in just about any neighborhood store.

Law enforcement loves technology like this. If you ever want to go off the grid, dump your cell phone and don't use any form of electronic payment, because it leaves a digital path. Investigators with the motivation, time, and resources will use it to find you and secure you for your statement or your arrest.

We ran the numbers for Valentin's EBT card and discovered he used it to buy groceries twenty miles from the scene of the shooting, at a bodega on Fourth Avenue in Brooklyn, right next to a subway.

We now had an approximate location where our suspect might be hiding out, so I called the U.S. probation officer handling his case, David Mulcahy, who produced a T-Mobile number for his client. Detective Simeon and I crossed our fingers that our guy hadn't had the sense to get rid of the handset. Valentin's phone was able to "roam" amongst the hundred or so transmission towers that were situated within a four-mile radius of the deli's address.

Across the USA, various police departments and federal agencies now make over 1.3 million Pen Register Trap and Trace requests per year, and these figures are rising steadily, forcing T-Mobile, Sprint, AT&T, and the other players to train dedicated teams which work 24/7 to keep up with the applications. Once he had seen our paperwork, the Honorable Eugene Oliver, Jr., of the Criminal Division Bronx Supreme Court signed the order for one more. We sent that on to T-Mobile on January 20 and they promptly handed over the records for that phone.

We pinged Valentin's details to a cell tower location very close to the deli where our suspect had bought his food. It was highly likely that he was somewhere in the neighborhood, lying low close to the train and the grocery store. Our fugitive's options were limited, and so, too, his options to make money, which meant he would commit further crimes and put others in harm's way. His circumstances and the risks attached marked him out for special attention. *It's Danny time.*

Movies show cops calling in SWAT every time they corner a collar, but in reality Homicide serves its own warrants most of the time. Guns are our last option—pepper spray and the threat of the telescopic baton are usually enough to discourage most suspects. For guys who like to shoot first and ask to see our warrants later, we have a different approach.

I picked up the phone and called the nearest thing the NYPD had to a Wild West sheriff: Detective Danny Rivera, a veteran cop who worked with the Bronx VFS—the borough's Violent Felony Squad—a small, elite team, who chased fugitives at large in the city and beyond. In many ways they played a role similar to that of the U.S. Marshals. It was one of the most dangerous assignments on the Job and, given the profile of the people they pursued, many of Danny's team were ex-military with an uncompromising attitude towards the fugitives they tracked down.

"This Valentin? No problem, Luke. We'll get him for you," our resident tough guy predicted with relish as I passed on the details, his appetite for flight and fight clear to see. Danny Rivera had never let me down in all the years we'd worked together, and five days later Carlos Valentin was arrested by Bronx VFS at 345 50th Street in Brooklyn, literally two minutes' walk from the bodega where he'd used his welfare card.

We established that the woman our witnesses believed was our shooter's sister was actually Valentin's girlfriend, Chrissy Moran. Her statement broadly corroborated the evidence of others outside the apartment that day, which put Abisay Rivera totally in the clear, or so I thought.

Zevon might have given up on pinning charges on PO Rivera, but his boss, a Captain Armstrong, was more determined. Zevon told me that Armstrong contacted ADA Ed Talty at the Bronx DA's office and said that he still suspected that Abisay may have driven her brother to Brooklyn after the murder. The details suggested otherwise, and I explained that the information from T-Mobile showed Valentin's phone following the path of the subway line to where the VFS found him, which pointed to him fleeing by train rather than in a car.

Armstrong's attitude was pretty commonplace amongst members of the Rat Squad, who usually wanted to put you in the picture until the facts counted you out of it.

Maria Rivera's case on the assault charges was assigned to ADA Melissa Beck, who agreed that she'd stabbed the Blood in self-defense. If Maria, not Valentin, had pulled out the pistol, she may well have beaten that charge, too. But the law is very strict on felons taking guns to knife fights, and when the case came to trial eighteen months later Carlos Valentin was convicted of manslaughter.

Whenever he does get out, the probation service will be waiting to drop a warrant on him and send him right back inside for breaking his parole on the initial drugs sentence.

The Man will always catch you, even if it's sometimes on the rebound.

CHAPTER NINETEEN

BE AFRAID, SCOOBY DOO

Sometimes all it takes is modern technology and a modern cowboy to locate a perp, but I never could have imagined that it would take two years, three police departments, three federal agencies, a luxury cruiser, a helicopter, a private jet, and millions of dollars to find one particular man . . . and that this would be the starting point of my final case in the NYPD.

November 26, 2009, eight p.m. Middle America collapses in front of the TV for a sacred annual tradition that's just as beloved as sweet potatoes, Snoopy specials, and kids impersonating the Pilgrim Fathers—a three-hour fix of padded collisions suitable for all the family, courtesy of the gladiators from the National Football League.

All over New York pumpkin pie is pushed aside as the Giants on the road in Colorado seek to annihilate the home team, the Denver Broncos. It's the first Thanksgiving fixture between these two teams in almost a decade. This year's prime-time show even has an added edge not usually permitted on network television as the Denver coach Josh McDaniels swears on air. "All we're trying to do is win a fucking game!" The network broadcasters are dumbstruck, and a million moms scramble for the mute button. "We apologize for ever airing anything like that, absolutely," their red-faced executive producer Eric Weinberger says in the media postmortem. "Especially on Thanksgiving."

Just off Creston Avenue in the Bronx, the Giants' game is kicking off as a black Honda Accord pulls up to the curbside in front of a local clothing store: Boutiqua 31. The engine is running and the driver watches anxiously as his passenger, a black Hispanic male aged about thirty, jumps out and draws a handgun. He pulls the trigger repeatedly, emptying the entire magazine into the people standing by the window, sending other passersby scattering like skittles as they dive for cover.

It's all over in less than ten seconds. The gunman jumps back into the getaway car, which pulls away in a belch of smoke and a squeal of rubber, leaving three victims bleeding to death on a blanket of broken glass.

Detectives from the 52nd Precinct got word later that the shooter's likely boss, Levit "Scooby Doo" Fernandini, was spotted cruising around the neighborhood in the Honda just as the football fans sang along to "The Star Spangled Banner." Levit was engaged in a battle of wills with other local drug lords for sole control of the multimillion-dollar cocaine and marijuana market operating on these corners. Outside Boutiqua 31—a known front for dealing—Julio Rodriguez (forty-five), Segundo Trinidad (fifty-five), and Carlos Lorenzo (twenty-five) lay motionless in a pool of blood while officers out of the 52 and EMS responded to the 911 calls flooding the switchboard. In cop terminology, all three vics are "likely"—likely gangsters or likely to be shot, you could say either.

Life, like professional sports, is all about hanging tough and beating the odds. Julio Rodriguez managed to beat them this time. But Trinidad and Lorenzo succumbed to their injuries, leaving us with a double homicide, an attempted murder, and a perp who would most likely go to ground. That's how it usually worked out, but I'd soon learn that my final case would prove far different from any I'd investigated up to that point in my career.

The shooter was soon identified as Hector "Hec" Garcia, a five-foot-nine-inch, twenty-six-year-old Bronxite of Puerto Rican extraction, who had just gotten out of federal prison for dealing drugs just yards from where he'd murdered his two latest victims. His years inside had taught Hector a lesson: if you are going to risk doing the time, make sure that the crime pays.

He had recently been promoted to lieutenant in Levit's organization, which was turning over around a hundred million dollars a year importing and dealing marijuana and coke. If you were to give Señor Garcia an official title, it'd be described as a communications troubleshooter, and he took this title literally. The Creston Crew gang was engaged in a hostile takeover, and Hec was the man chosen to deliver Levit's message—this usually came down the barrel of a 9mm pistol.

Five days before Thanksgiving, Levit's lieutenant had attempted to take out Clive Woolery, who worked for a Jamaican gang on the corner of Jerome Avenue and 193rd, close to St. James Park. It was where the second graders on the swings had been replaced by dealers pushing coke to the thieves and prostitutes who had claimed the streets as their own. Woolery was lucky and in follow-up interviews identified Hector as the man who'd tried to murder him. But in this neighborhood shootings are almost run-of-the-mill unless someone dies, so the squad detectives added the investigation to their other cases, little realizing that they had stumbled on a major criminal conspiracy.

But now we had two bodies, Woolery would have made it three, and if any more piled up the media would start to take note and the NYPD Brass would be on the phone to Lieutenant O'Toole demanding to know what the hell was going on.

Twenty hours later our suspect took it up another level. Ronaldo Perez sat at a traffic light, which seemed to be taking forever to turn green. He was on his way to St. James Park to meet some addicts who wanted to score. He sat drumming his fingers on the wheel and didn't spot the man approaching the car. He didn't see the pistol being raised and didn't even realize that he had been shot until the wave of pain attacked every fiber in his body and he heard the sound of his own voice screaming in agony. Hector hopped into a waiting Accord, which was driven off at speed by James "Mint" Rivera. This time, though, there was a police car in pursuit.

Lights flashing, sirens screaming, several RMPs quickly responded to the borough-wide alert, starting a high-speed chase which continued right through the Bronx for several miles, putting kids and pedestrians at risk. It ran up into the next county, where a Westchester Police Department cop who had joined in the hunt was hospitalized from his attempts to block the assailant's car. The driver and passenger bailed out and made good their escape, but left a raft of evidence tying them to the hit. Hector Garcia's prints were found inside the Honda and on the spare magazine for his pistol, which he had left on the floor. The gun he'd dumped out the window as they'd sped through Yonkers was also recovered, so it seemed that we had an open-and-shut case. All we needed to do now was find Hector Garcia. It couldn't be that difficult, could it?

"Luke, how do you like taking this over? This . . . what's-his-name . . . Garcia? Yeah. Hector Garcia. Three-time loser. This ass-hole is a problem. Unfortunately, he's our problem. You know what? I think we have a RICO case here," Lieutenant O'Toole mused, shifting his weight in his seat and leaning forward to hand me the case folder. "Get a task force together. Bring the feds in if they are interested. They have the manpower, and the money, and it's our turf, so cooperate. Put your other cases to one side, and concentrate on this until you get this bastard's nuts in a vise."

RICO refers to the Racketeer Influenced and Corrupt Organizations Act, which came out of congressional hearings in response to Mob control of gambling in the 1950s and 1960s and was passed into law under President Richard Nixon in 1970. It covers twenty-seven federal and eight state crimes, encompassing everything from bribery to loan-sharking and prostitution committed in the preceding ten-year period. The beauty of RICO is that, like the Triggerlock cases I worked on when I first came to Homicide, it's a federal statute and it assumes that everyone involved is acting as part of a criminal enterprise. In past decades it has been used to great effect against organizations as diverse as the Hell's Angels and the Catholic Church.

The next day I called the feds, or to be specific the assistant U.S. attorney for the Southern District of New York, Jessica Masella, and set up an appointment. AUSA Masella was a sweetheart soccer mom off-hours, but on the clock was fast gaining a reputation as a courtroom killer. Determined, dedicated, and diligent, she would not even consider taking a case unless she believed she would win. Her confidence was typical of federal prosecutors who were recruited from the front ranks of the top law schools in the country.

Masella was based in the Criminal Division, or the Gang Unit, as we call it on the Job, out of the Silvio V. Mollo Federal Building in downtown Manhattan—which also houses the

Secret Service and the U.S. Marshals Service. So a couple of days later, accompanied by O'Toole and Detective Victor Gomez, who'd caught the original shootings, we headed downtown.

We got quickly down to business and Jessica Masella listened intently as I outlined what we had on the case so far. O'Toole added his comments, and she paused for a moment to think through her options. The woman was spoiled for choice. It was clear that the drugs were being taken across state boundaries, and we had reason to believe our coke was coming through Puerto Rico—most of the gang had close family links there and it acted as a crucial conduit into the U.S. mainland for the South American cartels. The Creston Crew's weed probably originated in Mexico, which meant the ATF, the DEA, and of course the FBI would all be interested in chasing down our killer and his accomplices.

All of these agencies would go on to play a key part in this investigation but the attorney suggested that the Bureau, as the FBI is known, should play the lead role.

"Luke, do you know Roberto Riveros? Or Brandon Waller? They are with Group C-30 in the FBI. Excellent field agents. I've worked with these guys before, and the more I think about what you have here, the more I feel it's something we can work on together. I think we should set up a meeting with them and hear what they have to say, but I can tell you now that this is tailor-made for RICO and our office."

I had no problem with working with any feds Masella suggested, and O'Toole agreed, so another meeting was arranged with the duo who I would get to know very well over the following two years.

Special Agent Brandon Waller was the GI Joe of our operation, an expert in tactical situations who enjoyed nothing more than a shoot-out or an armed standoff, cut from the same cloth as my old pal Danny Rivera of the VFS.

Rob Riveros, who was of Chilean extraction, was more laid-back but just as sharp as his colleague and was equally intrigued by what we laid on the table.

When I put forward the NYPD's view it was clear that we were all on the same page—which is very important with inter-agency task forces, where egos and territorial jealousies can ruin any chance you have of success—and we all shook hands on the deal. Operation Creston Avenue Takedown, as it was officially designated, was now up and running.

There was only one thing left to do: deputize me as a de facto fed. And on May 10, 2010, already a seventeen-year veteran of the NYPD, I was presented with my new credentials.

The feds had the funding, manpower, and technology which would help to crack this case, but in addition to our own significant resources we had something that they lacked: local knowledge; and even better, we had a snitch. In fact we had probably the best snitch I ever worked with, a confidential informant who could give us chapter and verse on how Levit's organization was structured and operated, since he helped set it all in place.

Our CI was a parolee who had approached Detective Murphy from the 52 telling him that he was willing to provide the NYPD with invaluable intelligence on more than two dozen of Levit Fernandini's coconspirators, so Murphy introduced him to Detective Gomez and myself.

Our source, whom we code-named "Little," had been a member of the gang for years, but had become increasingly worried by their readiness to turn to violence as a first resort and was disgusted by the beatings he'd watched Levit and his lieutenants dole out to other members for relatively minor indiscretions.

Levit was also infamous for shooting people on a whim; concerned that he might be next, our snitch had cut his ties. His replacement was Hector, the man we were now searching for.

Little's decision to finally pluck up the courage to leave the organization was prompted by his boss's reaction to his complaints about another of his lieutenants, Angel "Julito" Diaz, a career criminal with twenty-seven convictions for robbery and gun possession. The inappropriately named Angel had become unpredictable, inflicting beatings on other members of the organization without permission, and Little feared either a coup or another murder, which would bring unwanted police attention to their activities. Little approached Levit and suggested that he show leadership by sorting the situation out.

Levit listened, thought it over, and agreed. He decided to delegate, so he clasped Little on the shoulder, looked him in the eye, and ordered his right-hand man to put a bullet in the back of Julito's head. Little refused. Their relationship was never the same.

What is utterly clear is that Levit Fernandini was despicable, dangerous, and without any moral inhibition—to this day we don't really know how many people he sent to a premature grave.

In 2007 the head of the Creston Crew was arrested for shooting at a rival dealer named Daniel Negron four times in a dispute over drugs, money, and territory. It's actually very difficult to shoot someone with a pistol unless you are standing close by and they are standing still, so the bullets failed to find their mark. Negron survived and initially identified the man who had pulled the trigger, before suddenly changing his mind, retracting his earlier statement, and assuring the squad DTs that he had just remembered that it wasn't his old pal Levit who had tried to turn him into a sieve after all. The case against Fernandini collapsed, and he was released to carry on his dealing and killing, but it was only in one of my chats with Little that the real story emerged.

He explained that the gang leader effectively bought his way out of an attempted murder charge by giving Negron twenty grand to smooth things over between them, but the really chilling part was that Fernandini later confided to his lieutenant that he deeply regretted the move. Not the attempted murder, Little was quick to emphasize, but his decision to pay off Negron for his silence. Levit was just sorry he hadn't simply strung him along and finished Negron off with a fresh magazine, saving himself the twenty G's.

Little and I had countless face-to-face chats, and from the first meeting I was impressed with what the man had to offer. I quickly completed the paperwork necessary to sign him up as a CI, keeping Masella up to speed, and called in Agents Waller and Riveros on the following interviews.

Confidential informants get paid, some as much as a grand a week, tax-free, from our specially earmarked budget, and the department actually has shopping lists of what they will pay for. To Bronx Homicide a gun is worth about a hundred dollars. A kilo of coke is more valuable, maybe netting a snitch a thousand dollars. You can get me an AK assault rifle? The rate goes through the roof, into thousands. Crime may pay, but preventing it does, too.

Intelligence is crucial to police work. The Job has very strict procedures for dealing with registered confidential informants, meaning that Little's details were only shared with myself, O'Toole, and the CI section of the NYPD. To this day I cannot reveal his real name, or even write it down, nor can I tell it to a judge. Our man was assigned a code—in this case CI 007 000115—and a code name.

Our new recruit, who had chosen his own code name "Little," had made a smart move deciding to switch from dealing drugs to selling information about other people dealing drugs. He knew very well that putting a major player like Fernandini behind bars for life would make him safer; it would also pay.

Well spoken and articulate, the only really obvious clues to Little's criminal past were his numerous tattoos. If his life had taken another turn he would probably have made a good cop, or indeed an excellent federal agent, asking the questions instead of answering them.

We began developing a file of those who made up the Creston Crew, starting with names and aliases, which I checked off old DD5 arrest reports and the NYPD's NITRO, or the Narcotic Investigation and Tracking of Recidivist Offenders system, to give it its full title. (NITRO was rolled out in 2006 to replace the old mainframe computer databases which up to then allowed us to save complaints on everything from drug dealing to public moral offenses, such as prostitution; these are now compiled and networked into similar programs maintained by other law enforcement agencies, the intelligence constantly updated by investigators and Field Teams working on other cases.)

We also started to tag the names of Creston Crew dealers and associates and began to build up photo databases of everyone involved, which were worked into a series of giant banners and hung on the office wall, showing how the players interacted, with lots of arrows leading to and from the various branches, every one eventually pointing to Levit Fernandini at the top of the tree.

The gang's main base of operations was 2600 Creston Avenue, so we photographed everyone who entered or left the address, or even hung around outside for longer than a minute or two, putting books together on people whom we considered suspects. In many cases we simply lifted the picture from the mug shot on their arrest report, and if that failed we could run their driver's license or welfare card, copying-and-pasting the image into our files. If we still needed a head-and-shoulders, FBI agents would run the Con Ed truck trick, dressing as utility workers and discreetly taking pictures while they pretended to inspect perfect power cables, or covertly photographing our targets from inside vans marked up with the logos of a local pizza company.

We had to use an array of tactics in this case, and I caught a break when we realized that Levit's landlord had security cameras trained on the hallways and corridors of 2600 Creston, a common feature in both commercial and residential buildings in New York. The security was handled by SecureWatch 24, a Manhattan-based company specializing in property protection and management, its cameras' data streamed through a secure website to their customers' laptops. I rang the company, introducing myself as an NYPD detective, and learned that Levit had, unsurprisingly, decided not to pay the bill to have the activities of his dealers filmed.

My very next call was to the landlord. "Sure. We got cameras in the building, Detective, through those SecureWatch people. But the damn cheapskate tenants I got? Won't pay the fees. So I had to cancel," he explained.

"Well, you know the NYPD like to be proactive in the community and stop crime before it happens if we can. How about, oh . . . how about if, say, we pick up the tab? Would you have any objection?" I suggested.

"None at all. That's great. Go right ahead," he replied, his mood immediately lifting.

I passed on the details and the Bureau wrote the check, giving us access not only to 2600 Creston Avenue but to all the company's cameras in the five boroughs. Our focus was on Levit Fernandini, though. Now that every deal his people made was captured on our hard drives, we were well on our way to closing down the Creston Crew—for good.

CHAPTER TWENTY

LITTLE BY LITTLE

The two men stand at opposite sides of the hotel room, sizing each other up. One has a gun; the other has money and wants to buy a gun. One of the two will soon go back to prison for a very long time.

The bigger of the two, a three-hundred-pound, three-time loser named Roberto "Indio" Rosa, cradles a rusting Arminius Titan Tiger .38, a cheap, chunky "truck gun," in one hand, click-clacking the ammunition for it between the fingers and thumb of his other hand. The other is Little, who is wearing digital recording equipment hidden under his clothes. Little seals the deal when he flashes a thick wad of buy money, the serial number of each bill carefully recorded on our database, which we handed him thirty minutes earlier as Agent Waller kitted him out for our covert recording.

On the streets, or in a hotel room, you can't trust an ex-con. It's something Rosa will be reminded of when he is charged with a 924E felony, under U.S. Code 18, which for a loser like him could mean twenty years without parole.

Back in the office we unhook Little from the hidden microphone and camera before I voucher the gun and take it to be swabbed for DNA and fingerprints. I organize for a Triggerlock detective to do the complaint against Rosa, but take no action against him for the time being. It's another piece of leverage we hold in our efforts to take down Fernandini and apprehend the hit man Hector Garcia. When it suits us we will pick Indio up, sit him in a chair, and tell him he has a choice. Give up your homeys or take the fall for the gun sale—and by the time you are released from federal prison people won't be using revolvers anymore. They'll be using lasers.

What Rosa had said on the wire had given me more than I could hope for, warning Little that if he appeared anywhere around 2600 Creston he was risking his life because Levit wanted him dead. Within a week we were reminded of just how much danger our CI was always facing. My phone rang. It was a familiar voice, but it was the first time I had ever detected panic behind the words.

"Detective Waters? It's me. Got bad news. Real bad. Man, you gotta do something! Indio just called me. It's 'bout to go down. He's gonna whack a guy, and he wants me to help him."

Normally unflappable, Little was close to losing it.

"Okay, calm down, buddy. Take a breath. Nobody is going to get whacked. Who has Rosa got this beef with? Who's he going to kill?"

"Scooby. He's going over to kill Levit Fernandini."

The leader of the Creston Crew might end up in a morgue by the end of this shift unless we stepped in and arrested everyone, killing our case stone-dead at a cost of thousands of man-hours and hundreds of thousands of dollars, while the other members of the gang would melt into the background.

It's debatable whether planet earth would be a better place without gangsters like the leader of the Creston Crew, and nobody in the Bronx precincts or Group C-30 would lament his eventual passing, but we all took on a duty to protect the public and uphold the laws of the United States. We could not allow this murder to take place. Some reasons were moral, others practical. Power abhors a vacuum. The gang leader's death would not solve anything, because if Rosa pulled off the hit it would simply put some other figure, from inside the Creston Crew or another organization, in the position he now occupied, and a year from now we would have to start our investigation against the new power broker.

I tried to calm Little down, telling him that he was still the key to our case and he must convince his buddy Rosa to change his mind and leave Levit alone, at least for the time being.

"I dunno, Detective Waters. Indio ain't too smart. Scooby disrespected his woman, and he's real mad about that. Plus, the homey's afraid that Lev will pop him . . ."

"Look, you have to stop him or stall him. One way or another you have to make sure he does not shoot Fernandini."

We got Little to come into our office, and I told him to call Rosa back right away, while the FBI and I listened to every word. Rosa was still highly agitated, and Riveros rolled his eyes when the man on the other end of the line asked Little to be his wheelman for the hit. Our CI played it smart, and played Indio, too, eventually getting him to agree to postpone the assassination and let Little know when he decided to go through with it, which meant we would at least have a heads-up on the possible future shooting.

Levit's drug empire was centered on Creston Avenue, but another of his bases, an apartment on Clarence Avenue eight miles away in leafy Eastchester, was also coming up on the wiretaps—ones which had been put in place by the New York Organized Crime Drug Enforcement "Strike Force."

On November 21, 2010, several members of Strike Force, curious to see what was going on inside the apartment, used the direct approach and politely knocked on the door.

Inside, the cops and agents found two of the gang, who were placed in cuffs while their visitors searched the joint, quickly finding $276,000 in shoe boxes. The money was neatly parceled into bundles of ones, fives, twenties, and fifties, along with an off-the-shelf digital bill counter, the sort of gadget now on sale in your local Walmart, which would whirr through a thousand bills in under a minute.

The seizure barely made a dent in Levit's bank balance, and back on the wires the following day the feds picked up his boys congratulating themselves on taking such an easy hit, crowing at the small quantities of drugs that we had swept up. The more than a quarter of a million dollars seized by the cops and agents? Less than one day's takings, according to the relieved gangsters, their admissions proving the importance of RICO statutes in proving a criminal conspiracy.

Multiply $250,000 by 365 and you get some idea of the sums of money Levit and his friends were generating. With $90 million or so on the line, right and wrong go out the window.

Our undercover buys continued while I reached out to the Violent Felony Squad to try to flush out Hector Garcia, who was keeping a lower profile than Salman Rushdie. Meanwhile, I got a call from DT Andy Bonan from Queens Vice, who, along with DT Mauricio Cortes, was working with Strike Force. Two of our subjects were crossing links with his case.

On May 20, 2011, Strike Force members approached a man, Richard Gonzalez Santiago, on West Forty-fifth Street. He differed little from the tourists and office workers who thronged nearby Times Square, but they placed him under arrest. To judge by his heavy suitcases, the suspect looked like any other holidaymaker, but the cop popped the catches and found seventy-nine pounds of cocaine wrapped in plastic. Estimated street value: approximately $1.5 million.

"Big Times Square Drugs Bust" screamed the *New York Post* the next day, but the reality behind the column inches was that our DTs and the agents knew what Santiago was packing. He had been under surveillance ever since his flight had landed at JFK from Puerto Rico, but we'd allowed him to pass through customs to pick up his contacts, one of whom, Linda Perez, was also coming up on our wires.

The collar had been on the radar for several years and was wanted in New York, as well as by the feds in Philly. Santiago had risked a return to meet with another of Fernandini's lieutenants, Francisco Rivera. On April 13, Vic Gomez and I arrested Linda Perez at 2600 Creston Avenue, where she was charged under U.S. Code 21, Section 812, for the thirty-six kilos of the drug under law deemed to be in her possession and was remanded, without bail.

When Little had refused to shoot Angel Diaz, Levit's lieutenant, Levit had instead hired two outside hitters to carry out the contract, and on June 12, 2006, they walked up to a group of people outside 2592 Creston Avenue and opened fire, catching their target in the face, to the horror of a twenty-two-year-old woman and two older teenagers standing near him, who were also caught in the crossfire.

The victims were rushed to Jacobi Medical Center and St. Barnabas Hospital, where the male victim was pronounced

DOA. But Levit's freelancers had got their wires crossed and instead had succeeded in murdering a twenty-seven-year-old father named Christopher "Gremlin" Santiago.

After the shooting Levit told Little he wanted to meet him for a face-to-face, and they agreed to Orchard Beach on Long Island Sound—a man-made facility, part of the enormous Pelham Bay Park, which is many times the size of its more famous Manhattan cousin, Central Park, and is all but deserted outside of the summer months.

The beach, complete with millions of tons of sand, miles of boardwalk, and several basketball and handball courts, dates back to the 1930s, promoted as the "Riviera of New York," and is a popular spot with families, sun worshippers, and gangsters who want to "off" a rival, so Little was understandably nervous as he sat down for a chat with the murderous and possibly psychopathic gang leader whom he'd defied only a couple of days earlier.

Levit claimed he wanted to smooth things over between them, and while Little gazed out at sunlight glinting on the broken bottles on Rat Island, he listened to his boss's fairy stories about how he'd had nothing to do with the botched hit. Little was thinking he was glad he had a way out.

I had never stopped looking for Hector Garcia, whose actions had led to the launch of Operation Creston in the first place, and I was in regular contact with members of the VFS. If we hooked Hector it would free us up to concentrate solely on the other members of the gang, but although Danny Rivera and his team had been chasing him for months, putting pressure on their own snitches, their efforts had come to nada.

The best lead we had was an address at 26 Pennyfield, a private waterfront apartment in a small development in Throgs

Neck, a quiet, respectable part of the Bronx borough, located on a peninsula just a hundred yards from the prestigious Maritime College of SUNY—the State University of New York.

The home was one of several financed by Levit with the millions he was laundering through drug dealing. He had chosen well, because even though Danny had cruised past the joint, he was adamant that proper surveillance techniques wouldn't work, so Waller and I sat down to chat to the VFS and agreed that we needed a different perspective on our suspect's possible hiding place—about ten thousand feet in the air. I reached out to NYPD Aviations, based at Floyd Bennett Field over in Flatbush, Brooklyn, to arrange a helicopter flyover of Pennyfield and the college campus to see if we could spot a good place to set up an OP—an observation post.

One of Waller's and Riveros's colleagues, FBI Special Agent Rachel Kolvek, accompanied us on the trip. Our pilot was one of my closest pals on the Job, Sergeant John O'Hara, and he went through the usual preflight safety checks, telling us to strap into our seats and don our headsets, before taking off for the peninsula, which we reached in about ten minutes.

O'Hara hovered over the location and it was pretty clear why the VFS had come up empty-handed so far. As well as offering panoramic views of the East River, Long Island Sound, and the Throgs Neck Bridge, the balconies of our three-story target apartment were also the perfect place to spot any potential surveillance. Agent Kolvek tapped my arm to get my attention and pointed at a sailing boat cruising Long Island Sound, her forefinger and thumb forming an "okay." The water, which was about eighty yards from the apartment's balcony, would offer us the only real chance to set up surveillance.

Back in the office I rubbed my hands together, looking for-

ward to a spin in a 150-mile-per-hour cigarette boat, as we prepared to set up the surveillance at Pennyfield, but Waller turned
penny-pincher and burst my bubble. We stood at the jetty a
couple of days later staring at something more practical and
comfortable: a mid-sized luxury fishing craft that the Bureau
had kitted out with cameras, binoculars, and other equipment,
which we checked before heading on to Long Island Sound and
up to the mouth of the East River towards our target apartment.

We spent the next few days and nights offshore, taking
turns staring through telephoto lenses in the hope of catching
the merest glimpse of Hector, but countless hours of bobbing
up and down produced no sighting. Soon after, I got a tip that
he might be up in Boston, where his wife, with whom he had a
child, was staying. The VFS wasted no time in following up on it
and drove up to meet Hector's old lady—but they got nothing.
"I ain't seen Hector in weeks. And I don't know where he at,"
Mrs. Garcia told Rivera at the door.

With no warrant to search the house, the cop had little
choice but to leave his card. I applied for Pen Register Trap and
Trace for the two numbers we knew had been used by Hector,
just to be on the safe side. We sat down with the feds and Gomez
to work out where we'd go from there. How could we turn up
the heat on Levit, somehow force his hand and get him to lead
us to Hector?

CHAPTER TWENTY-ONE

SCOOBY DOO, WE GOT YOU

The members of the Violent Felony Squad take a perp's continuing freedom as a personal affront. Danny Rivera and his
team were becoming frustrated by the fact that they had been
unable to get any firm leads on Hector Garcia's location. If we
could take him down it would blow open the whole gang and
help us nail Levit "Scooby Doo" Fernandini. Although they'd
been chasing Hector for months and months, putting pressure
on their own snitches, the VFS's efforts had come to nada. But
I had an idea.

I suggest that it's time to do a little wallpapering. Detective
Vic Gomez and I could cover every foot of Creston Avenue with
"Wanted" posters of Hector, offering a two-thousand-dollar
Crime Stoppers reward for information leading to his capture.
Our chances of actually catching him this way are virtually nil,
but the real idea is to raise up his pals. Without realizing their
phones are "wired," they might just ring him and tell him that
The Five-O are on his case again—allowing the FBI to trace the
location of our hit man's cell phone. "Hey, why not, Luke?" FBI
Agent Waller says with a shrug. "It might work. Let's run it and
see where it takes us."

"What do you think, Rod?"

The other agent laughs at the simplicity of the plan, but is all for it. "Me? Hey, you know that I'm all about the teamwork, guys. Yeah, buddy, if you think it's worthwhile, we can try it." Riveros and Waller hit the wires. Gomez and I take to the streets. We're not long into the operation when I spot a short, dark-haired female aged about thirty trying hard to look casual, her cell phone in hand, watching our every move. I recognize her immediately from the giant poster plastered over one wall of the FBI field office. It's Karina Olivera—Levit's girlfriend—a most trusted member of his gang. She is clearly conducting a little countersurveillance, a common move when we stake out a perp.

I walk towards her, smiling, trying to appear as casual as I can.

"Excuse me, miss. Could you take one of these flyers? We're looking for the guy pictured."

"Sure, Office-ah. Thank you. Can I get a few of those? Maybe I'll recognize this boy."

"Of course. Thanks for your help, have as many as you like," I reply.

Olivera walks away with a small bundle of posters stuck under her arm, her cell phone glued to her ear once more. One hour and one coffee later, my cell phone chimes. If my hunch has proved right, our break has come early. It's Riveros.

"Luck o' the Irish, Luke. It worked, it worked!" he says gleefully. "Your girl just called Levit, and he reached out to his amigo, pronto. Pack your bags, buddy. We're off to the Caribbean."

Our wiretaps revealed the precise location where the call was received as 15-10 Calle Calais in Carolina, San Juan, Puerto Rico. The teams sat down and worked out how best to apprehend Hector without tipping him and Levit off that the FBI were on their tail.

After weighing the pros and cons, we decided to see if we could use the Bronx district attorney to go through the motions of prosecuting our hit man for one of the murders he had committed back in Creston, rather than applying for a federal warrant, which might get out and tip off Levit.

I rang Ed Talty, now heading the DA's Homicide Division, a clever attorney whom I had worked with a lot down the years, and asked him for a solid favor. I told him that we would eventually "writ" our suspect over to the feds, and that he could drop his charges, but I didn't even hint that I was working as part of a task force on a federal case, because there would be little in it for his office.

Talty agreed to hand the case over to his ADA Nancy Barko, the veteran prosecutor whom I had worked with before. She brought Hector's case before a grand jury, in absentia, where he was charged with second degree murder, second degree attempted murder, and assault in the second degree. Supreme Court Judge George Villeras agreed with our evidence and signed a New York State warrant for his arrest.

We spent the next day getting the paperwork arranged for our flight arranged and obtaining the signatures allowing us to carry our pistols on the aircraft. Victor and I headed to the airport in good time for Flight 707 to San Juan and we bumped into William "Gonzo" Gonzalez, one of the two VFS guys who would back us up on the manhunt. We were browsing the magazines in the gift shop when I noticed what Gonzalez had brought along for the trip.

"Jesus, Gonzo! What do you want that thing for?" I asked in amazement, staring at the MP5 submachine gun peeking out from under his jacket.

"Eh? This? Firepower, buddy, firepower. Ain't nobody gonna get the jump on Gonzo, bro. I'll sit on it on the plane," he responded, eyes glinting as he lightly fingered the trigger.

We left on different flights, but I am guessing Detective Gonzalez got an upgrade to first class that morning without even having to say a word. Gomez and I touched down at Luis Muñoz Marín International Airport, and barely had we left the front gates before I was saying a prayer of thanks that Gonzo and his equally well-armed VFS colleagues were with us for the operation.

San Juan had police cruisers on every corner, lights ablaze, and armed cops standing to one side, hands on hips, pistols prominently displayed in holsters to show the local gangsters that the PD were ready to fight fire with firepower. The homicide rate there was about a thousand per year. What should be the fun capital of an island paradise was just like the Bronx, but on a really, really bad day. The FBI had just finished one of the biggest investigations into police corruption in its history, ending with a three a.m. raid across Puerto Rico. In total, eighty-nine local cops and several corrections officers were arrested and charged with offering to protect undercover federal agents posing as drug dealers looking to hire muscle.

In San Juan we trusted nobody, and I slept with one eye open for the couple of nights we spent there. Agents Riveros and Waller dressed down and left their sharp suits back in the Big Apple. They told anyone who asked that they were NYPD detectives and left the talking to me. From our hotel, I picked up the phone and reached out for help to the DEA agents from the Caribbean Division and the U.S. Marshals, along with a few trustworthy members of the local police. But like DA Ed Talty back in the Bronx, they had no idea that this was an interagency task force. Even if we caught him, just one throwaway comment in front of Hector could result in his alerting Levit Fernandini and potentially ending the investigation. Any leak would see his associates dump their phones, grab whatever cash they could, and kill anyone likely to sell them out, before dropping off the map.

Though we knew where Hector was staying, cell phone towers are rare enough in the mountains of semirural Puerto Rico—meaning we could only get an approximate location for his phone. We needed much more before we could swoop. The DEA and Marshals were friendly and cooperative and willing to wait for me to give the go-ahead. But the hours dragged on into a day, then turned into a second, and we still awaited confirmation of our target's location.

As patience waned, frustration levels rose, and all eyes turned to me.

U.S. Marshal Tim Callahan, just arrived from Mexico, set off into the countryside on foot to see if he could pin the signal down. He carried a backpack with a portable tracking device but had little success. Any vehicle with a larger rig approaching Hector's hacienda would be spotted immediately, so for an accurate fix we ramped it up—literally. Back in the Bronx we'd used helicopters and offshore boats to track Hector, but Callahan had a better idea. He offered to loan us his jet.

"Luke, this is getting us nowhere. I have a pilot and a U.S. Marshals plane on the runway in Tampa. I'm going to call him up and get him to fly on a direct path over this address. If Garcia is there we should get a hit on the phone." Callahan made the call and ultimately won the day. The pilot had to stall until the local rainstorms lifted but soon the jet took off from Florida on its two-hour flight to our coordinates.

Federal agencies often call on U.S. military aviation for backup, but the paperwork involved can take days when only minutes are available. Callahan's assistance that day was critical and prompt.

251

We used that time to make one final check on the equipment and climb into our SUVs parked up close to the University of Puerto Rico. On its campus, some students were studying forensics and criminal justice; one mile away we hoped our killer was busy studying the latest episode of *MTV Cribs*—not peering through the blinds ready to bolt or blast his way out.

Inside the jeeps the atmosphere was quiet and tense. All of us wore ballistic helmets and Kevlar body armor. Between the DEA and the U.S. Marshals, we had enough small arms to start a Central American revolution. The agents were checking and rechecking 9mm MP5s, 5.56mm M4 assault rifles, and Remington 12-gauge pump-action shotguns. In addition, we all had various semiautomatic pistols, as did the local Puerto Rican police accompanying us.

We sat in silence. Four miles above us the Triggerfish signal locator hurtled towards Hector at hundreds of miles per hour. Callahan hung on at the end of the line, waiting for the news which would dictate the success, or failure, of this entire mission. Suddenly he was animated.

"He's there! The pilot got a hit on the phone! He's in the house. Go, go, go!"

Our convoy took off at speed and in less than two minutes we'd reached the location. As the first truck hit the driveway, several of our guys piled out and charged towards the door. They advanced behind ballistic shields with their weapons drawn in case anyone inside decided to fight it out. I was in the second SUV, just seconds behind, and we arrived in time to see Hector stumble out the back door and run for the hills. Racing behind him came maybe two dozen cops and agents, all screaming at him to surrender.

With over twenty guns aimed at his head our hitter

decided the odds, for once, weren't in his favor: 539 days after shooting two people dead in New York, Hector Garcia raised his hands before being knocked onto his knees, handcuffed, and placed under arrest. I waved the warrant in his face as he coughed through the dust kicked up by our boots and was put in the jeep.

His girlfriend, Monica Callow, was terrified. She was also restrained for our safety, but we had no intention of charging her. We chose to leave her alone in the house, frightened and confused, as we took Hector to the Extradition Office in San Juan. We were guessing and hoping she'd call Levit's wire-tapped cell and read him the name off the NYPD card I'd placed in her hand.

Thirteen hundred miles away, FBI agents in downtown Manhattan listened on their headsets and they were on the phone in minutes with good news. Monica had just rung Levit to tell him Hector'd been popped by the Po-Po. The same technique we'd used handing out the Crime Stoppers flyers in Creston Avenue had worked here, too—but in a slightly more high-tech, jet-set way.

Back in New York the wires were humming. Levit was highly agitated, already calling his lieutenants and his lawyer to tell them the bad news about Hector. Right then Garcia was a heck of a lot calmer than his soon-to-be-former boss, sipping a Coke in our custody.

There was little to be gained from leaning on our prisoner, so I pulled up a chair and asked him if there was anything else that I could do. I told him we could draw up a cooperation agreement with the Bronx DA. I made no mention of the FBI—the warrant we'd served was the one from DA Talty.

I took a photo of Hector from my jacket pocket and turned

it faceup. I slid it across the table next to his half-empty can and looked him in the eye.

"Yo—I am not that man, the man you cops think I am," he said, taking another gulp and returning my stare. "I gotta take orders, jus' like you. I got a wife, man. I got a kid, and my homeys know where my family is at, up in Boston. I don't do as I'm told, I'm dead. I talk to the Five-O, and they dead. I gotta jus' do my time, like a man."

He did not realize that he was saying exactly what I wanted to hear. Hector's only concern was his family's safety, not his loyalty to his boss, so when we got the others behind bars, Hector should cooperate and help us keep them there.

We left our prisoner in the care of the local cops, and Gomez and I went to sample some local rum to celebrate. The next day we flew back to JFK and set up a meeting with O'Toole, Masella, and the others involved to bring them up to speed. Two years after he'd shot up Boutiqua 31, the killer responsible was finally in custody. But Levit and the other members of the Creston Crew, although unnerved by the arrest of their key enforcer, had no idea that it was anything other than an NYPD operation.

I went down to meet with ADA Nancy Barko and tell her how we'd got on. She was delighted that Hector was in custody, but she, too, had no idea of any federal law enforcement involvement in his location and arrest. She grew more animated during our conversation at the prospect of prosecuting him for the double homicide. But our focus remained on Levit and his crew.

Taking down multiple targets involves huge planning, even more so when organized by the feds, so a lot of calls and meetings took place over the following days. Even the smallest detail was not left to chance, as the Job coordinated with the local

FBI field office, resulting in a big boost for agents' smiles and air miles all over the country as they packed their famous blue jackets with the bold yellow letters and flew in from Washington, D.C., Boston, and cities in other states to back up the local field offices with the simultaneous raids which would take place in New York, Florida, Texas, and Puerto Rico.

The tactical commanders decided that six a.m. on Wednesday, July 13, 2011, would be Zero Hour. The early start was carefully chosen, as there was every chance that the targets would resist, many of them facing life in prison with little to lose by shooting it out. At about a dozen addresses in the Bronx, police cars, FBI SUVs, and trucks full of federal SWAT team members quietly pulled up to the perimeter as dawn approached. It would be the last daybreak Levit Fernandini ever saw as a free man.

Snipers were set in position on nearby rooftops and FBI helicopters hovered overhead, searchlights trained on the back doors and yards should anyone try to bail out the rear. Nearby our mobile command centers—large articulated trucks—coordinated the joint police and federal operation, the captains sitting inside sipping their cappuccinos. At six a.m. exactly we got the call to move in, and I joined tens of police officers and agents who swarmed on 2600 Creston Avenue. The raid was led by members of the FBI Regional SWAT team and NYPD ESU, who stormed the building. We screamed at the dazed residents to lie on the floor and cooperate or they would be shot.

Levit Fernandini, for years the most ruthless and terrifying man on the Bronx streets, complied without a whimper. Faced with an army of assault rifles, half blinded by arc lights dancing along the walls, he and his crew did exactly as ordered. They were handcuffed, placed under arrest, and given their Miranda warnings. We recovered several firearms in the raid, but not one shot, to my knowledge, was fired. In the days that followed, Hector Garcia unveiled information which led to me deciding to end my career in the NYPD.

But for now there was still the matter of that email from Sergeant John Griffin blinking in my in-box, telling me that Nancy Barko was looking for a copy of the Puerto Rico warrant and wanted to have a chat about "jurisdiction . . ."

CHAPTER TWENTY-TWO

DON'T FORGET TO DUCK

With Hector Garcia safely incarcerated, ADA Nancy Barko is taking her exclusion personally.

"Why were you not up-front with me on this Garcia case, Luke? You have made me look pretty stupid here!" Nancy barks.

"Look, I made an agreement with Ed Talty, and I kept it, Nancy," I testily respond. "We asked you for a solid favor, and you were kind enough to do it for us. How did I deceive you?"

"You know what you did! You didn't tell us about the other cases, or that the feds were involved. You never intended letting us prosecute," she hits back.

"I wasn't obliged to, Nancy. And even if I wanted to, I couldn't do that, as you know."

Barko and Talty continue to seethe. But they don't have a case in any sense of the word.

In 1985 I was an illegal alien, oversalting the pretzels and sliding pints along the bar of O'Reilly's Pub on West 31st Street to off-duty cops and serving sandwiches to off-the-books construction workers. Meanwhile, downtown a guy called Sol Wachtler was handing down sentences. As chief judge of the New York Court of Appeals, he was a key figure in both judicial and Republican political circles, a go-getter and a trendsetter. Combined with his efforts to make spousal rape a criminal offense and his determination to reform the grand jury system, he was a darling of the tabloids.

Sol, it seemed, was destined for the governor's mansion. Twenty-five years later he was remembered mostly for his one-liners. Well, his one-liners, and the fact that he was certainly out there.

Discussing the growing power of the DA in the Big Apple, Judge Wachtler once told Maria Kramer of the *New York Daily News* that the DAs were now so powerful that, by and large, they could indict a ham sandwich. Seven years later, he was arrested by the FBI on charges of extortion, racketeering, and blackmail. It emerged that he was stalking his former girlfriend, Joy Silverman, a wealthy heiress whose trust fund he administered, and threatening to kidnap her daughter—while dressed up as a cowboy.

The unfortunate man was suffering from bipolar disorder, his daily cocktail of amphetamines, tranquilizers, and antidepressants perhaps explaining his bizarre behavior, and maybe his comments about the Bronx DA's office, too.

Robert Johnson was a new arrival when Wachtler traded in his spurs for an orange uniform, and a quarter of a century later he still presided over a bigger cowboy outfit than the former chief judge ever owned.

The Bronx DA's office had become synonymous with cost overruns, inefficiency, and laziness for as long as I served in the department. The tabloids gleefully reported the fact that Johnson's attorneys lagged 10 percent behind the citywide averages in prosecuting violent offenders and took almost twice as long to file complaints in court as their counterparts across the city—declining to take on cases which would rank as straightforward prosecutions in other boroughs. When they did go to trial before a jury, Johnson's team of ADAs won fewer than half their cases.

So I suppose I could see why Nancy Barko, as one of the longest-serving ADAs, was put out about being kept in the dark about the true nature of the Garcia case. But that certainly didn't excuse the Bronx DA's office from trying to convict one of our principal targets in the Creston Crew for a murder he never committed, which I only discovered when Masella and I sat down with our prisoner and his lawyer.

For Hector our meeting was a welcome change of scenery and routine, and with Levit and the other gangsters under lock and key, his wife and child were now safe from a revenge hit, so he willingly described his role in the Creston Crew and the inner workings of the entire organization. It served to corroborate facts we already knew and confirmed other details which we had surmised but could not absolutely ascertain. This was a real help for Masella in preparing her RICO case. Hector's days of shooting people were behind him, but he had one final bombshell to drop.

"I gotta tell you something. I capped one guy you dunno about. Me and Rafi Reyes killed the homey. I had a .357 and he got hisself a .32. I remember 'cos that was just before the Five-O got Rafi with three pieces for blasting that bouncer at the Umbrella Club," he declared.

Our prisoner was referring to a 2009 shooting at an expensive Washington Heights dance spot whose clientele ranged from well-dressed hip-hop, house, and salsa fans to high-end hookers as well as gangbangers like Hector, Reyes, Angel "Julito" Diaz, and Anthony "Fat Boy" Torres.

Three handguns along with a number of casings were found

after the Umbrella Club shooting, and these were run through the ATF and FBI-sponsored Integrated Ballistics Identification System—IBIS—made up of Brasscatcher and the similar Bulletcatcher programs, which allow technicians to check the resulting magnified high-resolution pictures against previously recovered evidence of the same caliber. Their computers got a positive hit and, combined with prints and other evidence, this helped the ADA to convict Raphael Reyes for his part in the crime. He was serving a stretch in Rikers, but now Hector had revealed that his old friend had helped him with the murder of Derek "Gotti" Moore. "This other homey, we shot him in his head. Levit want this Gotti dead, so we both capped him," Hector explained helpfully.

Masella looked in my direction, but this new confession had come as just as much of a shock to me as it clearly was to her. Garcia went on to describe not only his role in this murder, but also his route to it, from the Cross Bronx Expressway to the crime scene, detailing how he and the other hitter waited for their quarry on Leland Avenue and shot him at point-blank range with two weapons: a powerful .357 Magnum revolver and a much less powerful .32-caliber pistol, a defensive handgun which fires a significantly smaller bullet.

Masella was delighted to have potentially solved another homicide as part of our RICO case, but was concerned that these details were emerging so late, and she asked me to get over to Simpson Street to check the case folders without delay.

An hour later Hector was back in the cell block with his homeys and I was over at Homicide with my files, staring at paperwork which was about to further damage the already tarnished reputation of the DA's office. There was only one problem with the shooting which Hector had confessed to carrying out.

It was not an unsolved homicide. According to the thick file in front of me, Derek "Gotti" Moore had been killed by a thirty-three-year-old New Yorker named Luis Vignold, who had spent the last two years on remand in Rikers, and his case was about to come to trial.

ADA Christiana Stover, on behalf of the People of New York, would allege that on August 31, 2009, at 8:55 p.m., in front of 1512 Leland Avenue, the accused approached his victim, a twenty-two-year-old black male and Bloods gang member, and shot at him half a dozen times, two rounds catching him in the head, one of which traveled to his brain, killing him almost instantly.

It was a curious situation.

Jumping to conclusions is dangerous in police work, and it was possible that Hector, realizing he was facing life anyway, was simply holding up his hands to another crime as a favor to the real shooter, but my instincts told me otherwise, so I picked up the phone and called Christiana Stover to discuss the contradictions between her charges and our confession.

The ADA and I had never gotten on, a personality clash which was not resolved by her recent marriage to Detective Jimmy McSloy, one of my longtime colleagues in Homicide, who'd just "got grade"—been promoted to D2, a boost in pay and status. I had been assured that the promotion was mine, and the wound was still raw: I was angry at being overlooked—I had a strong record as a detective and consistently excellent evaluations—but I wasn't exactly surprised. Office politics is part of any large organization, and the NYPD is no exception. Playing favorites is part of playing the game on the Job. I hadn't complained when my Irishness had gotten me looked after by the Brass, and although I felt frustrated, hurt, and unappreciated because of the recent lack of promotion, when I sat down and thought about it over the weeks to come, I realized that there was little point holding a grudge. Life isn't fair. The trick is to make it work unfairly in your favor. I would move on—literally.

Meanwhile, Vignold would face life in prison for a crime he may not have committed, so I contacted Stover. She seemed unimpressed by the questions I had and waved aside the issues raised by Hector's surprise confession.

"Mr. Vignold was identified by a witness on the street who saw him pull the trigger, Detective," Stover replied, referring to the DD5 arrest reports I had in front of me, which showed that an eyewitness did indeed finger the guy, making no mention of an accomplice.

"I don't know what Hector Garcia's motivation is, but there was only one shooter on this, and I am confident that Mr. Vignold was the man who killed our victim."

My conversation with Stover quickly over, I reviewed the details again. Detective work is about facts which either fit or don't. Molding them can lead to miscarriages of justice.

The ADA was so certain that I initially started to second-guess my assessment, and I went through the reports line by line, which chronicled a typical street shooting and solid follow-up work by the 43 Detective Squad and Bronx Homicide.

Moore had been taken in for dealing, robbery, and escape from a detention facility in the past and ended up running with pretty dangerous criminals who had been arrested for crimes including attempted murder. The victim seemed to have changed his lifestyle little, according to one witness who confirmed that Gotti was a dealer, and word was the shooting was a message from rivals who wanted to control the trade on the block where he and his pals peddled drugs.

The accused, Luis Vignold, was not an angel by any means, with several convictions down the years, but his rap sheet was no worse than those of a lot of young males in the ghetto. He also lived just around the corner from the gang members who were rivals to Moore and the Bloods. Vignold and Hector looked somewhat alike, though Vignold was lighter in skin color.

Both were Hispanic males, aged about thirty at the time of the murder, with close-cropped hair and short beards. Our shooting took place as darkness started to fall and under streetlights, so it could be a case of mistaken identity on behalf of the main witness. In Vignold's statement, he said that he fled when the shots rang out. Another possibility was that the whole thing could be a malicious complaint. It wouldn't be the first time someone tried to use the PD to settle an old score. Half of the tip-offs you get on dealers are rip-offs by other criminals who want to take them out of the game and control the corners themselves.

However, none of this really mattered. All that concerned cop or prosecutor were cold, hard facts. Did the evidence point to Vignold as the shooter, or someone else?

Reading through the files, it seemed to me that the evidence against our alleged shooter as trial approached was fairly thin. In light of a confession by an avowed killer, with seemingly nothing to gain from adding another homicide to his long list of charges, it now appeared flimsy.

Hector had also provided details about the case which he could not be expected to know had he not been there or been briefed in detail by someone who was present—notably his declaration that he and Reyes had shot Gotti with two hand-guns, a .357 and a .32, from close range, while the witness talked about only one shooter. Now, if the deceased had been hit with bullets from both weapons, as Hector claimed, it should show up in the autopsy conducted after his death, so I drove over to have a chat with Dr. James Gill, the deputy chief medical examiner for Bronx County.

Gill was a highly experienced doctor in his early fifties, an associate professor in pathology at Yale Medical School and New York University School of Medicine, regarded as an expert witness on this subject, having conducted autopsies on countless gunshot victims and even written about firearms deaths by law enforcement.

He knew the importance of his findings on all parties involved in the shooting, and the seriousness of the questions I raised. Gill confirmed that the deceased was shot in the right side of the head, leaving an entry hole of three-eighths of an inch, which fragmented upon impact and entered the victim's brain, killing him. He found that Moore was also shot in the right cheek, leaving a hole of one-eighth of an inch, the bullet seriously wounding him before lodging in his face, where it was recovered during the postmortem.

Our expert was confident that the evidence was clear and that, just as Hector had said, our subject was shot by two very different weapons, of two different calibers, at close range, one of them fitting the profile of a round from a .357 Magnum.

I reported these findings back to Stover, but she was unmoved and remained adamant that she was right, dismissing any suggestion that the People were about to go to trial in a few weeks' time to convict an innocent man of attacking Moore. In my years on the Job I never saw a hitter use two such different weapons in a killing.

I returned to the U.S. attorney's office and Masella, Rob Riveros, and Brandon Waller sat down with me to discuss the ME's findings and other paperwork we had on hand. We reviewed the evidence again, line by line, and talked through the various possibilities, trying to make a case against Vignold, but we all reached the same conclusion: Hector's confession and the medical evidence were compelling. The man on remand was innocent.

"I think the best thing we can do here is to let me handle this part of the case, Luke," Masella said decisively, and went away to consult with her superiors, after which another meeting was arranged downtown with Hector and his lawyer and AUSA Tim Kasulis, myself, Waller, Riveros, and, this time, ADA Stover, who brought the original crime-scene photographs for clarification.

Once more our hit man walked us through the shooting, explaining how Levit ordered him and Reyes to kill Derek Moore, and how they drove to the scene of the hit, sitting in their car until their victim appeared.

Our prisoner continued to outline the incident in minute detail, including an accurate description of everything Moore had been wearing when he was shot, without any prompting from his lawyer or anyone else present.

Stover's demeanor in the presence of the U.S. attorneys had thawed considerably, but even with the shooter sitting in front of her the prosecutor stuck to her guns, insisting that the evidence pointed to Luis Vignold as our killer.

Masella was tactful and showed Hector a photo of Derek Moore, while the other attorney passed over the CSU photographs.

"Yeah, that's the guy we shot—'Gotti,'" Hector said, without a moment's hesitation.

There was no way to explain his familiarity with these details and no suggestion that he knew Stover's target, Vignold, or that Vignold was somehow involved with Hector in killing Moore.

His only confusion was with our reluctance to accept that he and his buddy Rafi had whacked the guy.

"That's what I tryin' to tell you. This is the homey we killed, and those are pictures of where we shot him. What don't y'all understand?" he asked, staring at the photo in front of him once more.

That's when the ADA asked him to reenact how he shot the victim.

Riveros looked at Waller. Waller looked at me. I looked at Masella. Masella looked at Kasulis.

Hector looked at all of us in amazement. I tried not to laugh. It wasn't the time or the place—a man's freedom was at stake. But the scene was pretty amusing, since it's not every day that a coldhearted killer is asked to get in touch with his inner mime for the benefit of the feds, attorneys, and a city cop.

I shrugged my shoulders, and with a sigh, Hector did as he was instructed, making a pretend pistol from his forefinger and thumb and pointing it at an invisible body on the carpeted floor. He was about to shout "Bang! Bang!" when Tim Kasulis raised his hand, thankfully calling a halt to the farce as Hector prepared to shoot an imaginary victim in the face.

"Enough. I think we have seen enough here."

Hector and his lawyer were ushered to another office, as, for the first time in our discussions, Stover conceded ground.

"Well . . . uh . . . okay. I can go back to Ed Talty and talk to him about these new developments. Perhaps we can release Mr. Vignold on bail while the detectives investigate Mr. Garcia's story in greater detail."

Kasulis and Masella both shook their heads.

"No. The Bronx DA will order the immediate release of Mr. Vignold, Counselor. He has no case to answer, based on this evidence," Kasulis concluded, his tone as polite as ever but the finality clear for everyone in the room to hear.

Stover had no choice but to comply. There was no time to be lost. Rikers is probably the most dangerous place in New York, but fortunately Vignold seemed to have survived his ordeal in one piece and was finally released.

The Bronx DA's office had come within an inch of throwing its full weight and resources behind pursuing a prosecution which, on a bad day, with a careless jury and a distracted judge, could well have seen an innocent man sentenced to life imprisonment for a crime he did not commit.

The Creston Crew takedown had proved to be a turning point for me, both personally and professionally.

I hadn't told anyone in my office yet, but I had decided to pull the pin, take my pension, and retire. Any lingering doubts I might have harbored disappeared with all that had happened on the Luis Vignold case. I felt like my face simply didn't fit in at Bronx Homicide anymore.

I had been told I was next up for grade, and not getting the promotion was more than simply disappointing: it filled me with a deep unease and a lack of faith in the system I had sworn to uphold.

Anybody who thinks the Job won't be the same without them is more naive than I was in my earliest days, mistaking baseball superstars for barstool regulars on Long Island. I have seen countless cops come and go during my years; unless you are close friends or work with them for an extended period, their faces soon fade. We are all replaceable, and Luke Waters is no different.

There was still time to knock back a few drinks over in Kennedy's, where in many ways it had all started for me. The place hadn't changed too much in the intervening two decades. Nor, I would hope, had I. A few pounds heavier, a lot balder, but the same person in every way that really counted.

I had pulled the pin while I could still make that claim to the guy looking back at me in the shaving mirror every morning.

My going-away party was a quiet affair, attended by the old gang from down through the years, along with the FBI agents and federal lawyers I had come to know well towards the end of my time. I was presented with framed certificates from the Bureau, acknowledging me for my work in bringing down the Creston Crew and on other operations. As I accepted the congratulations, I caught the eye of Paul Hurley, who loudly declared that no certificate from the head of the FBI could convince him that I was not still an idiot from Finglas who should have stuck to being a barman and made something of himself.

Hurley's son, Desmond, and my kids, Tara, Ryan, and David, all have been born in this country, meaning they will never face a battle for a green card. They are Irish-American in every sense of the word, comfortable in both cultures, little aware of the opportunities which holding dual citizenship will confer upon them in the future.

Hurley had stayed behind the bar and made a success of it, but I had no real regrets about the decisions I'd made. I put about a thousand lawbreakers behind bars in my time carrying a badge, and although I made plenty of mistakes, I never took a dime I wasn't entitled to, never set a perp up for a crime he did not commit. Not once did I have to pull the trigger off the range.

Best wishes shared with all present, I stepped out onto Fifty-seventh Street and felt dizzy for a moment, as the whiskey and fresh Midtown Manhattan air combined. A hand reached out to steady me. It was Sergeant John O'Hara, whose skills as a pilot and instincts as a cop had been honed over three decades. He stood in the doorway, offering a final handshake.

"So that's it, eh, buddy? Tell me this, Detective Waters, looking back, would you change anything?"

I paused for a moment, but I didn't really need to think about my reply.

"You know what, Sarge? Not a thing. I'm going to miss the circus, but I'm not going to miss the clowns. Even so, I wouldn't change a bit of it. How about you? Would you do anything differently?"

"Me? Sure I would!" O'Hara replied with a snort.

"Really? What so, John? What would you do differently?"

O'Hara looked at me with a deadpan expression.

"Well, you know the time that asshole Larry Davis shot me, back in '86?"

"'Course. You'd have shot first?"

"No . . . but I'd have ducked, buddy."

There are a lot of fantasies when you join the NYPD, but few fanfares when you exit the stage. And for me there were no songs playing softly in the background, just the best words of advice anyone ever got on the Job—the kind of advice, unfortunately, most will never hear.

Theo Kojak couldn't have said it better.

When the punches, bullets, or recriminations start to fly, keep smiling, baby, and stand your ground.

But don't forget to duck.

ACKNOWLEDGMENTS

To my wife, Susan, for her support throughout my career, and to our children, the light of my life, Tara, Ryan, and David. I strive now to be the husband and father that the Job sometimes prevented me from being.

I write with fond regard for my parents, Vincent and Sheila, and my brothers and sisters Vincent, Thomas, Sheila, Lucy, and Bernadette: you mean more to me than I will ever be able to express.

To my best friend, Paul Hurley: thanks for bullying me into joining you in New York City thirty years ago!

I would like to thank everyone at Simon & Schuster for their hard work and determination. Thanks too to Plunkett PR for your help and advice.

To the outstanding men and women in Bronx Homicide, who truly live up to our motto, "The Best Detectives in the World": know that your pictures are still on my wall, and your stories will forever be in my heart.

Special thanks are due to my commanding officer, Lieutenant Sean O'Toole, the sharpest knife in the drawer, and to all the heroes who pinned on a badge during my time, in particular Sergeant John O'Hara and Detective Danny Rivera, who raced towards the sound of gunfire as others ran from it.

ACKNOWLEDGMENTS

I am grateful to the staff at the Bronx Medical Examiner's Office, particularly Dr. James Gill and Dr. Carolyn Kappen: you truly do God's work.

My thanks also to the best and brightest law enforcers I worked with, the tough and talented agents of Group C-30, FBI. To the U.S. Attorney's Office SDNY, the crème de la crème of the nation's law schools: your professionalism and dedication were both a revelation and an inspiration.

I am especially grateful to Frankie Pellegrino (Rao's Restaurant) for his incredible love and support through my journey and for always helping me.

Finally, I would like to thank and acknowledge the following people who helped and advised on *NYPD Green*: Ed Conlon, Dr. Pat Wallace, and Dr. John J. McGrath (TCI College of Technology).

About the Author

Luke Waters was born in Finglas on Dublin's Northside. He initially planned on following in his grandfathers' and brother's footsteps in joining An Garda Síochána, but instead, in 1985, America beckoned. After some time as a barman, he enrolled in the NYPD, working his way from rookie through Narcotics, before becoming a Homicide detective. Luke retired from the NYPD in 2013 and now lives in County Cavan with his wife and three children.